DIY Home to Trust Transfer Guide

Step-by-Step Instructions to Move Your Property into a Living Trust and Avoid Probate Without a Lawyer

Bethuel Oliver McKnight

First Edition: 2025
ISBN: 978-1-7642720-2-5

DISCLAIMER

This book provides general information about property transfers to living trusts and is intended for educational purposes only. The information contained herein does not constitute legal advice and should not be relied upon as a substitute for consultation with qualified legal professionals.

No Attorney-Client Relationship: Reading this book does not create an attorney-client relationship between the author, publisher, and reader. No confidential relationship is established through the use of this book or its accompanying materials.

State Law Variations: Property transfer laws vary significantly between states and change frequently. While this book attempts to provide current information for all states, readers must verify current requirements with local authorities and legal professionals before proceeding with any property transfer.

Individual Circumstances Vary: Every property transfer situation involves unique factors that may affect the appropriateness of DIY approaches. Readers must evaluate their individual circumstances and seek professional guidance when situations exceed the scope of general guidance provided in this book.

Risk Acknowledgment: Property transfers involve legal and financial risks. Errors in deed preparation, recording procedures, or legal compliance can result in significant financial losses, title problems, or legal complications. Readers assume all risks associated with DIY property transfers.

Professional Consultation Recommended: This book identifies numerous situations requiring professional legal assistance. Readers are strongly encouraged to consult with qualified attorneys when facing complex situations, high-value properties, or any circumstances involving uncertainty about legal requirements or procedures.

Limitation of Liability: The author and publisher disclaim all liability for any damages, losses, or legal complications arising from the use of information contained in this book. This limitation applies to direct, indirect, consequential, and punitive damages.

Compliance with Laws: Readers are responsible for compliance with all applicable federal, state, and local laws. This book does not guarantee compliance with current legal requirements and cannot account for all possible variations in local procedures.

Professional Licensing: The author does not provide legal services through this book and is not rendering legal advice to readers. Legal advice can only be provided by licensed attorneys familiar with specific state laws and individual circumstances.

Updates and Changes: Laws and procedures change frequently. While efforts are made to provide current information, readers must verify all information with appropriate authorities before relying on it for actual property transfers.

When in Doubt, Seek Professional Help: This disclaimer emphasizes that professional legal consultation is always the safest approach for property transfers involving significant assets, complex situations, or any circumstances where readers feel uncertain about procedures or requirements.

By using this book and its accompanying materials, readers acknowledge understanding of these limitations and agree to assume full responsibility for their property transfer decisions and outcomes.

Table of Contents

Chapter 1: Why Transfer Your Home to a Trust Yourself

Sarah Martinez stared at the attorney's estimate: $4,800 for a simple trust transfer of her Phoenix home. After paying for her daughter's college tuition and dealing with her husband's recent medical bills, nearly five thousand dollars felt like a mountain she couldn't climb. Yet she knew putting her home in a trust was the right thing to do - she'd watched her neighbor's family spend eight months and twelve thousand dollars in probate court just to settle a simple estate.

"There has to be another way," she told herself, sitting at her kitchen table surrounded by legal documents she barely understood. That night, she discovered something that changed everything: she could legally transfer her home to her living trust herself, without an attorney, for less than $200 in fees.

Six weeks later, Sarah completed her DIY trust transfer successfully. She saved $4,600 and gained something equally valuable - the confidence that comes from understanding and controlling her own financial future. Her story isn't unique. Thousands of homeowners across America are discovering they can handle this crucial estate planning task themselves, saving substantial money while protecting their families' inheritance.

The Real Cost of Professional Help

Let's talk numbers, because that's where this conversation gets interesting. The average attorney fee for transferring a home into an existing trust ranges from $2,000 to $6,000, depending on your location and property complexity. In high-cost areas like California's Bay Area or Manhattan, fees can reach $8,000 or more. Even in smaller markets, you'll rarely pay less than $1,500.

Here's what you're actually paying for: document preparation (maybe 2 hours of work), deed recording (often handled by a paralegal), and the attorney's liability insurance. The actual legal complexity? In most straightforward cases, it's surprisingly minimal.

Compare that to the DIY approach. Your total out-of-pocket costs typically include:

- County recording fee: $15-$75
- Documentary transfer tax (if applicable): $0-$200
- Notary fee: $10-$25
- Certified copies: $15-$40

Total DIY cost: Usually under $300, often much less.

The math is compelling, but money isn't everything. The real question is whether you can handle this process safely and effectively. The answer, for most homeowners in most situations, is yes - if you understand what you're doing and when to step back.

When DIY Makes Perfect Sense

Tom and Linda Harrison owned their Colorado home free and clear. They'd established their living trust three years earlier and wanted to transfer their property into it. Their situation was textbook simple: one property, two owners (married couple), clear title, no liens, and Colorado's straightforward recording requirements.

Tom, a retired engineer, appreciated systematic processes. He spent two weekends researching the requirements, downloaded the proper forms from the county recorder's office, and carefully prepared their quitclaim deed. The entire process took him about eight hours spread over three weeks. His total cost: $47.

"I've built airplane engines," Tom laughed. "I figured I could handle a property deed."

The Harrisons represent the sweet spot for DIY trust transfers. They had:

- An existing, properly drafted living trust
- A straightforward property situation
- The time and patience to do it right
- Access to clear, reliable information
- A backup plan (they knew their attorney's phone number)

The Complexity Spectrum

Not every situation is right for the DIY approach. Property transfers exist on a complexity spectrum, and understanding where your situation falls is crucial for success.

Simple scenarios perfect for DIY include:

- Single-family residence with clear title
- Married couple transferring to joint trust
- No mortgage or mortgage with major lender
- Property in a DIY-friendly state
- Standard ownership structure

Moderate complexity situations where DIY is possible but requires extra care:

- Properties with existing mortgages
- Co-owned properties with unmarried owners
- Investment or rental properties
- Properties in states with additional requirements
- Situations involving recent divorces or title issues

High complexity scenarios where professional help is strongly recommended:

- Commercial properties or unusual property types
- Properties with existing title problems
- Situations involving disputed ownership

- Tax-deferred exchanges or seller financing
- Properties in states with attorney-required processes

The key is honest self-assessment. If your situation involves multiple complications or you're uncomfortable with any aspect of the process, the attorney fee represents good value for peace of mind.

Your Personal Capability Assessment

Before you decide to handle this yourself, you need to evaluate whether you're the right person for the job. This isn't about intelligence - it's about fit. Some brilliant people struggle with bureaucratic processes, while others find them straightforward.

Consider your comfort level with:

Administrative tasks: Do you handle your own tax returns? Have you ever recorded a document with a government office? Are you comfortable following detailed instructions precisely?

Detail orientation: Can you proofread carefully? Do you double-check important documents before signing? Are you good at catching small errors that could cause big problems?

Time availability: Do you have 4-8 hours to spread over several weeks? Can you work during business hours when recorder offices are open? Are you willing to start over if you make a mistake?

Stress tolerance: How do you handle uncertainty? Can you work through problems without getting overwhelmed? Are you comfortable taking reasonable risks when you've done your homework?

Learning style: Do you learn well from written instructions? Can you break complex processes into manageable steps? Are you willing to research unfamiliar terms and concepts?

Margaret Chen, a busy pediatrician in Austin, realized she wasn't the right fit for DIY. "I can handle complex medical procedures," she explained, "but I hate paperwork and I never have time to do it carefully. For me, paying the attorney was worth every penny because I knew it would be done right the first time."

Contrast that with David Rodriguez, a high school history teacher who transferred his family's San Antonio home successfully. "I'm used to breaking complex topics into understandable pieces," he said. "Plus, I had summer vacation to work on it. The process reminded me of grading papers - attention to detail is everything."

The Three-Tier State System

Your location dramatically affects your DIY success odds. After analyzing trust transfer requirements across all 50 states, a clear pattern emerges: states fall into three distinct tiers based on complexity, requirements, and DIY-friendliness.

Tier 1 states make DIY transfers relatively straightforward. These include Texas, Florida, Nevada, Arizona, and 15 others. They typically offer:

- Simple recording processes
- Clear fee structures
- Minimal additional forms
- Good online resources
- Transfer-on-death deed options

Tier 2 states add moderate complexity but remain DIY-feasible for most homeowners. Illinois, Ohio, Michigan, and about 20 others require:

- Additional documentation
- More complex tax forms
- Higher fees
- Some specialized knowledge
- Extra attention to detail

Tier 3 states present significant challenges that push many homeowners toward professional help. California, New York, Pennsylvania, and New Jersey feature:

- Extensive additional requirements
- Complex tax implications
- Multiple agency interactions
- Specialized forms and procedures
- Higher error risks

Living in a Tier 3 state doesn't automatically disqualify you from DIY success, but it does raise the bar considerably. You'll need more time, greater attention to detail, and stronger comfort with bureaucratic processes.

Time Investment Realities

Let's be realistic about time commitment. Most successful DIY trust transfers require 6-10 hours of actual work spread over 2-4 weeks. Here's how that typically breaks down:

Week 1: Research and Planning (2-3 hours)

- Understanding your state's requirements
- Gathering necessary documents
- Assessing your specific situation
- Determining if DIY is appropriate

Week 2: Document Preparation (2-4 hours)

- Preparing the new deed
- Completing required forms
- Double-checking all information
- Getting documents notarized

Week 3: Filing and Recording (1-2 hours)

- Submitting documents to recorder

- Paying fees
- Tracking processing
- Obtaining certified copies

Week 4: Follow-up Tasks (1-2 hours)

- Notifying mortgage company
- Updating insurance policies
- Filing property tax forms
- Organizing completed paperwork

Most people underestimate this time commitment initially. Plan for the high end, not the low end, especially if you're in a Tier 2 or Tier 3 state.

Risk Assessment Framework

Every DIY project involves trade-offs between cost savings and risk exposure. Trust transfers are no different. Understanding and managing these risks is crucial for making an informed decision.

Low-risk elements you can typically handle safely:

- Document preparation in straightforward situations
- Basic research and information gathering
- Simple recording processes
- Standard notification procedures

Medium-risk elements requiring extra care:

- Complex deed preparation
- Tax implication analysis
- Multiple-owner situations
- Mortgage company interactions

High-risk elements where professional help often pays for itself:

- Title problems or ownership disputes

- Complex family situations
- Business property transfers
- Situations with tax consequences
- Any scenario where you're unsure about legal requirements

The framework helps you identify when you're operating outside your comfort zone. A few high-risk elements don't necessarily disqualify DIY, but they should make you more cautious and thorough in your preparation.

Success Stories from Real Families

Beyond Sarah's story from our opening, consider these additional examples of successful DIY transfers:

The Johnsons of Tampa completed their transfer in two weeks for $38. Both retired teachers, they appreciated the learning experience and felt proud of mastering a new skill. "We learned more about our property ownership in those two weeks than we had in 15 years of homeownership," Marie Johnson reflected.

Single mother Lisa Park in Denver handled her transfer while working full-time and raising two teenagers. She tackled the project in 30-minute increments over six weeks, using her lunch breaks for research and weekends for document preparation. Her total cost: $73. "I was motivated by knowing I was protecting my kids' inheritance," she explained.

The Kowalski brothers in Phoenix successfully transferred their inherited family home into their joint trust. Despite initial concerns about their different last names and the property's history, careful preparation and attention to detail led to smooth completion. Total time: 12 hours over four weeks.

These aren't exceptional people - they're regular homeowners who took the time to understand the process and execute it carefully.

When Professional Help Makes Sense

13

Even DIY advocates recognize situations where attorney involvement is wise. Consider professional help when:

Your property situation is complex, involving multiple owners with different interests, business entities, or unusual ownership structures.

You're uncomfortable with any aspect of the process, from document preparation to government interactions.

Your state falls in Tier 3 with extensive additional requirements that push beyond your comfort zone.

You've identified multiple risk factors that compound the complexity of your situation.

You simply prefer the peace of mind that comes with professional handling, and the cost fits your budget.

There's no shame in choosing professional help. The goal is protecting your family's interests, not proving you can do everything yourself.

Making Your Decision

Standing at this crossroads, you need to balance several factors: cost considerations, personal capabilities, time availability, risk tolerance, and state requirements. Here's a decision framework to help:

Choose DIY if:

- Your situation is straightforward
- You're in a Tier 1 or Tier 2 state
- You have adequate time and patience
- Cost savings significantly impact your budget
- You're comfortable with moderate risk and complexity

Choose professional help if:

- Your situation involves multiple complicating factors

- You're in a challenging Tier 3 state
- Time constraints prevent careful attention to detail
- You're uncomfortable with risk or uncertainty
- The attorney fee doesn't strain your budget

Consider a hybrid approach if:

- You want to handle simple parts yourself
- You need professional guidance on specific issues
- You want to prepare documents but have them reviewed
- You're comfortable with most aspects but uncertain about some

Many attorneys offer limited-scope representation, helping with specific questions while letting you handle routine tasks. This can provide professional guidance at a fraction of full-service costs.

The path forward depends on your unique combination of circumstances, capabilities, and preferences. The next chapters will give you the knowledge and tools to succeed if you choose the DIY route, along with clear guidance about when to step back and seek professional help.

Your Investment in Knowledge

Whether you ultimately handle this transfer yourself or hire an attorney, understanding the process benefits you. Informed property owners make better decisions, ask better questions, and avoid costly mistakes. The time you spend learning about trust transfers isn't wasted - it's an investment in your financial literacy and family protection.

Sarah Martinez, whose story opened this chapter, put it best: "Even if I'd decided to hire an attorney, knowing what I learned made me a better client. I understood what needed to happen and could ask the right questions. Knowledge is never wasted when it comes to protecting your family's future."

The $5,000 question isn't really about money - it's about empowerment. Taking control of your estate planning, understanding your options, and making informed decisions based on your specific situation and capabilities.

Key Takeaways from Your Cost-Benefit Analysis

The financial case for DIY trust transfers is compelling for many homeowners, with potential savings ranging from $1,500 to $8,000 depending on your location and situation complexity. However, money represents just one factor in your decision.

Success depends on honest assessment of your personal capabilities, understanding your state's requirements, and recognizing when complexity pushes beyond DIY appropriateness. The three-tier state system provides a framework for evaluating your location's DIY-friendliness, while the risk assessment helps identify situations requiring professional guidance.

Time investment runs 6-10 hours over 2-4 weeks for most successful DIY transfers. This represents a significant commitment that requires planning and patience, but the financial savings often justify the investment.

Most importantly, this isn't an all-or-nothing decision. Hybrid approaches combining DIY execution with professional guidance can provide cost savings while maintaining professional oversight where it's most valuable.

The next chapter will ground you in trust fundamentals, ensuring you understand the foundation concepts essential for successful property transfer, regardless of which path you ultimately choose.

Chapter 2: Trust Basics Every Homeowner Needs to Know

Standing in her lawyer's office three years ago, Janet Pearson felt completely lost. Terms like "grantor," "trustee," and "corpus" flew around the room while she nodded politely, pretending to understand. She signed documents creating her living trust but walked away with only a vague sense of what she'd actually done.

Now, preparing to transfer her Phoenix townhome into that same trust, Janet realized she needed to truly understand what she was working with. "I can't make smart decisions about something I don't really get," she told her sister. Over the next few weeks, Janet invested time learning the fundamentals. What she discovered wasn't complicated - it was actually quite logical once someone explained it in plain English.

Janet's experience reflects a common problem: many homeowners create trusts without understanding the basic mechanics. This knowledge gap becomes problematic when it's time to fund the trust or make management decisions. You don't need a law degree to grasp trust fundamentals, but you do need clear explanations without the legal jargon.

What Is a Living Trust and How Does It Work

Think of a living trust as a legal container designed to hold your assets during your lifetime and distribute them after your death. Unlike a will, which only takes effect when you die, a living trust operates while you're alive and provides continuous asset management.

Here's the basic setup: You create a trust document that establishes three key roles. The **grantor** (that's you) transfers ownership of assets into the trust. The **trustee** manages those assets according to the trust's instructions. The **beneficiaries** receive the assets according to the trust's terms.

In most living trusts, you wear all three hats initially. You're the grantor who creates and funds the trust, the trustee who manages the assets, and the primary beneficiary who retains complete control and use of everything. This arrangement continues until you die or become incapacitated, at which point your successor trustee takes over management duties.

The magic happens in the ownership structure. When you transfer your home to your trust, you're not giving it away - you're changing how you hold title. Instead of "Janet Pearson" owning the house, now "Janet Pearson, Trustee of the Pearson Family Trust dated March 15, 2021" owns it. Janet still lives there, maintains it, and makes all decisions about it, but the legal ownership structure has changed in a way that provides significant benefits.

This ownership change creates what estate planning professionals call "probate avoidance." Since the trust, not you personally, owns the asset, there's nothing in your individual name requiring probate court involvement when you die. Your successor trustee can immediately take control and distribute assets according to your instructions, without court oversight, delays, or public proceedings.

The Two Types Every Homeowner Should Understand

Living trusts come in two basic varieties: revocable and irrevocable. The difference between them is crucial for homeowners considering trust transfers.

Revocable Living Trusts represent the overwhelming choice for homeowners transferring their primary residence. "Revocable" means you can change, modify, or completely cancel the trust at any time. You retain complete control over all assets, can buy or sell property freely, and pay taxes exactly as you did before creating the trust.

From the IRS perspective, revocable trusts are "transparent" - they essentially don't exist for tax purposes. You report all income and expenses on your personal tax return using your Social Security number. No separate tax returns, no additional complexity, no immediate tax consequences.

The flexibility of revocable trusts makes them perfect for homeowners. You can:

- Sell your house and buy another without trust complications
- Refinance mortgages in your individual name if needed
- Change beneficiaries or distribution instructions anytime
- Add or remove assets from the trust freely
- Maintain complete privacy (unlike wills, trusts avoid public probate records)

Irrevocable trusts work differently. Once you transfer assets into an irrevocable trust, you generally can't take them back or change the trust terms. This permanent transfer can provide significant benefits - asset protection from creditors, estate tax reduction, Medicaid planning advantages - but comes with substantial trade-offs.

For homeowners considering primary residence transfers, irrevocable trusts usually make sense only in specific circumstances: significant estate tax concerns, Medicaid planning needs, or asset protection requirements. These situations typically warrant professional guidance because the stakes and complexity levels increase dramatically.

The vast majority of homeowner trust transfers involve revocable living trusts, so that's our focus throughout this book.

Trustee Roles and Responsibilities

19

Understanding trustee duties is essential because you'll initially serve as your own trustee, and you'll eventually name someone else to take over. The role carries legal obligations that shouldn't be taken lightly.

As **initial trustee** of your own trust, your responsibilities include:

- Managing trust assets prudently and in the beneficiaries' best interests
- Keeping accurate records of all trust transactions
- Filing any required tax returns (though for revocable trusts, this typically means your normal personal return)
- Following the trust document's instructions for asset management and distribution
- Avoiding conflicts of interest between your personal interests and trust interests

In practice, since you're also the primary beneficiary, these duties rarely create problems. You're managing your own assets for your own benefit, so conflicts are minimal.

Successor trustees face more complex responsibilities. When you die or become incapacitated, your successor trustee must:

- Take immediate control of trust assets
- Notify beneficiaries of your death and their inheritance rights
- Manage assets during the transition period
- Pay your final debts and taxes
- Distribute assets according to trust instructions
- Provide accountings to beneficiaries
- Handle any disputes or legal challenges

Choosing the right successor trustee is crucial. You need someone who is:

- Trustworthy and financially responsible
- Organized enough to handle detailed record-keeping
- Available and willing to serve when needed
- Young enough to outlive you

- Geographically accessible to manage local assets like real estate
- Capable of making tough decisions under pressure

Many people name their adult children as successor trustees, but this isn't always wise. Consider whether your intended successor has the necessary skills, time, and temperament. Professional trustees (bank trust departments or trust companies) offer expertise and objectivity but charge ongoing fees that can significantly impact smaller estates.

Beneficiary Designations Made Simple

Beneficiary planning in trusts can be straightforward or complex, depending on your family situation and goals. Most homeowners transferring their residence use simple structures, but understanding your options helps you make informed decisions.

Primary beneficiaries are the people who inherit your assets when you die. Common approaches include:

- Spouse as sole beneficiary, with children inheriting when both spouses die
- Children as equal beneficiaries, inheriting immediately when you die
- Specific percentage splits among multiple beneficiaries
- Contingent beneficiaries who inherit if primary beneficiaries predecease you

Remainder beneficiaries receive assets after the primary beneficiaries' interests end. This typically applies in situations where spouses receive lifetime income or use of assets, with children inheriting the remainder eventually.

For straightforward family situations, simple beneficiary structures work best. Married couples often leave everything to each other, then to children equally. Single parents typically leave assets directly to children, with siblings or other relatives as contingent beneficiaries.

Complex beneficiary arrangements - special needs trusts, generation-skipping provisions, charitable remainder interests - require professional drafting and ongoing management. If your situation involves these elements, focus on understanding the basics while working with qualified professionals for implementation.

Key Terms and Definitions

Grantor or Settlor: The person who creates and funds the trust (that's you)

Trustee: The person responsible for managing trust assets and following trust instructions

Beneficiary: The person or entity entitled to receive trust benefits or assets

Trust Corpus or Principal: The assets owned by the trust (your house, once transferred)

Pour-over Will: A will that transfers any forgotten assets into your trust after death

Funding the Trust: The process of transferring assets from your individual ownership into the trust

Trust Certificate or Abstract: A shortened version of your trust document used to prove the trust's existence without revealing private details

Successor Trustee: The person who takes over trustee duties when you die or become incapacitated

Revocation: Your right to cancel the trust and take back all assets (in revocable trusts)

Distribution: The process of transferring assets from the trust to beneficiaries

These terms appear repeatedly in trust documents and real estate transfer paperwork. Understanding them prevents confusion and helps you communicate effectively with professionals when needed.

Common Misconceptions Debunked

Homeowners often arrive at trust transfers with significant misconceptions that can lead to poor decisions or unnecessary worry. Let's address the most common myths:

Myth: Transferring my house to a trust means I no longer own it. Reality: You absolutely still own your house. You've simply changed the legal form of ownership from individual to trust ownership, while retaining complete control as trustee.

Myth: I'll need my trustee's permission to sell or refinance. Reality: Since you are the trustee, you need no one's permission. You maintain complete control over all decisions affecting your property.

Myth: Trust ownership will affect my property tax exemptions. Reality: In most states, transferring your primary residence to your own revocable trust doesn't affect homestead exemptions or other property tax benefits. Some states require simple notification forms, but the benefits continue.

Myth: My homeowner's insurance won't cover a trust-owned property. Reality: Insurance companies regularly cover trust-owned properties. You may need to notify your insurer and possibly add the trust as an additional insured party, but coverage continues.

Myth: I can't get a mortgage on trust-owned property. Reality: Most major lenders routinely make loans secured by trust-owned real estate. Some may require you to temporarily transfer the property back to individual ownership for closing, then immediately return it to trust ownership.

Myth: Creating a trust eliminates estate taxes. Reality: Revocable living trusts provide no estate tax benefits. For tax purposes, you still own everything personally. Trusts avoid probate, not taxes.

Myth: Trusts are only for wealthy people. Reality: Anyone owning real estate can benefit from probate avoidance, privacy, and the management continuity that trusts provide. These benefits aren't limited by wealth levels.

Myth: Once I transfer my house to the trust, I can't change anything. Reality: With revocable trusts, you can modify terms, change beneficiaries, add or remove assets, or completely revoke the trust anytime you want.

How Property Flows Through Trust vs. Probate

Understanding the difference between trust asset distribution and probate proceedings helps illustrate why homeowners choose trust transfers.

Traditional probate process for real estate involves:

1. Filing will and death certificate with probate court
2. Court appointment of personal representative (executor)
3. Public notice to creditors and potential heirs
4. Inventory and appraisal of all estate assets
5. Payment of debts and taxes
6. Court approval for real estate sales or distributions
7. Final accounting and distribution to heirs
8. Court closure of estate (typically 6-18 months minimum)

Trust distribution process works differently:

1. Successor trustee takes immediate control upon your death
2. Private notification to beneficiaries (no court involvement)
3. Trust document provides distribution authority
4. Assets distributed according to trust instructions
5. No court supervision or approval required

6. Process typically completed within weeks or months

The contrast is striking. Probate involves court supervision, public proceedings, lengthy timelines, and significant costs. Trust distributions happen privately, quickly, and with minimal expense.

Consider the Petersons of Sacramento, whose father died owning his home individually. The probate process took 14 months and cost over $8,000 in court fees and attorney costs. During probate, the family couldn't sell the house, access rental income, or make major repairs without court approval.

Compare that to the Chen family in San Jose, whose mother had transferred her home to her living trust. When she died, their successor trustee (the oldest daughter) took immediate control. Within six weeks, they'd sold the house, paid final expenses, and distributed inheritance to all siblings. Total professional fees: $1,200 for escrow and real estate services.

Both families achieved the same result - transferring family real estate to the next generation. But the trust structure made the process faster, cheaper, and more private.

Trust Management During Your Lifetime

Once you've transferred your home to your trust, day-to-day management remains exactly the same. You continue living in the house, maintaining it, paying taxes and insurance, and making all decisions about its use. The trust ownership is largely invisible in your daily life.

However, certain administrative aspects require attention:

Financial accounts and records should reflect trust ownership. Update your property tax records, insurance policies, and mortgage accounts to show the trust as owner. Most institutions handle this with simple forms, though some may require trust certificates or other documentation.

Major transactions like sales, refinancing, or substantial improvements require you to sign documents in your capacity as trustee. Instead of "Janet Pearson," you'll sign as "Janet Pearson, Trustee of the Pearson Family Trust dated March 15, 2021."

Record keeping becomes slightly more complex. While you don't need separate accounting for revocable trusts, maintaining clear records of trust assets and transactions helps your successor trustee and provides documentation if questions arise.

Trust document storage deserves careful consideration. Your successor trustee will need the original trust document and related paperwork. Many people keep originals in safe deposit boxes or fireproof safes, with copies in easily accessible locations.

Communication with family about trust arrangements prevents confusion and conflict later. Your successor trustee and beneficiaries should know the trust exists, understand their roles, and know where to find necessary documents.

The Foundation for Success

Trust fundamentals aren't complicated, but they are essential. Understanding these basics allows you to make informed decisions about property transfers, ask intelligent questions when you need help, and avoid costly mistakes.

Janet Pearson, whose confusion we discussed at the beginning, successfully completed her townhome transfer six months after taking time to understand her trust. "Once I got the basics," she reflected, "everything else made sense. I felt confident because I understood what I was doing and why."

That confidence - based on solid understanding rather than blind faith - is your goal. The mechanics of property transfer build on these foundational concepts. Trustees transfer assets, grantors fund trusts, and beneficiaries eventually inherit - but first, you need to know which category your state falls into and what specific requirements you'll face.

Key Takeaways from Trust Fundamentals

Living trusts serve as legal containers holding your assets during life and distributing them at death, with revocable trusts providing the flexibility most homeowners need for primary residence transfers. The three-role structure - grantor, trustee, beneficiary - typically starts with you filling all positions until your death or incapacity activates successor management.

Understanding trustee responsibilities, both your current duties and your successor's future obligations, helps you make informed decisions about trust management and successor selection. Beneficiary designations can be straightforward for simple family situations but may require professional guidance for complex arrangements.

Common misconceptions about trust ownership often create unnecessary anxiety, but the reality is that revocable trust ownership preserves your complete control while providing probate avoidance and privacy benefits. The contrast between trust distribution and probate proceedings illustrates the primary advantages motivating most homeowners to pursue trust transfers.

Daily trust management remains largely invisible, but certain administrative updates and record-keeping practices help ensure smooth operation during your lifetime and efficient transition to your successors.

The next chapter introduces the three-tier state complexity system, helping you understand how your location affects the DIY feasibility of your trust transfer project.

Chapter 3: The Three-Tier Complexity System

When Michael Torres started researching trust transfers, he assumed the process would be the same everywhere. After all, he reasoned, property law is property law, right? That assumption nearly cost him $3,000 in attorney fees he didn't need to spend.

Michael lived in Nevada, a state with some of the most homeowner-friendly trust transfer laws in the country. His neighbor, concerned about Michael's DIY plans, shared horror stories from his brother in California, where transfer requirements are significantly more complex. The neighbor's warnings sent Michael straight to an attorney's office.

Fortunately, that attorney was honest enough to explain that Nevada's straightforward requirements made Michael's situation perfect for DIY. "If you lived in California or New York, I'd say hire me," the attorney explained. "But in Nevada, with your simple situation, you're just paying for peace of mind you don't really need."

Michael's experience highlights a crucial reality: your location dramatically affects your DIY success probability. States vary enormously in their requirements, from ultra-simple to bewilderingly complex. Understanding where your state falls on this spectrum is essential for making an informed DIY decision.

The Three-Tier System Explained

After analyzing trust transfer requirements across all 50 states plus the District of Columbia, a clear pattern emerges. States cluster into three distinct groups based on their DIY-friendliness, required documentation, fee structures, and overall complexity levels.

This isn't random variation - it reflects different philosophical approaches to property transfers and government involvement in real estate transactions. Some states prioritize simplicity and low costs to encourage property transfers. Others impose extensive documentation requirements, multiple agency involvement, and significant fees that can make professional assistance worthwhile even for simple situations.

The three-tier system helps you quickly assess your state's DIY-friendliness and set appropriate expectations for your transfer project.

Tier 1: The DIY-Friendly States

Eighteen states earn top marks for homeowner-friendly trust transfer requirements. These states generally feature simple recording processes, reasonable fees, minimal additional documentation, and excellent online resources. If you live in a Tier 1 state, DIY success rates exceed 90% for straightforward residential transfers.

Texas leads the pack with incredibly simple requirements. Transfer your home to your trust by preparing a quitclaim deed, getting it notarized, and recording it with your county clerk. Total fees typically run $25-$40. Texas also offers Transfer-on-Death (TOD) deeds as an alternative to trust transfers, providing multiple options for probate avoidance.

Florida combines simple processes with excellent county resources. Most Florida counties provide detailed instructions and form templates online. Recording fees stay reasonable (usually $10 for the first page plus $8.50 per additional page), and documentary stamp taxes don't apply to transfers into your own revocable trust.

Nevada, Michael's state from our opening story, requires only basic deed preparation and recording. No additional forms, no transfer taxes, no special requirements. The entire process typically takes two weeks and costs under $50.

Arizona offers similar simplicity with the added benefit of some of the lowest recording fees in the nation. Many Arizona counties charge just $18 to record a deed, making it extremely cost-effective for DIY transfers.

Other **Tier 1 states** include: Alabama, Alaska, Arkansas, Colorado, Georgia, Idaho, Louisiana, Montana, New Mexico, North Dakota, South Dakota, Utah, West Virginia, and Wyoming.

These states share common characteristics that make DIY transfers straightforward:

- Single recording location (county recorder/clerk)
- Simple deed requirements (usually just quitclaim or warranty deed)
- No additional state-level forms or approvals
- Documentary transfer taxes either don't exist or don't apply to trust transfers
- Reasonable recording fees (typically $15-$75)
- Good online resources and customer service

Tier 2: The Moderate Complexity States

Twenty-three states fall into the moderate complexity category. These states add layers of documentation, higher fees, or additional requirements that increase DIY difficulty without making it impossible. Success rates for DIY transfers in Tier 2 states run 70-85% for straightforward situations.

Illinois typifies Tier 2 complexity. Beyond basic deed preparation, you'll need to complete a Property Transfer Declaration, calculate transfer taxes (even though they don't apply to trust transfers, you still need to document the exemption), and navigate county-specific requirements that vary significantly across Illinois's 102 counties.

Ohio requires additional documentation including a Conveyance Fee Statement and, in some counties, a Residence and Familial Interest form. Transfer taxes don't apply to trust transfers, but you must complete forms documenting your exemption. Recording fees vary widely by county, ranging from $25 to $120.

Michigan adds a Property Transfer Affidavit requirement and mandates that certain transfers be reported to the state Treasury Department. While trust transfers are exempt from the state's real estate transfer tax, you need to document this exemption properly to avoid problems later.

Virginia requires a Grantor Tax Certificate even for tax-exempt transfers, plus additional disclosures depending on the property type and location. Some Virginia localities impose additional requirements or fees beyond state mandates.

Other **Tier 2 states** include: Delaware, Hawaii, Indiana, Iowa, Kansas, Kentucky, Maine, Maryland, Massachusetts, Minnesota, Mississippi, Missouri, Nebraska, New Hampshire, North Carolina, Oklahoma, Oregon, South Carolina, Tennessee, Vermont, Washington, and Wisconsin.

Common **Tier 2 characteristics** include:

- Multiple forms beyond the basic deed
- Transfer tax calculations (even when taxes don't apply)
- Some county-specific variations in requirements
- Higher recording fees (typically $50-$150)
- More complex exemption documentation
- Potential for multi-agency interaction (county recorder, state revenue, local assessor)

Tier 3: The Complex States

Nine states and the District of Columbia create significant DIY challenges through extensive requirements, high fees, complex procedures, or multiple agency involvement. While DIY success is still possible, it requires substantial additional time, attention to detail, and comfort with bureaucratic complexity.

California presents the most daunting requirements. Trust transfers require:

- Basic deed preparation and recording
- Preliminary Change of Ownership Report (PCOR)
- Documentary transfer tax calculation and exemption documentation
- Potential property tax reassessment considerations
- Homestead exemption preservation procedures
- Possible additional local requirements depending on city/county

California's PCOR process alone can confuse experienced real estate professionals. The form asks detailed questions about the transfer circumstances, property characteristics, and tax implications. Errors can trigger property tax reassessments or create title problems years later.

New York requires completion of Form TP-584 (Combined Real Estate Transfer Tax Return and Credit Line Mortgage Certificate), even for tax-exempt trust transfers. The form is complex, the instructions are confusing, and errors can result in significant delays or financial penalties.

Pennsylvania imposes both state and local transfer taxes, plus requires multiple disclosure forms that vary by municipality. While trust transfers may qualify for exemptions, documenting these exemptions properly requires understanding complex state and local regulations.

New Jersey combines high fees with extensive documentation requirements. Recording fees can exceed $200, and various disclosure forms add complexity for even simple residential transfers.

Other **Tier 3 states** include: Connecticut, Massachusetts (borderline Tier 2/Tier 3), Rhode Island, and the District of Columbia.

Tier 3 characteristics typically include:

- Extensive additional documentation requirements
- High fees (often $150-$500+)
- Multiple agency interactions required
- Complex tax calculation and exemption procedures
- Significant penalties for errors
- Limited online resources or confusing guidance

State-Specific Cost Expectations

Understanding your potential costs helps you evaluate whether DIY savings justify the effort required. Costs vary dramatically by tier and specific location within states.

Tier 1 typical costs:

- Recording fees: $15-$75
- Notary fees: $5-$25
- Document preparation: $0 (DIY)
- Total: Usually under $100

Tier 2 typical costs:

- Recording fees: $50-$150
- Additional form fees: $10-$50
- Notary fees: $10-$25
- Certified copies: $15-$40
- Total: Usually $85-$265

Tier 3 typical costs:

- Recording fees: $100-$300
- State/local forms: $25-$100
- Professional document review (recommended): $300-$800
- Notary fees: $15-$35
- Certified copies: $20-$50
- Total: Often $460-$1,285 (including professional review)

These ranges reflect typical straightforward residential transfers. Complex situations, unusual property types, or locations with higher-than-average fees can push costs significantly higher.

Documentary Transfer Tax Implications

Documentary transfer taxes represent one of the most confusing aspects of real estate transfers. These taxes, imposed by state or local governments, typically apply when property changes hands for consideration (money). However, transfers to your own revocable living trust usually qualify for exemptions.

Understanding these taxes matters because even exempt transfers often require documentation proving the exemption applies. Errors in this documentation can create expensive problems later.

States without documentary transfer taxes include most Tier 1 states plus some Tier 2 locations. These states make transfers simpler because you don't need to calculate taxes or document exemptions.

States with transfer taxes but clear exemptions for trust transfers include California (despite other complexities), New York, Pennsylvania, and others. You'll need to complete forms and understand exemption requirements, but the process is generally manageable.

States with unclear or complex exemption procedures create the most problems for DIY transfers. Some states require specific language in deeds, others demand separate exemption applications, and a few delegate decisions to local officials who may interpret requirements differently.

The key is understanding your state's specific approach and ensuring you comply with both the tax calculation requirements (even if no tax is owed) and the exemption documentation procedures.

Red Flags Requiring Professional Help

Certain warning signs suggest your situation has moved beyond appropriate DIY territory, regardless of your state's tier classification. These red flags often compound complexity beyond what the tier system captures:

Title problems including liens, judgments, boundary disputes, or ownership questions require professional resolution before any transfer attempt.

Multiple ownership structures involving business entities, partnerships, or unusual co-ownership arrangements add legal complexity that benefits from professional guidance.

Recent life events including divorce, death of co-owner, or significant financial changes can create complications requiring professional attention.

Complex family situations involving blended families, estranged relatives, or potential inheritance disputes benefit from professional drafting and guidance.

Time pressure situations where you need immediate completion may justify professional assistance even for otherwise simple transfers.

Mortgage complications including specialized loans, pending modifications, or lender concerns may require professional navigation.

These red flags don't automatically disqualify DIY attempts, but they should make you more cautious about proceeding without professional consultation.

State Complexity Assessment Checklist

Before committing to DIY, honestly evaluate your situation using this comprehensive checklist:

Location Assessment:

- Which tier does your state fall into?
- Are you in a county with additional requirements?
- Do local municipalities impose extra fees or forms?
- Are online resources readily available for your jurisdiction?

Situation Complexity:

- Do you own the property individually or jointly?
- Is there an existing mortgage?
- Are there any title issues or liens?
- Is this your primary residence or investment property?
- Do you have a properly drafted living trust?

Personal Capability:

- Do you have 8-15 hours available over 3-6 weeks?
- Are you comfortable with detailed paperwork and government forms?
- Can you work during business hours when offices are open?
- Do you have a reliable backup plan if problems arise?

Risk Tolerance:

- Can you handle potential delays or complications?
- Are you comfortable taking responsibility for accuracy and compliance?
- Do you have financial cushion for unexpected fees or professional help?
- Would errors or problems create significant stress for you?

Cost-Benefit Analysis:

- What would professional assistance cost in your area?
- How much can you realistically save with DIY?
- Does the potential savings justify the time and effort required?
- Are there non-financial benefits (learning, control) that matter to you?

Honest answers to these questions provide a realistic assessment of your DIY prospects.

Making Your State-Specific Plan

Once you understand your state's tier classification and your personal situation, you can develop a realistic action plan tailored to your specific circumstances.

For Tier 1 state residents with straightforward situations, DIY success is highly likely. Focus on understanding your specific county's requirements, gathering necessary documents, and allowing adequate time for careful completion. Professional consultation probably isn't necessary unless you encounter unexpected complications.

For Tier 2 state residents, success depends more heavily on your personal capabilities and situation complexity. Consider starting with thorough research of your state's specific requirements, possibly including a brief consultation with a local attorney to understand the process and identify potential pitfalls. Many Tier 2 situations benefit from DIY preparation with professional review before filing.

For Tier 3 state residents, carefully weigh the complexity against potential savings. Consider hybrid approaches like professional document preparation with your own filing, or complete DIY with professional review before submission. Pure DIY in Tier 3 states works best for people with strong administrative skills, plenty of time, and high comfort with complex processes.

Resources for State-Specific Research

Each state provides official resources for property transfer requirements, though the quality and accessibility vary significantly. Start with these reliable sources:

County Recorder/Clerk websites often provide the most practical, up-to-date information about local requirements, fees, and procedures. Many offer form templates and step-by-step instructions.

State revenue department websites explain transfer tax requirements, exemptions, and necessary forms. Even if you qualify for exemptions, understanding the underlying tax structure helps ensure proper compliance.

State bar association websites sometimes offer consumer resources explaining property transfer basics and providing attorney referral services for complex situations.

Real estate professional associations in your area may provide consumer education materials about transfer requirements and common problems.

Title company websites serving your area often include helpful resources about local transfer requirements, since they handle these transactions professionally.

The key is using multiple sources to verify information and understand both state and local requirements that may apply to your situation.

Success Stories Across the Tiers

Real examples from each tier illustrate how location affects DIY experiences:

Jennifer Walsh in Austin, Texas (Tier 1) completed her transfer in 10 days for $32. She prepared a simple quitclaim deed using a template from the Travis County Clerk's website, had it notarized at her bank, and mailed it to the courthouse with a check. Two weeks later, she received her recorded deed in the mail. "It was almost disappointingly easy," she laughed.

Robert Kim in Columbus, Ohio (Tier 2) needed three weeks and $127 to complete his transfer. Beyond the basic deed, he completed Ohio's Property Transfer Declaration and calculated transfer tax exemptions. He made two trips to the Franklin County Recorder's office - once to ask questions and once to file documents. The extra complexity was manageable with careful preparation.

Maria Santos in Los Angeles County, California (Tier 3) spent six weeks and $340 completing her DIY transfer. She needed to prepare the deed, complete California's complex PCOR form, calculate documentary transfer taxes, and coordinate with both the county recorder and assessor's offices. Despite the complexity, she saved over $3,000 compared to attorney fees. "It was challenging, but doable if you're patient and detail-oriented," she reported.

These examples show that DIY success is possible across all tiers, but the required investment of time and attention increases significantly as complexity rises.

Key Takeaways from State Complexity Analysis

The three-tier state system provides a framework for assessing DIY feasibility based on your location, with Tier 1 states offering the highest success probability and Tier 3 states requiring the most preparation and attention to detail. Your state's classification affects time investment, cost expectations, and the likelihood of needing professional assistance.

Documentary transfer tax requirements vary significantly by state, with many locations requiring extensive documentation even for exempt transfers. Understanding these requirements early in your planning prevents costly errors and delays during the transfer process.

Red flags indicating situations beyond appropriate DIY complexity can arise regardless of state tier, making honest assessment of your specific circumstances essential for success. The complexity assessment checklist helps evaluate both location-based and situation-specific factors affecting your DIY prospects.

State-specific research using reliable official sources provides the detailed information needed for successful completion, though the quality and accessibility of these resources varies significantly by location.

Success stories from all three tiers demonstrate that DIY completion is possible across different complexity levels, but time investment and attention requirements increase substantially as state complexity rises.

The next chapter provides the detailed preparation framework needed before beginning any trust transfer, regardless of your state's complexity level.

Chapter 4: Pre-Transfer Preparation Checklist

David Chen learned the hard way that rushing into a trust transfer without proper preparation creates far more problems than it solves. Eager to complete the process quickly, David printed a generic quitclaim deed from the internet, filled it out based on his understanding of the requirements, and recorded it with the county.

Three months later, David discovered his mistakes. The deed contained his property's legal description from 15 years ago, before a boundary line adjustment. His mortgage company received no notification and started asking uncomfortable questions about unauthorized title changes. His homeowner's insurance policy didn't reflect trust ownership, potentially creating coverage gaps.

"I spent more time fixing my mistakes than I would have spent doing it right the first time," David reflected. After working with an attorney to correct the problems, David's total cost reached $2,400 - more than many people pay for complete professional handling from the start.

David's experience illustrates why preparation represents the most crucial phase of any DIY trust transfer. The time you invest upfront gathering documents, verifying information, and understanding requirements determines whether your transfer proceeds smoothly or creates expensive complications.

Document Collection List

Successful trust transfers require multiple documents, some obvious and others easily overlooked. Starting with a complete collection prevents delays and ensures accuracy throughout the process.

Essential trust documents form the foundation of your transfer:

Your **original living trust document** (or a certified copy) provides the legal authority for the transfer and contains the exact trust name and date you'll need for the deed. Trust names must appear exactly as written in the original document - even minor variations can create title problems.

Trust amendments or restatements, if any exist, may affect the trust name, trustee designations, or transfer authority. Outdated information from superseded documents causes confusion and potential legal problems.

Pour-over will and other estate planning documents help confirm the transfer fits your overall estate plan and doesn't inadvertently contradict other arrangements.

Current property deed represents the most critical document in your collection. This deed, recorded when you purchased your property or last transferred it, contains the exact legal description, ownership structure, and title information you'll need for accurate transfer preparation.

Locating your current deed can challenge homeowners who haven't seen it since closing. Check these sources:

- Your closing documents from purchase (look for a recorded deed with county stamps)
- Title company or attorney files from your purchase
- County recorder/clerk online records (most counties now provide online access)
- Title insurance company that handled your purchase
- Your mortgage lender's files

Property tax records provide backup information about legal descriptions and ownership details, plus confirm your property's assessed value and tax status. Annual tax statements typically include abbreviated legal descriptions that can verify deed accuracy.

Survey and title documents from your purchase help confirm property boundaries, easements, and title conditions that might affect the transfer. While you probably won't need these for simple transfers, having them available helps resolve questions that might arise.

Mortgage-related documents become essential if you have existing financing:

- Original promissory note and deed of trust/mortgage
- Current account statements showing lender contact information
- Loan modification agreements, if any
- Home equity line of credit documents
- Any correspondence about previous ownership changes

Insurance policies require updating after transfer, so gather:

- Current homeowner's insurance policy and declarations pages
- Umbrella liability policies that might cover the property
- Contact information for your insurance agent or company

HOA documents, if applicable, may contain restrictions on ownership transfers or require notification of ownership changes. Review your CC&Rs and HOA bylaws for any relevant provisions.

Property Deed Location and Review

Your current property deed contains information essential for accurate transfer preparation. Understanding how to read and interpret this document prevents costly errors.

Locate your recorded deed by searching county records using your name and property address. Online record systems make this easier than ever, though some counties still require in-person searches. You need the most recent deed showing how you currently hold title.

Verify the grantees (that's you) are listed exactly as you intend to sign the new deed. Names must match precisely, including middle initials, suffixes, and designations. "John Smith" and "John A. Smith" are different for legal purposes.

Check the legal description carefully. This technical description of your property's boundaries and location must transfer exactly to your new deed. Even small errors can create title problems or delay recording.

Legal descriptions typically use one of three formats:

- **Metes and bounds:** Precise boundary measurements and directions
- **Lot and block:** Reference to recorded subdivision plats
- **Government survey:** Township, range, and section references

Don't attempt to abbreviate or "simplify" legal descriptions. Copy them word-for-word, including seemingly redundant phrases and technical terminology.

Examine the current vesting (how you hold title now) to understand your ownership structure. Common forms include:

- **Sole ownership:** "John Smith, a single man"
- **Joint tenancy:** "John Smith and Mary Smith, husband and wife, as joint tenants"
- **Tenancy in common:** "John Smith and Mary Smith as tenants in common"
- **Community property:** "John Smith and Mary Smith, husband and wife, as community property"

Your current vesting affects how you transfer to the trust and what new vesting language you'll use.

Note any exceptions or restrictions mentioned in the deed, such as easements, covenants, or liens. These typically transfer with the property and should be referenced in your new deed.

Title Verification Process

Clean title - meaning clear ownership without problematic liens or claims - is essential for successful trust transfers. Title problems must be resolved before attempting any transfer.

Order a current title report from a title company if you want professional verification of your title status. While not required for simple transfers, title reports reveal potential problems you might not discover otherwise. Costs typically range from $200-$400, but peace of mind may justify the expense.

Review your title insurance policy from your purchase. This policy, which you paid for at closing, protects against certain title defects and provides information about known issues affecting your property.

Search for liens and judgments that might affect your property. Common problems include:

- Unpaid property taxes or assessments
- Contractor liens from recent work
- Homeowner association liens
- IRS or state tax liens
- Civil judgment liens
- Mortgage liens not properly released

Check for recent changes in ownership, liens, or legal description since your purchase. Boundary line adjustments, easement grants, or lien releases may have changed your title situation.

Verify ownership percentages if you own property with others. Joint tenancy typically assumes equal ownership, but tenancy in common can involve unequal shares that affect transfer requirements.

Confirm spouse rights in community property states or states with dower/curtesy interests. Some states require spousal consent for property transfers, even to revocable trusts.

Most title problems are resolvable, but they require attention before transfer. Simple issues like unreleased mortgage liens may need only paperwork and phone calls. Complex problems involving boundary disputes or ownership claims require professional assistance.

Mortgage Lender Notification Requirements

Existing mortgages add complexity to trust transfers, even though federal law generally protects your right to make such transfers. Proper lender notification helps prevent problems and maintains good relationships.

Review your mortgage documents for specific provisions about ownership changes. Look for:

- Due-on-sale clauses (present in most mortgages)
- Transfer restrictions or notification requirements
- Specific language about trust transfers
- Lender contact information for ownership changes

Understand Garn-St. Germain Act protection for trust transfers. This federal law prohibits lenders from calling loans due solely because you transfer your primary residence to your own revocable living trust. The protection applies when:

- The property is your primary residence (not investment property)
- You remain the trust beneficiary
- The trust is revocable
- You continue making payments as agreed

Prepare notification letter to your mortgage company explaining the transfer. Include:

- Your loan number and property address
- Explanation that you're transferring to your own revocable living trust
- Reference to Garn-St. Germain Act protection

- Request for any specific forms or procedures they require
- Your contact information for questions

Send notification before recording your deed if possible. Some lenders prefer advance notice, and early communication helps resolve any concerns or requirements they might have.

Expect various lender responses to your notification:

- Many lenders acknowledge the notice and request no further action
- Some require specific forms or additional documentation
- A few may request trust certificates or legal opinions
- Occasional lenders mistakenly claim you need their permission (you don't)

Document all communications with your lender. Keep copies of letters, emails, and records of phone conversations. This documentation helps resolve disputes and provides evidence of proper notification.

Consider refinancing implications if you're planning to refinance soon. Some lenders prefer properties in individual ownership for new loan underwriting, though most will work with trust-owned properties.

Insurance Company Coordination

Homeowner's insurance policies typically continue coverage for trust-owned properties, but notification and possible policy updates ensure uninterrupted protection.

Contact your insurance agent before completing the transfer. Explain that you're transferring your home to your own revocable living trust and ask about their requirements for continued coverage.

Expect standard procedures from most insurance companies:

- Simple notification form acknowledging the ownership change
- Possible addition of the trust as an "additional insured" party
- Updated declarations page reflecting trust ownership
- Confirmation that coverage terms remain unchanged

Understand potential complications with some insurers:

- Occasional requirement for new underwriting (rare for trust transfers)
- Questions about trustee liability coverage
- Requests for trust certificates or documentation
- Possible premium adjustments (usually minimal)

Update policy information to reflect trust ownership once the transfer is complete. Ensure your policy shows:

- Trust as property owner
- Your continued status as insured party
- Unchanged coverage limits and deductibles
- Updated contact information if needed

Consider umbrella liability coverage if you carry broader liability policies. These policies may also require notification of trust ownership changes.

Review coverage adequacy while you're updating policies. Trust transfers provide good opportunities to reassess coverage limits and ensure adequate protection.

Critical Timeline Considerations

Timing matters significantly in trust transfers. Rushing creates errors, while excessive delays can allow circumstances to change in ways that complicate the process.

Plan for 4-6 weeks minimum for simple transfers in Tier 1 states. More complex situations or challenging states may require 8-12 weeks. This timeline includes:

- Document gathering and preparation: 1-2 weeks
- Deed preparation and review: 1-2 weeks
- Recording and processing: 1-2 weeks
- Follow-up notifications and updates: 1-2 weeks

Consider seasonal factors that might affect timing:

- County offices may have reduced hours during holidays
- Summer vacation schedules can slow processing
- End-of-year rush periods may create delays
- Weather conditions might affect mail delivery or office access

Coordinate with life events that could complicate matters:

- Pending home sales should be completed before trust transfers
- Refinancing plans may require coordination with transfer timing
- Major renovations involving permits might benefit from delayed transfers
- Tax planning considerations may affect optimal timing

Plan for contingencies including potential delays or complications:

- Document errors requiring correction and re-recording
- Questions from recorder offices requiring additional information
- Lender concerns needing resolution
- Title problems discovered during the process

Avoid rush situations that increase error risks. Last-minute estate planning or urgent family situations may justify professional assistance rather than DIY approaches under time pressure.

Co-Ownership Issues Identification

Properties owned by multiple people present additional complexity that requires careful consideration before attempting trust transfers.

Married couples generally face straightforward transfers, especially in community property states. However, consider:

- Whether both spouses should be trustees
- How beneficiary designations should be structured
- State-specific spousal consent requirements
- Differences between joint tenancy and community property

Unmarried co-owners face more complex decisions:

- Whether all owners transfer to one trust or separate trusts
- How to handle different ownership percentages
- What happens if co-owners disagree about the transfer
- Whether existing tenancy in common arrangements should change

Family partnerships or LLCs owning property require professional guidance for trust transfers. These entity ownership structures create legal and tax complexities beyond DIY scope.

Recent inheritance situations may involve co-ownership among siblings or other relatives who need to coordinate transfer decisions and possibly resolve disagreements about property management.

Divorce-related ownership issues require careful attention to court orders, separation agreements, and spouse consent requirements before any transfer attempts.

Investment partners sharing ownership for business purposes should consult professionals about trust transfer implications for partnership agreements and tax consequences.

Most co-ownership situations remain manageable for DIY transfers, but they require additional planning and sometimes coordination among multiple parties with different interests and priorities.

Pre-Transfer Document Checklist

Before proceeding with deed preparation, verify you have collected and reviewed all necessary documents:

Trust Documents:

- ✓ Original living trust document or certified copy
- ✓ Any amendments or restatements
- ✓ Pour-over will and related estate planning documents

Property Documents:

- ✓ Current recorded deed showing your ownership
- ✓ Recent property tax statements
- ✓ Survey or title documents from purchase (if available)
- ✓ HOA documents with transfer restrictions (if applicable)

Mortgage Documents:

- ✓ Original loan documents
- ✓ Current mortgage statements with lender contact information
- ✓ Home equity line documents (if applicable)
- ✓ Previous correspondence about ownership changes

Insurance Information:

- ✓ Current homeowner's insurance policy
- ✓ Umbrella liability policies affecting the property
- ✓ Insurance agent/company contact information

Verification Complete:

- ✓ Legal description verified against current deed

- ✓ Names and ownership structure confirmed
- ✓ Title problems identified and resolved
- ✓ Lender notification requirements understood
- ✓ Insurance update procedures confirmed
- ✓ Timeline planned with adequate cushion for delays

This comprehensive preparation prevents most problems that derail DIY trust transfers. The time invested upfront pays dividends in smoother processing and reduced stress throughout the transfer process.

Preparation Success Stories

Contrast David Chen's rushed approach from our opening story with Sarah Williams' methodical preparation in Denver. Sarah spent three weeks gathering documents, verifying information, and understanding Colorado's requirements before preparing her deed.

Sarah discovered her property deed contained an error - her middle initial was wrong, creating a technical name discrepancy. She corrected this with a simple affidavit before proceeding with the trust transfer. Her mortgage company required a specific notification form, which she obtained and completed in advance. Her insurance agent needed only a phone call to confirm coverage would continue seamlessly.

Sarah's trust transfer proceeded without problems. Total time from start to finish: five weeks. Total cost: $65. Most importantly, she completed the process with confidence, knowing she'd addressed all requirements properly.

"The preparation was actually the hardest part," Sarah reflected. "Once I had everything organized and understood what I was doing, the actual transfer was straightforward."

Key Takeaways from Pre-Transfer Preparation

Thorough document collection forms the foundation of successful DIY trust transfers, with particular attention to locating and understanding your current property deed's exact legal description and ownership structure. Title verification helps identify and resolve potential problems before they complicate the transfer process.

Mortgage lender notification, while not always legally required, maintains good relationships and prevents problems, with federal Garn-St. Germain Act protection generally safeguarding your right to transfer primary residences to revocable trusts. Insurance company coordination ensures uninterrupted coverage and proper policy updates reflecting trust ownership.

Critical timeline considerations require planning 4-6 weeks minimum for simple transfers, with additional time needed for complex situations or challenging state requirements. Co-ownership situations add complexity that requires careful coordination and sometimes professional guidance.

The comprehensive preparation checklist helps ensure all necessary documents are gathered and verified before beginning deed preparation, preventing most problems that can derail DIY transfers.

Proper preparation, while time-consuming upfront, creates the foundation for smooth, successful trust transfers and prevents costly errors that rushed approaches often generate.

The next chapter begins the actual transfer process with detailed guidance on creating or working with your existing living trust.

Chapter 5: Creating Your Trust

Rebecca Martinez sat in her kitchen staring at a pile of trust documents her attorney had prepared three years earlier. She'd paid $2,800 for what looked like a thick stack of legal papers she barely understood, and now she needed to transfer her Phoenix home into this mysterious entity called "The Martinez Family Trust."

The problem? Rebecca couldn't figure out what she actually owned. The trust document was 47 pages of dense legal language that might as well have been written in ancient Greek. She knew she was supposed to be the trustee, but what did that really mean? Her daughter Lisa was listed as a beneficiary, but so was her son Mark, who hadn't spoken to her in two years after a family argument.

"I feel like I bought a car without knowing how to drive," Rebecca confided to her neighbor. That conversation led Rebecca to spend the next month truly understanding what she'd created three years earlier. The knowledge transformed her from a confused trust owner into someone who could confidently manage her estate planning affairs.

Rebecca's story reflects a common challenge: many homeowners have trusts but don't really understand what they own or how these legal tools work. If you're in Rebecca's position - owning a trust but feeling confused about it - this chapter will help you understand what you have and how to use it effectively. If you don't have a trust yet but know you need one, we'll help you understand the basics and recognize when you need professional help.

Trust Creation Overview

Creating a living trust involves establishing a legal relationship between you (the grantor), your chosen trustees, and your designated beneficiaries. Think of it as creating a legal container that will hold your assets according to your specific instructions.

The trust document itself serves as the instruction manual for this container. It explains who can put things in, who manages what's inside, and who gets everything when you're gone. But unlike a will, which only works after you die, your trust starts working immediately and continues operating through your lifetime and beyond.

Most people create revocable living trusts because they offer maximum flexibility during your lifetime while providing significant benefits after death. "Revocable" means you can change your mind about anything - trustees, beneficiaries, terms, or even the trust's existence. You retain complete control over everything you put into the trust.

The basic structure involves several key components that work together to create a comprehensive estate planning tool. Your trust document establishes the rules, names the players, and provides detailed instructions for managing and distributing your assets. It also includes provisions for what happens if you become incapacitated and can't manage your affairs.

Modern trust documents typically run 25-50 pages because they need to address numerous scenarios and possibilities. They include standard legal language that has been tested in courts over decades, plus specific provisions tailored to your family situation and goals. While the length can seem overwhelming, most of the content deals with unusual situations you'll probably never encounter.

Professional vs. DIY Trust Creation

Here's the reality about trust creation: most people benefit from professional assistance with the initial drafting. Unlike property transfers, which involve filling out standardized forms, trust creation requires customizing legal language to your specific situation, family dynamics, and goals.

Professional trust drafting typically costs $1,500-$4,000 for straightforward family situations. This investment usually includes:

- Initial consultation to understand your goals and family situation
- Custom document drafting tailored to your state's laws
- Review and revision of draft documents
- Final document preparation and execution
- Basic instructions for trust funding and management

DIY trust creation using online services or software costs $100-$500 but involves significant limitations and risks. While these tools have improved dramatically in recent years, they can't replicate the judgment and customization that experienced attorneys provide.

Consider professional drafting if you have:

- Significant assets requiring tax planning
- Complex family situations (blended families, estranged relatives, special needs children)
- Business ownership or unusual assets
- Concerns about family disputes or will contests
- Questions about your state's specific trust laws

DIY approaches might work for people with:

- Simple family structures (married couples with adult children)
- Straightforward asset portfolios (house, bank accounts, investments)
- Limited budgets for professional services
- Strong confidence in following detailed instructions

The key distinction is that trust creation sets the foundation for decades of asset management and family inheritance. Errors in property transfers are usually fixable with additional paperwork. Errors in trust documents can create permanent problems affecting your family for generations.

Selecting Trustees and Successors

Trustee selection represents one of your most important trust decisions. You're choosing the person who will manage potentially hundreds of thousands of dollars and make decisions affecting your family's financial future.

Initial trustees for most people are simple choices: you name yourself (and your spouse, if married) as the initial trustees. This arrangement gives you complete control over trust assets during your lifetime while establishing the legal structure for future management.

Some people worry about serving as their own trustee, thinking it creates conflicts of interest. Actually, the opposite is true for revocable trusts. Since you're also the primary beneficiary, managing trust assets in your best interests naturally serves the trust's purposes. You're not managing someone else's money - you're managing your own money using a trust structure.

Co-trustees can provide backup management and shared decision-making, but they also complicate routine transactions. Banks, investment companies, and real estate professionals sometimes require all trustees to sign documents, making simple tasks more cumbersome. Most people start with individual trustees and add co-trustees only if specific circumstances require shared management.

Successor trustee selection requires much more careful thought. This person steps in when you die or become unable to manage the trust yourself. They'll handle everything from paying your final bills to distributing inheritance to your beneficiaries.

Look for successor trustees who possess several key qualities:

Trustworthiness tops the list because successor trustees gain access to all your assets with minimal oversight. Choose someone whose integrity you trust completely, even under pressure or family conflict.

Financial competence doesn't require professional expertise, but your successor should understand basic money management, record-keeping, and investment principles. They'll be managing potentially substantial assets for months or years.

Organizational skills are essential because successor trustees must handle detailed paperwork, tax returns, legal requirements, and beneficiary communications. Disorganized people often create chaos during already-difficult family situations.

Availability and longevity matter because successor trustees need time to handle trust administration properly. Choose someone young enough to outlive you but mature enough to handle the responsibility. Geographic proximity helps with local asset management like real estate.

Family dynamics awareness helps successor trustees navigate relationships among beneficiaries, especially if tensions exist between family members. Some families benefit from neutral successor trustees who aren't involved in family conflicts.

Common successor trustee choices include:

- Adult children, typically the oldest or most financially responsible
- Siblings or other family members who know your wishes
- Trusted friends who understand your values and family situation
- Professional trustees like bank trust departments or trust companies

Professional trustees offer expertise and objectivity but charge ongoing fees (typically 1-2% of trust assets annually) that can significantly impact smaller estates. They make sense for large trusts, families with significant conflict, or situations requiring specialized expertise.

Many people name multiple successor trustees in order of preference, creating backups if their first choice becomes unavailable. Others name co-successor trustees to share responsibility, though this approach requires people who work well together.

Beneficiary Designation Strategies

Beneficiary planning determines who inherits your assets and under what conditions. Simple family situations allow straightforward designations, but complex families require more careful planning.

Primary beneficiaries receive the main benefits from your trust. Common approaches include:

Spouse-first plans leave everything to your surviving spouse, with children inheriting only after both parents die. This approach works well for stable marriages with shared values about inheritance. It provides maximum flexibility for the surviving spouse while ensuring children eventually inherit.

Direct-to-children plans distribute assets immediately to children when you die, bypassing the surviving spouse. This approach sometimes makes sense in second marriages where you want to protect inheritance for children from your first marriage. However, it can create financial hardship for surviving spouses who expected to inherit.

Split arrangements give some assets to your spouse and others to children immediately. For example, you might leave your house to your spouse but split investment accounts between your spouse and children. This approach provides immediate inheritance to children while supporting your spouse.

Age-based distributions control when beneficiaries actually receive their inheritance. Instead of giving everything to your 25-year-old son immediately, you might distribute one-third at age 25, one-third at 30, and the remainder at 35. This approach protects young beneficiaries from potentially poor financial decisions.

Contingent beneficiaries inherit if your primary beneficiaries die before you. Common contingent arrangements include:

- Children as contingent beneficiaries if your spouse predeceases you
- Grandchildren as contingents if your children predecease you
- Siblings or other relatives as final contingents
- Charitable organizations as ultimate beneficiaries

Special considerations for beneficiary planning include:

Minor children can't inherit property directly, so trusts must include provisions for managing their inheritance until they reach adulthood. You'll need to name guardians for minor children and trustees to manage their money.

Adult children with problems - addiction, financial irresponsibility, legal troubles - may benefit from restricted inheritance arrangements that provide support without enabling destructive behavior.

Children with disabilities often need special needs trust provisions that preserve government benefits while providing supplemental support. These arrangements require professional drafting to avoid disqualifying beneficiaries from essential programs.

Estranged family members present difficult decisions about inclusion or exclusion from inheritance. Completely disinheriting close relatives sometimes invites legal challenges, but including people you don't trust can create other problems.

Pour-Over Will Importance

Your trust works in partnership with a specialized will called a "pour-over will" that catches any assets you forgot to transfer to your trust during your lifetime. This backup document ensures your estate plan works completely, even if your trust funding wasn't perfect.

Pour-over wills contain several essential provisions that protect your estate plan's integrity:

Asset transfer provisions direct your executor to transfer any individually-owned assets into your trust after death. If you forgot to transfer your car, bank account, or other property to your trust, the pour-over will fixes this oversight by moving those assets into your trust for distribution according to trust terms.

Guardian nominations for minor children appear in your will, not your trust. Courts look to wills for guardian preferences, making this one of the few essential functions that trusts can't handle directly.

Personal effects distribution often works better through will provisions than trust language. Your will might say "I leave all my personal effects to my spouse" while your trust handles major financial assets.

Executor appointment names the person responsible for handling probate proceedings, if any become necessary. Often this person is the same as your successor trustee, but they serve different roles with different responsibilities.

Final instructions about funeral arrangements, organ donation, or other personal matters traditionally appear in wills, though these preferences can be expressed in separate documents or letters to your family.

Pour-over wills still require probate if they actually receive significant assets, but they provide essential backup protection for your estate plan. Many people never use their pour-over will because they successfully transfer all major assets to their trust during lifetime. But having this backup protection provides peace of mind and catches inevitable oversights.

Complex Family Situations Requiring Professional Help

Certain family situations push trust planning beyond DIY appropriateness, regardless of your confidence or cost concerns. These situations involve legal complexity, family dynamics, or financial considerations that benefit significantly from professional guidance.

Blended families with children from previous relationships often create competing inheritance interests that require careful legal planning. Second marriages raise questions about supporting the new spouse versus protecting inheritance for children from the first marriage. Professional guidance helps balance these competing interests while minimizing family conflict.

Special needs family members require specialized trust provisions that preserve government benefits while providing supplemental support. Medicaid, SSI, and other programs have strict asset limits that can be triggered by poorly-planned inheritance. Special needs trusts require professional drafting to avoid disqualifying beneficiaries from essential programs.

Significant wealth involving estate tax planning, generation-skipping transfers, or charitable giving arrangements requires professional expertise that goes far beyond basic trust creation. These situations involve ongoing tax obligations and complex legal requirements that DIY approaches can't handle safely.

Business ownership complicates trust planning because business assets require specialized handling, valuation considerations, and potential tax elections. Professional guidance helps integrate business succession planning with family estate planning.

Family conflicts involving likely inheritance disputes, estranged relatives, or financial disagreements benefit from professional drafting that anticipates potential legal challenges. Attorneys can include specific provisions that reduce contest risks and protect your intended distributions.

Asset protection concerns involving potential creditor claims, lawsuit risks, or professional liability require specialized trust structures that go beyond basic revocable trust planning. These situations often benefit from irrevocable trust strategies that provide enhanced protection.

Geographic complications involving property in multiple states, foreign assets, or beneficiaries living abroad require coordination of different legal jurisdictions and tax systems.

If your situation involves multiple complicating factors, the cost of professional trust creation often proves wise investment compared to the potential costs of fixing problems later. Attorneys can also provide limited assistance for specific issues while letting you handle routine aspects yourself.

Trust Funding Beyond Real Estate

Creating your trust document is only the first step - you must also transfer assets into the trust to make it functional. This process, called "funding the trust," typically involves retitling various assets from individual ownership to trust ownership.

Bank accounts and CDs usually transfer easily using forms provided by financial institutions. You'll need to provide a copy of your trust document (or trust certificate) and complete change of ownership paperwork. Most banks handle trust accounts routinely and can explain their specific procedures.

Investment accounts including brokerage accounts, mutual funds, and retirement accounts require different approaches. Taxable investment accounts typically transfer to trust ownership easily. Retirement accounts (401k, IRA) usually should NOT be transferred to trusts during your lifetime because this creates immediate tax consequences. Instead, name your trust as beneficiary of retirement accounts.

Life insurance policies should typically name your trust as beneficiary rather than transferring ownership to the trust. This approach provides death benefit proceeds to your trust for distribution according to trust terms while avoiding potential tax complications from trust ownership of the policies.

Vehicles and personal property can transfer to trust ownership, but many people leave these assets in individual ownership because they're relatively low-value and easy to handle through pour-over will provisions.

Business interests including partnerships, LLC memberships, and corporate stock require careful handling because business agreements may restrict transfers or require approval from other owners.

The key principle is that trust funding should include your major assets - particularly those that would otherwise require probate. Your house, significant bank accounts, and investment portfolios benefit most from trust ownership. Smaller assets can often remain in individual ownership for convenience.

Understanding What You Already Have

If you're like Rebecca from our opening story - owning a trust but confused about its contents - spend time reviewing your documents with fresh perspective. Most trust documents include several standard sections you can understand without legal training.

Article I typically establishes the trust name, initial parties (grantor, trustee, beneficiaries), and basic trust purposes. This section tells you what you created and who's involved.

Article II usually covers your powers as initial trustee, including your authority to buy, sell, invest, and manage trust assets. This section confirms that you retain complete control during your lifetime.

Article III often addresses what happens during your lifetime if you become incapacitated. It explains how successor trustees take over and what powers they have to manage your affairs.

Article IV typically covers distribution terms after your death - who gets what, when, and under what conditions. This section explains your inheritance plan.

Article V usually includes trustee powers and responsibilities, administrative provisions, and other operational details that help trustees manage the trust effectively.

Don't worry if some language seems confusing - trust documents use technical terminology that lawyers understand but doesn't affect your day-to-day relationship with your trust. Focus on understanding the big picture: who are your trustees and beneficiaries, what are your main goals, and how does the trust help achieve those goals.

Working With Your Existing Trust

Once you understand your trust's basic structure, you can work with it confidently to achieve your estate planning goals. Most trust management during your lifetime involves routine activities that don't require legal expertise.

Regular review of your trust terms helps ensure they still match your current situation and goals. Family circumstances change, relationships evolve, and financial situations shift over time. Annual reviews help you identify when trust amendments might be beneficial.

Asset management within your trust operates exactly like individual asset management. You buy, sell, invest, and spend according to your judgment and preferences. The trust structure doesn't limit your financial decision-making during your lifetime.

Record keeping for trust assets doesn't require separate accounting or complex procedures. For tax purposes, revocable trusts are transparent - you report all income and expenses on your individual tax return. However, maintaining good records helps your successor trustee and provides documentation if questions arise.

Communication with family about trust provisions helps prevent confusion and conflict later. Your successor trustee and beneficiaries should understand their roles and know where to find necessary documents when needed.

Professional assistance for specific questions or complex situations can supplement your DIY approach without requiring comprehensive professional management. Many attorneys provide limited consulting services for trust owners who want occasional guidance while handling routine matters themselves.

The goal is confident, informed trust ownership that supports your estate planning objectives while fitting comfortably into your daily financial management.

Key Takeaways from Trust Creation and Management

Trust creation typically benefits from professional guidance because it establishes the foundation for decades of asset management and family inheritance, with errors in trust documents potentially creating permanent problems that simple property transfer mistakes don't present. DIY trust creation may work for simple family situations with straightforward assets, but complex families or significant wealth usually justify professional investment.

Trustee selection involves naming yourself as initial trustee for maximum control, while choosing successor trustees requires careful evaluation of trustworthiness, financial competence, organizational skills, and family dynamics awareness. Professional trustees offer expertise but charge ongoing fees that impact smaller estates.

Beneficiary designation strategies range from simple spouse-first or direct-to-children approaches to complex age-based distributions and special needs arrangements. Pour-over wills provide essential backup protection by transferring forgotten assets into your trust and handling matters like guardian nominations that trusts can't address directly.

Complex family situations involving blended families, special needs members, significant wealth, business ownership, or family conflicts typically require professional assistance that goes beyond basic trust creation capabilities.

Trust funding extends beyond real estate to include bank accounts, investment portfolios, and life insurance beneficiary designations, while retirement accounts typically should name trusts as beneficiaries rather than transferring ownership during lifetime.

Understanding existing trust documents focuses on identifying key parties, distribution terms, and operational provisions rather than comprehending every technical detail, with regular review and good communication helping ensure your trust continues serving your evolving needs effectively.

The next chapter addresses the foundation of successful property transfers through comprehensive understanding of property deeds and their essential components.

Chapter 6: Property Deeds - Your Transfer Foundation

Tom Bradley thought he understood property ownership until he tried to read his deed. After purchasing his Denver home five years earlier, Tom had filed away his closing documents without much thought. Now, preparing to transfer the property to his living trust, Tom pulled out what he thought was his deed and stared at a document that might as well have been written in code.

"Legal description," "habendum clause," "appurtenant rights" - the terminology was completely foreign. Tom's deed referenced "Lot 12, Block 3, Mountain View Subdivision" but also included a paragraph of metes and bounds descriptions with compass headings and distances. Was his property 0.33 acres or 0.34 acres? The deed seemed to say both.

After two frustrating hours, Tom called his real estate agent from the original purchase. "Most people never really read their deeds," she explained. "But once you understand the basic structure, they make perfect sense. Let me walk you through yours."

That conversation transformed Tom's confusion into confidence. Within an hour, he understood exactly what he owned, how his ownership was structured, and what information he'd need for his trust transfer. More importantly, he learned to spot the common errors that derail many DIY property transfers.

Tom's experience reflects a fundamental challenge in property transfers: deeds contain essential information presented in technical legal language that intimidates many homeowners. Understanding your deed isn't optional for successful trust transfers - it's the foundation that determines whether your transfer succeeds or fails.

Deed Anatomy and Components

Property deeds follow standardized formats that have been refined over centuries of real estate practice. While the specific layout and terminology vary by state, all deeds contain certain essential elements that establish legal property transfers.

The caption or heading identifies the document type (warranty deed, quitclaim deed, grant deed), the state and county where the property is located, and sometimes the date of execution. This section immediately tells you what kind of deed you're reading and where it applies.

The parties section identifies the grantor (person transferring the property) and the grantee (person receiving the property). Names must appear exactly as they appear on the previous deed in the chain of title. Even small variations in spelling or middle initials can create title problems that require correction later.

The granting clause contains the legal language that actually transfers the property. Traditional phrases like "grant, bargain, sell and convey" or "quitclaim and release" have specific legal meanings that courts have interpreted for decades. Modern deeds often use simpler language like "conveys and warrants" or "grants," but the legal effect remains the same.

The consideration statement indicates what the grantee paid for the property. While actual sale prices often aren't disclosed (many deeds list consideration as "ten dollars and other valuable consideration"), this section must include some statement of consideration to make the transfer legally valid.

The legal description provides the precise boundaries and location of the property being transferred. This section requires absolute accuracy because even small errors can invalidate the transfer or create title disputes years later.

The **habendum clause**, beginning with "To Have and to Hold," defines the type and duration of ownership being transferred. Most residential deeds transfer "fee simple absolute" ownership - complete ownership with no restrictions or time limitations.

Reservations and exceptions list any rights being kept by the grantor or any limitations on the ownership being transferred. Common examples include mineral rights reservations, utility easements, or restrictions from previous deeds.

The warranty provisions (in warranty deeds) contain the grantor's promises about title quality and their obligation to defend the grantee against title challenges. These warranties provide legal protection for the new owner.

The signature block includes spaces for the grantor's signature, notary acknowledgment, and sometimes witness signatures depending on state requirements. Proper execution of this section is essential for recording the deed.

Recording information gets added by the county recorder's office, including recording date, document number, and filing information that becomes part of the permanent public record.

Understanding these components helps you read any deed confidently and ensures you include all necessary elements when preparing your trust transfer deed.

Quitclaim vs. Grant vs. Warranty Deeds

Different deed types provide different levels of protection and serve different purposes in property transfers. Choosing the appropriate deed type for your trust transfer affects both the legal protection you provide and the requirements you must meet.

Quitclaim deeds offer the least protection but maximum simplicity. The grantor essentially says "I'm giving you whatever interest I have in this property, but I'm not promising what that interest actually is."

Quitclaim deeds transfer only the grantor's actual ownership interest without warranties or promises about title quality.

For trust transfers, quitclaim deeds work perfectly because you're transferring property to yourself (as trustee). You know exactly what you own, so warranties about title quality are unnecessary. Most DIY trust transfers use quitclaim deeds because they're simple to prepare and meet all legal requirements for transfers to your own trust.

Grant deeds provide moderate protection by including implied warranties that the grantor actually owns the property and hasn't previously transferred it to someone else. Grant deeds also warrant that the property isn't encumbered by undisclosed liens or restrictions created by the grantor.

Some states prefer grant deeds for trust transfers, particularly California, where grant deeds are standard for most property transfers. However, the additional warranties typically aren't necessary for transfers to your own trust since you're not changing the actual ownership interest.

Warranty deeds (also called general warranty deeds) provide maximum protection through comprehensive warranties about title quality. The grantor promises not only that they own the property and haven't encumbered it, but also that the entire chain of title is clear and the grantor will defend against any title challenges.

Warranty deeds rarely make sense for trust transfers because the extensive warranties are unnecessary when you're transferring property to yourself. The additional warranty language also creates potential liability that serves no purpose in trust transfers.

Special warranty deeds limit warranties to problems created during the grantor's ownership period. The grantor warrants they haven't encumbered the property but doesn't guarantee against problems created by previous owners.

Trust transfer deed selection typically follows these guidelines:

- Use quitclaim deeds in states that allow them for trust transfers (most states)
- Use grant deeds in states like California where they're preferred for property transfers
- Use warranty deeds only if your state requires them or your title company recommends them
- Follow local customs and recorder office preferences when choosing between acceptable options

The key principle is using the deed type that provides appropriate protection while meeting your state's requirements and local customs. Since you're transferring to yourself, extensive warranties usually aren't necessary, making simpler deed types preferable.

Legal Description Importance and Accuracy

The legal description represents the most critical component of any property deed. Errors in legal descriptions can invalidate transfers, create title disputes, or result in transferring the wrong property entirely. Understanding and accurately copying legal descriptions is essential for successful DIY transfers.

Legal descriptions identify property using one of three basic systems:

Lot and block descriptions reference recorded subdivision plats that show the exact boundaries of individual lots. A typical lot and block description might read: "Lot 15, Block 3, Sunrise Subdivision, according to the plat recorded in Plat Book 25, Page 17, in the office of the County Recorder of Denver County, Colorado."

This system works well for most residential properties in developed subdivisions. The legal description references a specific recorded document (the subdivision plat) that contains detailed boundary information. Copying lot and block descriptions requires absolute accuracy in lot numbers, block numbers, subdivision names, and plat recording references.

Metes and bounds descriptions use precise measurements and compass directions to describe property boundaries. These descriptions typically start from a known reference point and describe the property boundaries by following specific compass headings for specific distances around the property perimeter.

A metes and bounds description might begin: "Beginning at a point on the south line of Main Street, 150 feet east of the southeast corner of the intersection of Main Street and Oak Avenue, thence south 89°45'30" east a distance of 75.5 feet..." These descriptions continue around the entire property boundary and return to the starting point.

Metes and bounds descriptions require extreme accuracy because small errors in angles or distances can result in descriptions that don't close (don't return to the starting point) or that describe the wrong property entirely. Never attempt to modify or "simplify" metes and bounds descriptions.

Government survey descriptions use the federal township and range system to identify property locations within six-mile-square townships. These descriptions typically reference sections (one-square-mile areas), quarter sections, or smaller subdivisions within sections.

A government survey description might read: "The Southwest Quarter of the Northeast Quarter of Section 15, Township 2 South, Range 68 West of the 6th Principal Meridian, Jefferson County, Colorado."

This system works well for rural properties and provides precise location references that surveyors can easily locate and verify.

Accuracy requirements for legal descriptions:

Copy exactly from your current deed without any changes, abbreviations, or "improvements." Legal descriptions use precise technical language that has been verified through surveys and title examination. Any changes, no matter how minor, can create title problems.

Include all punctuation exactly as it appears in the original. Periods, commas, quotation marks, and other punctuation marks are part of the legal description and must be copied precisely.

Maintain original formatting including line breaks, capitalization, and spacing. While these elements might seem cosmetic, they're part of the recorded legal description and should be preserved.

Double-check numbers including lot numbers, block numbers, distances, angles, and recording references. Transposed numbers are common errors that can result in describing the wrong property.

Verify subdivision names and recording references to ensure they match the original deed exactly. Subdivision names sometimes change over time, but legal descriptions reference the original recorded names.

Cross-reference with property tax records to verify that your legal description matches the property tax assessor's records. Discrepancies might indicate errors in your deed or changes that occurred after your deed was recorded.

The absolute rule for legal descriptions is: copy exactly, change nothing. Even changes that seem logical or helpful can create title problems that require professional correction later.

Chain of Title Considerations

Chain of title refers to the sequence of ownership transfers that brought the property to your current ownership. Understanding your position in this chain helps ensure your trust transfer maintains the integrity of property ownership records.

Title continuity requires that each deed in the chain properly transfers ownership to the next owner. Your name on your current deed must match exactly the name you use as grantor on your new trust transfer deed. Even small variations can create gaps in the chain of title.

Name consistency represents the most common chain of title issue in trust transfers. If your current deed lists you as "Robert J. Smith" but you plan to sign your trust deed as "Bob Smith," you've created a potential title problem. The legal solution involves using exactly the name from your current deed or preparing a corrective affidavit explaining the name variation.

Marital status changes can affect chain of title if your current deed shows different marital status than your current situation. If your deed lists you as "Mary Jones, a single woman" but you're now married, some states require acknowledgment of the marital status change in your trust transfer deed.

Previous corrections or modifications to your deed might affect how you prepare your trust transfer. If you've recorded affidavits correcting errors in your current deed, ensure your trust deed references your current legal name and ownership status.

Mortgage releases and other documents recorded since your current deed might affect your ownership situation. Refinancing, home equity loans, or lien releases could have changed aspects of your ownership that affect your trust transfer.

Title company involvement in your original purchase provides a resource for verifying chain of title issues. The title company that insured your purchase maintains records about your property's title history and can help clarify questions about proper names or ownership details.

The goal is ensuring your trust transfer deed properly continues the chain of title without creating gaps or inconsistencies that could cause problems for future owners or refinancing situations.

Common Deed Errors to Avoid

Experience shows that certain errors appear repeatedly in DIY property transfers. Understanding these common mistakes helps you avoid problems that could invalidate your transfer or create expensive corrections later.

Name errors top the list of common deed problems:

- Using nicknames instead of legal names ("Bill" instead of "William")
- Adding or omitting middle initials inconsistent with current deed
- Incorrect spelling of names
- Using current married names when current deed shows maiden names
- Omitting or incorrectly stating marital status

Legal description errors create serious title problems:

- Copying legal descriptions from property tax statements instead of current deed
- Attempting to "simplify" or abbreviate technical legal language
- Transposing numbers in lot numbers, block numbers, or measurements
- Omitting essential phrases or recording references
- Using outdated legal descriptions from old documents

Trust name errors affect the validity of your transfer:

- Inconsistent trust names between trust document and deed
- Omitting the trust date required for proper identification
- Incorrect trustee designations or missing trustee authority language
- Using informal trust references instead of exact legal names

Signature and notarization errors prevent proper recording:

- Signing names inconsistent with grantor names in the deed

- Missing or improper notary acknowledgments
- Incorrect notary commission information or expired notary credentials
- Missing signatures from all required grantors

Recording reference errors create confusion in public records:

- Incorrect recording information for referenced documents
- Omitting required recording references for subdivision plats or previous deeds
- Using outdated recording information that doesn't match current records

Consideration statement problems can affect deed validity:

- Omitting consideration statements entirely
- Using inappropriate consideration language for trust transfers
- Incorrectly stating consideration amounts that might trigger unnecessary taxes

Missing or incorrect reservations can create title problems:

- Failing to include mineral rights reservations from previous deeds
- Omitting utility easements or other restrictions that should transfer with the property
- Including inappropriate reservations that don't apply to trust transfers

Prevention strategies for common deed errors include:

Use your current deed as template for names, legal descriptions, and other technical information rather than trying to recreate this information from memory or other sources.

Triple-check all numbers including lot numbers, block numbers, distances, and recording references. Read these aloud or have someone else verify them to catch transposition errors.

Verify trust information against your original trust document to ensure exact consistency in trust names, dates, and trustee designations.

Review notary requirements for your state to ensure proper acknowledgment procedures and current notary credentials.

Have someone else proofread your completed deed to catch errors you might miss after working on the document extensively.

Name Formatting Requirements for Trust Transfers

Proper name formatting in trust transfer deeds requires attention to both the grantor designation (you individually) and the grantee designation (you as trustee). Errors in either designation can create title problems that require correction.

Grantor name formatting must match exactly the way your name appears on your current deed. If your current deed lists you as "Jennifer Anne Rodriguez, a married woman," you must use exactly that designation as the grantor in your trust deed. You cannot simplify it to "Jennifer Rodriguez" or change it to "Jennifer A. Rodriguez" without creating potential title problems.

Grantee name formatting for trust transfers follows specific conventions that identify you in your capacity as trustee. The standard format is: **"[Your exact name as it appears on your current deed], Trustee of the [exact trust name] dated [trust date]"**

For example: "Jennifer Anne Rodriguez, Trustee of the Rodriguez Family Trust dated March 15, 2021."

Critical formatting requirements for trust grantee designations:

Use your exact legal name as it appears on your current deed, not shortened versions or nicknames. If your current deed shows "Jennifer Anne Rodriguez," use that complete name in your trustee designation.

Include "Trustee of" language to establish your capacity. This phrase tells the world you're holding title in trust capacity, not individual capacity.

Use your trust's exact legal name as it appears in your trust document. Trust names must match precisely between the deed and the trust document. Even small variations can create title problems.

Include the trust date to distinguish your trust from other trusts with similar names. The date should match exactly the date your trust document was signed and notarized.

Avoid unnecessary additions like "and any successors in trust" or other language that isn't required for basic trust transfers. Keep the designation simple and accurate.

Examples of proper trust grantee formatting:

Single person: "Michael James Thompson, Trustee of the Thompson Living Trust dated April 2, 2023"

Married couple as co-trustees: "David Alan Chen and Susan Marie Chen, Trustees of the Chen Family Trust dated June 18, 2022"

Single trustee with full formal name: "Elizabeth Margaret O'Sullivan, Trustee of the O'Sullivan Revocable Living Trust dated September 5, 2021"

Common formatting errors to avoid:

Using informal names: "Mike Thompson, Trustee..." instead of "Michael James Thompson, Trustee..."

Omitting trust dates: "David Chen, Trustee of the Chen Family Trust" without the date

Incorrect trust names: Using "Chen Trust" instead of "Chen Family Trust" as shown in the trust document

Missing trustee designation: "David Chen" instead of "David Chen, Trustee of..."

Adding unnecessary language: "David Chen, Trustee of the Chen Family Trust dated June 18, 2022, and his successors and assigns"

Proper name formatting ensures clear title records and prevents confusion about your ownership capacity and authority. When in doubt, err on the side of being more formal and complete rather than abbreviated or informal.

Deed Comparison Chart and Verification Tools

Understanding the practical differences between deed types helps you choose the appropriate option for your trust transfer and state requirements.

Quitclaim Deed Characteristics:

- Transfers whatever interest grantor actually owns
- No warranties about title quality
- Simple preparation and execution
- Preferred for trust transfers in most states
- Lowest protection level but adequate for trust transfers
- Typically costs least in recording fees

Grant Deed Characteristics:

- Transfers fee simple ownership with limited warranties
- Warrants grantor owns the property and hasn't previously conveyed it
- Warrants no undisclosed encumbrances created by grantor
- Required or preferred in California and some other states
- Moderate protection level appropriate for most transfers
- Standard residential transfer deed in many western states

Warranty Deed Characteristics:

- Transfers fee simple ownership with comprehensive warranties
- Warrants entire chain of title quality
- Grantor agrees to defend against all title challenges
- Provides maximum protection but unnecessary for trust transfers
- Creates extensive liability for grantor
- Traditional deed type in many eastern and southern states

State preferences vary significantly:

- California typically requires grant deeds for property transfers
- Texas commonly uses warranty deeds but allows quitclaim for trust transfers
- Florida accepts quitclaim deeds for most trust transfers
- New York often uses quitclaim deeds for family transfers
- Check local customs and recorder office preferences

Legal Description Verification Worksheet:

Step 1: Locate Current Deed

- Find your recorded deed from property purchase
- Verify it shows your current ownership
- Check recording date and document number

Step 2: Extract Legal Description

- Copy legal description exactly as written
- Include all punctuation and formatting
- Note any referenced documents (plat books, etc.)

Step 3: Cross-Reference Property Tax Records

- Compare legal description with tax assessor records
- Verify property address matches legal description
- Check for any discrepancies requiring resolution

Step 4: Verify Names and Ownership

- Confirm your name matches exactly between deed and trust document
- Check marital status consistency
- Identify any name variations requiring correction

Step 5: Double-Check Technical Elements

- Verify all numbers (lot, block, measurements)
- Confirm spelling of subdivision names and references
- Check recording information for referenced documents

This systematic verification process catches most errors before they become expensive problems requiring professional correction.

Key Takeaways from Property Deed Understanding

Property deeds contain essential information presented in standardized formats that include parties, granting clauses, consideration, legal descriptions, and warranty provisions. Understanding these components helps you read any deed confidently and prepare accurate trust transfer documents.

Deed types provide different levels of protection, with quitclaim deeds offering simplicity appropriate for most trust transfers, grant deeds providing moderate warranties preferred in some states, and warranty deeds delivering comprehensive protection unnecessary for transfers to your own trust.

Legal descriptions require absolute accuracy with exact copying from current deeds, including all punctuation, formatting, and technical references. Chain of title considerations emphasize name consistency and proper continuation of ownership records without gaps or discrepancies.

Common deed errors involve names, legal descriptions, trust designations, and notarization problems that can invalidate transfers or create expensive correction requirements. Prevention strategies focus on using current deeds as templates and careful verification of all technical information.

Name formatting requirements for trust transfers demand exact grantor names from current deeds and proper grantee designations including trustee capacity, exact trust names, and trust dates. Proper formatting ensures clear title records and prevents confusion about ownership authority.

Deed comparison tools and verification worksheets provide systematic approaches to choosing appropriate deed types and ensuring accuracy before recording, preventing most problems that derail DIY property transfers.

The next chapter provides detailed step-by-step instructions for preparing your trust transfer deed with every detail correct for successful recording and title transfer.

Chapter 7: Getting Every Detail Right

Maria Gonzalez thought she'd done everything right. She'd carefully researched Colorado's trust transfer requirements, studied her current deed, and downloaded the proper quitclaim deed form from the Jefferson County Recorder's website. Maria spent three hours meticulously filling out the form, double-checking every detail against her original deed.

Two weeks after recording her deed, Maria received a letter from the county recorder's office. Her deed was being returned unrecorded due to "insufficient legal description." Confused and frustrated, Maria compared her deed to the original and couldn't spot the problem. Everything looked identical to her.

The issue, Maria discovered after calling the recorder's office, was subtle but critical. Her original deed included the phrase "TOGETHER WITH all appurtenances thereunto belonging" at the end of the legal description. Maria had assumed this was unnecessary legal boilerplate and omitted it from her trust deed. However, Jefferson County required complete legal descriptions including all appurtenant language from the original deed.

"I learned that 'unnecessary' legal language often isn't unnecessary at all," Maria reflected after correcting and re-recording her deed. "The safest approach is copying everything exactly, even if you don't understand why it's there."

Maria's experience illustrates why deed preparation requires meticulous attention to detail and conservative copying approaches. Small omissions or modifications that seem logical can invalidate your transfer or create recording problems that delay your entire process.

Step-by-Step Deed Completion Instructions

Successful deed preparation follows a systematic process that ensures accuracy while minimizing error risks. This step-by-step approach works for any deed type and adapts to different state requirements.

Step 1: Gather Required Materials

- Your current property deed (original or certified copy)
- Your living trust document
- Blank deed form appropriate for your state and deed type
- Property tax statement for reference
- Pen with black ink (required in most counties)
- Legal pad for notes and verification

Step 2: Choose Your Deed Form Source

- County recorder's office website (most reliable source)
- State bar association approved forms
- Reputable legal form providers
- Title company forms (often available upon request)

Avoid generic internet forms that aren't specific to your state and county. Recording requirements vary significantly by jurisdiction, and generic forms often lack required elements or include inappropriate language.

Step 3: Complete the Caption and Header Start with the document title and location information at the top of the deed form. This section identifies the document type and jurisdiction.

Document title: Ensure the form header matches your intended deed type (Quitclaim Deed, Grant Deed, Warranty Deed)

State and County: Fill in the state and county where your property is located (not where you live if different)

Recording space: Leave blank the area marked "For Recorder's Use Only" - this gets filled by the county when they record your deed

Step 4: Complete the Parties Section This critical section identifies who's transferring the property (grantor) and who's receiving it (grantee).

Grantor information must match exactly how your name appears on your current deed:

- Copy your name exactly, including middle initials, suffixes, and designations
- Include marital status exactly as shown on current deed
- Use identical formatting and punctuation

Example: If your current deed shows "Robert James Wilson and Patricia Ann Wilson, husband and wife," use that exact designation.

Grantee information designates you in your trustee capacity:

- Use the same name format as grantor section
- Add trustee designation: "Trustee of the [Trust Name] dated [Date]"
- Ensure trust name matches your trust document exactly

Example: "Robert James Wilson and Patricia Ann Wilson, Trustees of the Wilson Family Trust dated April 15, 2022"

Step 5: Insert Consideration Statement Every deed requires a consideration statement, even if no money changes hands in your trust transfer.

Standard consideration language for trust transfers:

- "For the sum of Ten Dollars ($10.00) and other valuable consideration"
- "For valuable consideration, the receipt of which is hereby acknowledged"
- "For good and valuable consideration"

Use whatever language your deed form provides. Don't modify or elaborate on consideration statements unless your state requires specific language for trust transfers.

Step 6: Add the Granting Clause The granting clause contains the legal language that actually transfers the property. Use the exact language provided in your deed form without modification.

Quitclaim deed language: "...does hereby quitclaim and release..." **Grant deed language:** "...does hereby grant..." **Warranty deed language:** "...does hereby grant, bargain, sell and convey..."

Don't attempt to modify granting clause language. These phrases have specific legal meanings that courts have interpreted for decades.

Step 7: Insert Legal Description The legal description represents the most critical and error-prone section of your deed preparation.

Copy exactly from your current deed:

- Include every word, comma, and punctuation mark
- Maintain original line breaks and formatting
- Don't abbreviate technical terms or substitute "simpler" language
- Include all referenced documents and recording information

Double-check critical elements:

- Lot and block numbers (if applicable)
- Subdivision names and plat references
- Metes and bounds measurements and angles

- Government survey references (township, range, section)

Include appurtenant language such as:

- "TOGETHER WITH all appurtenances thereunto belonging"
- "SUBJECT TO all easements and restrictions of record"
- Any other qualifying language from your current deed

Step 8: Add Habendum Clause (if required) Some deed forms include "To Have and to Hold" language that defines the type of ownership being transferred. If your form includes this section, complete it according to the form instructions, typically granting "fee simple absolute" ownership.

Step 9: Include Reservations and Exceptions Copy any reservations or exceptions from your current deed exactly as they appear. Common examples include:

- Mineral rights reservations
- Utility easements
- Subdivision restrictions
- Other limitations on ownership

Don't omit reservations thinking they're unnecessary - they're part of your property's title and must transfer with the deed.

Step 10: Prepare Signature Block The signature section requires careful attention to ensure proper execution and recording.

Grantor signature lines: Provide signature lines for all grantors (you) exactly as names appear in the grantor section

Date line: Include a line for execution date

Notary section: Ensure your form includes proper notary acknowledgment language for your state

Step 11: Final Review and Verification Before signing, systematically review your completed deed:

Verify all names match between grantor section, grantee section, and signature blocks

Check legal description word-for-word against your current deed

Confirm trust information matches your trust document exactly

Review consideration and granting language for completeness

Ensure all blanks are filled appropriately or marked "N/A" if not applicable

This systematic approach prevents most errors that cause deed rejection or title problems later.

Grantor and Grantee Formatting

Proper formatting of the grantor and grantee sections establishes clear title transfer and prevents confusion about ownership changes. These sections must be precise, complete, and consistent throughout the deed.

Grantor section formatting principles:

Exact name matching represents the most critical requirement. Your name as grantor must match exactly how it appears on your current property deed. This includes:

- Full legal names (not nicknames or shortened versions)
- Middle initials or full middle names as shown
- Suffixes like Jr., Sr., III
- Professional designations if included in original deed
- Marital status designations as they appear

Individual ownership example: Current deed shows: "Margaret Elizabeth O'Connor, a single woman" Grantor section should read: "Margaret Elizabeth O'Connor, a single woman"

Joint ownership example: Current deed shows: "David Alan Martinez and Rosa Marie Martinez, husband and wife, as joint tenants" Grantor section should read: "David Alan Martinez and Rosa Marie Martinez, husband and wife, as joint tenants"

Common grantor formatting errors:

- Using "David and Rosa Martinez" instead of full names with marital status
- Changing "Margaret Elizabeth O'Connor" to "Margaret E. O'Connor"
- Omitting marital status when it appears on current deed
- Using current marital status instead of status shown on current deed

Grantee section formatting for trust transfers:

The grantee section identifies you in your new capacity as trustee, following specific formatting requirements that establish proper trust ownership.

Individual to trust transfer example: "Margaret Elizabeth O'Connor, Trustee of the O'Connor Living Trust dated September 12, 2023"

Joint owners to trust transfer example: "David Alan Martinez and Rosa Marie Martinez, Trustees of the Martinez Family Trust dated February 8, 2022"

Critical elements of trust grantee formatting:

Use identical personal names as shown in grantor section - don't change spelling, initials, or format between sections

Include "Trustee" or "Trustees" designation to establish capacity

Use exact trust name from your trust document - even small variations can create title problems

Include complete trust date - month, day, and year as shown in trust document

Maintain consistency between deed and trust document in trust naming and dating

Examples of proper trust grantee designations:

Single trustee: "Jennifer Rose Thompson, Trustee of the Thompson Revocable Living Trust dated March 20, 2024"

Co-trustees: "Michael James Chen and Linda Sue Chen, Co-Trustees of the Chen Family Trust dated July 4, 2023"

Successor trustee situation: "Robert Paul Johnson, Successor Trustee of the Johnson Living Trust dated November 15, 2021"

Formatting consistency requirements:

Between grantor and grantee sections: Personal names must match exactly

Between deed and trust document: Trust names and dates must match exactly

Throughout the deed: Use consistent formatting in all name references

In signature blocks: Names must match grantor section exactly

This attention to formatting detail prevents title problems and ensures clear ownership records that future transactions can rely upon.

Critical Trust Designation Requirements

Trust designations in property deeds serve as the legal bridge between individual ownership and trust ownership. These designations must meet specific requirements to establish valid trust title and prevent future complications.

The standard trust designation formula follows this pattern: **"[Individual Name], Trustee of the [Complete Trust Name] dated [Trust Date]"**

Each element of this formula serves essential legal purposes:

Individual name component establishes who holds legal title to the property. This person has the authority to sign documents, make decisions, and manage the property on behalf of the trust.

"Trustee of" language establishes the capacity in which the individual holds title. This phrase tells the world that the individual owns the property not for personal benefit, but in trust for the benefit of trust beneficiaries.

Complete trust name identifies the specific trust that owns the property. Trust names must appear exactly as written in the trust document, including any descriptive terms like "Family Trust," "Living Trust," or "Revocable Trust."

Trust date distinguishes your trust from other trusts with similar names and provides a specific reference point for identifying the governing document. The date must match exactly the date your trust document was signed and notarized.

Examples of proper trust designations:

Single person trust: "Elizabeth Anne Rodriguez, Trustee of the Rodriguez Living Trust dated June 18, 2023"

Married couple trust: "John Michael Davis and Sarah Lynn Davis, Trustees of the Davis Family Trust dated September 3, 2022"

Formal trust name: "William Charles Thompson, III, Trustee of the William C. Thompson Revocable Living Trust dated December 10, 2024"

Common trust designation errors that create problems:

Incomplete trust names: Using "Smith Trust" instead of "Smith Family Living Trust" as shown in trust document

Incorrect dates: Using the date you signed the deed instead of the date the trust was created

Missing trustee designation: Using just your name without "Trustee of" language

Inconsistent formatting: Using different trust names between deed and other trust documents

Abbreviated references: Using initials or shortened versions of formal trust names

Trust designation verification checklist:

Compare with trust document to ensure exact name and date consistency

Verify trustee authority - confirm you're designated as initial trustee in trust document

Check successor provisions - if you're a successor trustee, ensure proper appointment documentation

Confirm joint trustee arrangements - verify whether you serve individually or jointly with spouse

Review amendment history - ensure you're using current trust name if amendments changed original name

Special situations requiring careful attention:

Amended trusts may have different names or dates than original trusts. Use the current operative trust name and date, but consider noting amendment history to prevent confusion.

Restated trusts typically retain original dates but may have updated names. Use the restatement date if the trust was completely restated, or original date if only amended.

Joint trustees must decide whether both serve together or individually. Joint service requires both signatures for all transactions, while individual service allows either to act alone.

Successor trustees must establish their authority through resignation documents, death certificates, or incapacity determinations before they can properly execute deeds.

The goal is creating clear, unambiguous trust designations that establish proper ownership records and provide sufficient information for future transactions, refinancing, or other dealings with the property.

Legal Description Transfer Process

Transferring legal descriptions from your current deed to your trust deed requires absolute precision and systematic verification. The legal description defines exactly what property you're transferring, making accuracy essential for valid ownership transfer.

The fundamental rule for legal descriptions: copy exactly, change nothing. This conservative approach prevents the common errors that invalidate property transfers or create title disputes.

Step-by-step legal description transfer:

Step 1: Locate the Complete Legal Description Find the legal description section in your current deed, typically appearing after the granting clause and consideration statement. Legal descriptions often begin with phrases like:

- "The following described real property..."
- "All that certain parcel of land..."
- "The land referred to herein..."

Step 2: Identify All Components Legal descriptions may include multiple parts that must be copied completely:

- Primary description (lot/block, metes/bounds, or government survey)
- Appurtenant language ("together with all appurtenances...")
- Exception language ("excepting therefrom...")
- Subject clauses ("subject to easements of record...")

Step 3: Copy Word-for-Word Transfer every word, number, and punctuation mark exactly as it appears:

- Include all commas, periods, and quotation marks
- Maintain original capitalization
- Preserve line breaks and spacing
- Don't substitute similar terms or "correct" apparent inconsistencies

Step 4: Verify Technical References Double-check all technical elements:

- Lot and block numbers
- Subdivision names and plat book references
- Recording information for referenced documents
- Measurements, angles, and compass directions (in metes/bounds descriptions)
- Township, range, and section references (in government survey descriptions)

Step 5: Include All Qualifying Language Copy all additional language that modifies or describes the basic legal description:

Appurtenant rights: "TOGETHER WITH all and singular the tenements, hereditaments and appurtenances thereunto belonging or in anywise appertaining"

Easement references: "SUBJECT TO easements, restrictions and reservations of record"

Mineral rights: "EXCEPTING AND RESERVING unto Grantor all oil, gas and mineral rights"

Access rights: "TOGETHER WITH right of ingress and egress over and across..."

Common legal description transfer errors:

Abbreviating technical terms: Changing "Southeast" to "SE" or "Township" to "Twp"

Modernizing language: Replacing "hereditaments and appurtenances" with "improvements and rights"

Omitting "unnecessary" language: Skipping phrases that seem redundant or outdated

Correcting apparent errors: Fixing typos or inconsistencies that appear in original deed

Simplifying complex descriptions: Breaking long descriptions into shorter, "clearer" sentences

Using property tax descriptions: Substituting abbreviated descriptions from tax statements

Quality control measures for legal descriptions:

Read aloud comparison: Read your copied description aloud while following the original to catch omitted words or phrases

Number verification: Have someone else verify all numbers (lot, block, measurements, recording references)

Professional review option: Consider having a title company or attorney review complex legal descriptions

Cross-reference verification: Compare your description with property tax records to ensure they describe the same property

Recording reference verification: Confirm that plat books, previous deeds, and other referenced documents exist and contain correct information

Special considerations for complex legal descriptions:

Multiple parcel descriptions require copying all parcels exactly as listed, maintaining original numbering or lettering systems

Condominium descriptions include unit numbers, building references, and common area designations that must be copied precisely

Metes and bounds descriptions require special attention to compass directions, distances, and curve calculations - never attempt to modify these technical elements

Historical language in older deeds may seem outdated but serves legal purposes - copy exactly without modernization

The legal description transfer process demands patience and precision, but this careful approach prevents most title problems that derail property transfers or create expensive correction requirements.

Consideration Statements

Every property deed must include a consideration statement indicating what the grantee paid for the property, even when no actual payment occurs in trust transfers. Understanding consideration requirements prevents deed invalidity and recording problems.

Legal purpose of consideration statements: Consideration demonstrates that the property transfer involves an exchange of value, making it a valid contract rather than a gift. While trust transfers don't involve actual sales, they require consideration statements to meet legal formalities for valid deed execution.

Standard consideration language for trust transfers:

Basic valuable consideration: "For good and valuable consideration, the receipt of which is hereby acknowledged..."

Nominal consideration: "For the sum of Ten Dollars ($10.00) and other valuable consideration..."

Receipt acknowledged: "For valuable consideration, the receipt and sufficiency of which are hereby acknowledged..."

Combined approach: "For the sum of Ten Dollars ($10.00) and other good and valuable consideration, the receipt and adequacy of which are hereby acknowledged..."

Trust transfer considerations are typically nominal because you're not actually selling your property. The consideration represents the legal formality required for deed validity rather than actual payment amounts.

State-specific consideration requirements:

Some states require specific language for trust transfers, such as:

- "For the purpose of placing title in trust..."
- "For estate planning purposes..."
- "To facilitate estate planning objectives..."

Documentary transfer tax states may require consideration statements that support transfer tax exemptions:

- "This transfer is exempt from documentary transfer tax pursuant to [specific statute]"
- "No consideration - transfer to grantor's revocable trust"

Property tax consideration in states that use consideration for assessment purposes:

- Some states require "full cash value" statements
- Others accept nominal consideration for family transfers
- A few require specific language to prevent property tax reassessment

Consideration statement errors to avoid:

Omitting consideration entirely - every deed requires some consideration statement

Using inappropriate amounts - stating actual property values when nominal consideration is sufficient

Including unnecessary tax references - adding transfer tax language unless required by your state

Contradicting deed purpose - using sale-oriented language for non-sale transfers

Creating tax complications - stating consideration amounts that might trigger unnecessary taxes or reporting requirements

Best practices for trust transfer consideration:

Use deed form language - if your deed form provides consideration language, use it without modification

Keep it simple - don't elaborate beyond what's required or provided in standard forms

Follow local customs - use consideration language that's customary in your area for similar transfers

Avoid actual values - don't state your property's actual value unless specifically required

Consider tax implications - ensure your consideration statement doesn't create unintended tax consequences

The goal is meeting legal requirements for deed validity while avoiding unnecessary complications or tax consequences that don't serve your estate planning objectives.

Signature Block Preparation

Proper signature block preparation ensures your deed can be executed validly and recorded successfully. The signature section must accommodate all required signatures and notarization according to your state's specific requirements.

Essential signature block components:

Grantor signature lines for every person listed in the grantor section:

- Provide individual signature lines for each grantor
- Include printed name lines under each signature line
- Match names exactly to grantor section designations
- Ensure adequate space for full signatures

Date line for execution date:

- "Dated this _____ day of _____, 2024"
- Some states require date completion, others allow blank dating
- Use execution date, not recording date

Notary acknowledgment section appropriate for your state:

- Use exact notary language required in your state
- Include spaces for notary signature, commission number, and seal
- Verify current notary acknowledgment requirements
- Some states have specific language for different types of transfers

Witness signature lines if required by your state:

- Most states don't require witnesses for deed execution
- Some states require witnesses in addition to notarization
- Check your state's specific requirements

Examples of proper signature block formatting:

Individual grantor example:

IN WITNESS WHEREOF, the undersigned has executed this deed on the date set forth below.

Dated: _____, 2024

_____
Margaret Elizabeth O'Connor

Joint grantors example:

IN WITNESS WHEREOF, the undersigned have executed this deed on the date set forth below.

Dated: _____, 2024

_____
David Alan Martinez

_____
Rosa Marie Martinez

Signature block preparation checklist:

Verify number of signature lines matches number of grantors exactly

Check name formatting matches grantor section exactly

Confirm notary section uses current language required in your state

Ensure adequate space for all signatures, dates, and notary information

Review execution requirements - some states require specific signature order or procedures

Plan notarization logistics - ensure all grantors can appear before notary simultaneously

Common signature block errors:

Wrong number of signature lines - not matching number of grantors

Name inconsistencies - signature block names don't match grantor section

Outdated notary language - using old acknowledgment forms that don't meet current requirements

Missing required elements - omitting commission numbers, seal spaces, or other mandatory notary information

Incorrect date formatting - using formats not recognized in your state

Insufficient space - cramping signatures or notary information into inadequate space

Execution best practices:

Schedule notary appointment in advance, ensuring all grantors can attend

Bring proper identification - government-issued photo ID for all signers

Use black ink - most counties require black ink for recording

Sign exactly as printed - match your signature to your printed name format

Don't date in advance - date the deed when you actually sign it

Obtain certified copies - get several certified copies when you record the original deed

Proper signature block preparation facilitates smooth execution and recording while ensuring your deed meets all legal requirements for valid property transfer.

Common Fatal Errors in Deed Preparation

Experience shows that certain deed preparation errors occur repeatedly and can invalidate your transfer entirely. Understanding these "fatal errors" helps you avoid problems that require expensive professional correction or complete deed re-preparation.

Name consistency errors represent the most common fatal mistake:

Grantor name variations between current deed and new deed create title gaps. If your current deed shows "Robert James Wilson" but your new deed shows "Bob Wilson," you've created a break in the chain of title that may prevent recording or create title insurance problems.

Grantee trust name errors include using informal trust names instead of exact legal names from trust documents, omitting required trust dates, or inconsistent naming between deed and trust document.

Signature inconsistencies occur when you sign the deed differently than your name appears in the grantor section, creating questions about signature validity.

Legal description errors can completely invalidate your transfer:

Incomplete copying of legal descriptions, omitting essential phrases or technical language that defines property boundaries or includes appurtenant rights.

Number transpositions in lot numbers, block numbers, measurements, or recording references can result in describing the wrong property entirely.

Abbreviating technical terms or "simplifying" legal language often creates descriptions that don't match public records or accurately describe your property.

Using outdated descriptions from old documents instead of current deed legal descriptions can create confusion about what property is actually being transferred.

Trust designation errors affect ownership validity:

Missing trustee capacity language - using just your name without "Trustee of" designation leaves unclear whether you're transferring to individual or trust ownership.

Incorrect trust dates - using deed execution date instead of trust creation date makes it impossible to identify the correct trust document.

Incomplete trust names - abbreviating formal trust names or omitting descriptive elements can create confusion with other similarly named trusts.

Execution and notarization errors prevent recording:

Missing signatures from all required grantors make the deed legally insufficient for property transfer.

Improper notarization including expired notary commissions, incorrect acknowledgment language, or failure to properly identify signers can prevent recording.

Dating problems such as impossible dates, dates before trust creation, or inconsistent dating between signature sections.

State-specific requirement errors:

Missing required forms that must accompany deeds in certain states, such as transfer tax returns or property transfer declarations.

Incorrect deed types - using warranty deeds where quitclaim deeds are required, or using inappropriate deed types for trust transfers.

Omitting mandatory language required by state statutes for specific types of transfers.

Prevention strategies for fatal errors:

Use current deed as template for all names, legal descriptions, and technical information rather than relying on memory or other sources.

Triple-check trust information against original trust documents to ensure exact consistency in names, dates, and designations.

Verify state requirements through county recorder websites or phone calls to ensure you're meeting all mandatory requirements.

Professional review option - consider having a title company or attorney review your completed deed before execution and recording.

Quality control checklist - systematically review every section of your completed deed against source documents and requirements.

Error correction procedures:

Minor errors discovered before recording can often be corrected by preparing a new deed with accurate information.

Errors discovered after recording may require corrective deeds, scrivener's affidavits, or professional assistance depending on the nature and severity of the error.

Title insurance claims may be necessary for errors that create title defects affecting property ownership or transferability.

The key to avoiding fatal errors is conservative, systematic deed preparation that prioritizes accuracy over speed and exact copying over perceived improvements or simplifications.

Warning: Critical Review Points Before Signing

Before executing your deed, conduct a final systematic review that catches errors while they're still correctable. This pre-signing checklist prevents most problems that cause deed rejection or title complications.

Grantor section verification:

- Names match current deed exactly, including middle initials and suffixes
- Marital status designations match current deed
- Spelling is identical to current property records
- All required grantors are included

Grantee section verification:

- Trust name matches trust document exactly
- Trust date matches trust creation date
- Trustee designation is complete and accurate
- Names are consistent between grantor and grantee sections

Legal description verification:

- Copied word-for-word from current deed
- All punctuation and formatting preserved
- No abbreviations or modifications attempted
- All appurtenant language included

Signature block verification:

- Correct number of signature lines for all grantors
- Names match grantor section exactly
- Notary section includes all required elements
- Date line is provided and properly formatted

State requirement verification:

- Correct deed type for your state and situation
- All required additional forms identified
- Proper consideration language included
- Recording requirements understood

This final review investment prevents most errors that derail DIY property transfers and ensures your deed accomplishes your estate planning objectives effectively.

Key Takeaways from Deed Preparation

Systematic deed completion following step-by-step procedures ensures accuracy while minimizing common errors that can invalidate transfers or prevent recording. Proper grantor and grantee formatting requires exact name matching from current deeds and precise trust designation language including complete trust names and creation dates.

Critical trust designation requirements follow the formula "[Individual Name], Trustee of the [Complete Trust Name] dated [Trust Date]" with each element serving essential legal purposes for establishing valid trust ownership. Legal description transfer demands word-for-word copying without modifications, abbreviations, or attempts to simplify technical language.

Consideration statements serve legal formality requirements rather than reflecting actual payment, with nominal consideration typically appropriate for trust transfers unless state laws require specific language. Signature block preparation must accommodate all grantors with proper notary acknowledgment sections meeting current state requirements.

Common fatal errors involve name inconsistencies, incomplete legal descriptions, missing trust designation elements, and execution problems that prevent valid recording. Prevention strategies focus on using current deeds as templates, systematic verification against source documents, and conservative copying approaches that prioritize accuracy over perceived improvements.

Final review procedures before signing provide the last opportunity to catch errors while they're still easily correctable, with systematic verification of all deed components against source documents and state requirements. This careful preparation approach prevents most problems that derail DIY transfers and ensures successful property transfer to trust ownership.

The next chapter guides you through the county recording process that makes your property transfer legally effective and part of the permanent public record.

Chapter 8: The Recording Process

Janet Morrison's hands shook slightly as she walked into the Maricopa County Recorder's Office in Phoenix, carrying her carefully prepared quitclaim deed in a manila folder. She'd spent weeks researching Arizona's requirements, preparing her deed with painstaking attention to detail, and gathering all necessary supporting documents.

The recording process felt like the moment of truth. Would the clerk accept her deed? Had she calculated the fees correctly? Were her documents properly prepared and notarized? Janet had invested too much time and energy to fail at this crucial final step.

Twenty minutes later, Janet walked out with a receipt showing her deed was officially recorded. The process that had seemed so intimidating was actually straightforward once she understood the requirements. "The clerk was helpful and professional," Janet reflected. "She answered my questions and made sure everything was correct before processing my deed."

Janet's successful recording experience illustrates that the recording process, while important, is typically the easiest part of DIY trust transfers. County recording offices handle thousands of property transfers every year, and their staff can guide you through the process if you arrive properly prepared with correct documents and fees.

The recording step transforms your private deed into a public record that provides legal notice of your property transfer. Until recording occurs, your deed transfer isn't legally complete or effective against third parties who might claim interests in your property.

County Recorder Office Procedures

County recorder offices (sometimes called County Clerk offices or Register of Deeds offices) maintain the official public records of property ownership for their jurisdictions. Understanding how these offices operate helps ensure smooth processing of your trust transfer.

Office organization and staffing: Most recorder offices separate different types of recordings into specialized departments. Real estate deeds typically go to the "Real Property" or "Deeds" department, while other documents like liens, mortgages, or court orders go to different sections. Larger counties may have separate windows or departments for different document types.

Staff members are usually county employees who understand recording requirements but aren't attorneys and can't provide legal advice. They can tell you whether your document meets recording requirements, but they can't help you prepare documents or advise you about legal consequences of recording decisions.

Standard recording procedures: When you arrive with your deed for recording, the process typically follows these steps:

Document review: Staff examines your deed to ensure it meets basic recording requirements including proper signatures, notarization, legal descriptions, and any required additional forms or fees.

Fee calculation: Staff calculates total recording fees based on document pages, deed type, and any applicable transfer taxes or additional charges.

Recording number assignment: Your deed receives a unique recording number that becomes its permanent identification in public records.

Indexing: Staff creates index entries under grantor and grantee names so future searchers can locate your deed.

Document processing: Your original deed gets microfilmed or digitally scanned and becomes part of permanent county records.

Return preparation: Most counties return your original deed with recording stamps, or you can request certified copies for your records.

Business hours and services vary by county:

- Most offices operate during standard business hours (8 AM - 5 PM, Monday through Friday)
- Some larger counties offer extended hours or Saturday services
- Many counties now accept documents by mail with proper procedures
- A few counties offer online recording for certain document types

Preparation for recorder office visits:

Call ahead to verify current procedures, fees, and any special requirements for trust transfers. Requirements can change, and phone calls prevent wasted trips for missing information or incorrect fees.

Bring required identification if you're submitting documents in person. Some counties require photo ID for document submission, especially for valuable property transfers.

Prepare exact fees in appropriate form - cash, cashier's check, or personal check depending on county policies. Many counties don't provide change for cash payments.

Allow adequate time for document review and processing. Simple recordings might take 15 minutes, while complex documents requiring staff review can take an hour or more.

Plan for potential complications such as staff questions about your deed, missing requirements you weren't aware of, or fee calculations that differ from your expectations.

County recorder staff limitations: Recording office employees can help with procedural questions but can't provide legal advice. They can tell you whether your deed meets recording requirements but can't advise you about:

- Whether you're using the correct deed type
- How to handle complex ownership situations
- Tax implications of your transfer
- Legal consequences of different deed language

Understanding these limitations helps you prepare appropriately and seek legal guidance for substantive questions while using county staff for procedural assistance.

Recording Fee Calculations

Recording fees vary dramatically by state and county, ranging from less than $20 in some Texas counties to over $200 in parts of California. Understanding fee structures helps you budget accurately and avoid surprises during recording.

Base recording fees typically include:

- First page fee: Usually the highest single charge, ranging from $10-$50
- Additional page fees: Often $2-$10 per page after the first
- Index fees: Some counties charge separately for indexing services
- Technology fees: Many counties add surcharges for computer system maintenance

Additional fees that may apply:

- **State transfer taxes:** Some states impose transfer taxes even on exempt transfers, requiring tax calculation and documentation
- **Local transfer taxes:** Cities or special districts may impose additional taxes

- **Document preparation fees:** Some counties charge for deed preparation assistance (not recommended for DIY transfers)
- **Certification fees:** Costs for certified copies of your recorded deed
- **Rush processing fees:** Extra charges for expedited processing when available

Fee calculation examples by state:

Texas (Collin County):

- First page: $25
- Additional pages: $5 each
- Typical quitclaim deed: $30-$35 total

Arizona (Maricopa County):

- Recording fee: $18
- Additional pages: $3 each
- Typical quitclaim deed: $18-$25 total

California (Los Angeles County):

- Recording fee: $75 first page, $3 additional pages
- Documentary transfer tax calculation required (though often exempt)
- Typical trust transfer: $75-$100 total

Florida (Orange County):

- Recording fee: $10 first page, $8.50 additional pages
- Documentary stamps may apply
- Typical trust transfer: $20-$40 total

Fee payment methods accepted vary by county:

- **Cash:** Accepted in most counties but often requires exact payment

- **Personal checks:** Usually accepted for amounts up to certain limits
- **Cashier's checks:** Always accepted and required for large amounts in some counties
- **Credit cards:** Accepted in some modern counties, often with processing fees
- **Money orders:** Generally accepted as cash equivalent

Fee calculation verification: Before visiting the recorder's office, call to verify current fees and accepted payment methods. Fee schedules change periodically, and phone verification prevents payment problems during recording.

Count your deed pages carefully, including all attachments and exhibits. Some counties charge for blank pages, while others only count pages with content.

Calculate estimated total fees including any transfer taxes, even if exempt, to ensure you bring adequate payment.

Documentary Transfer Tax Exemptions

Documentary transfer taxes, imposed by some states and localities on property transfers, typically don't apply to transfers into your own revocable living trust. However, many jurisdictions still require tax calculation and exemption documentation even when no tax is owed.

Understanding documentary transfer taxes: These taxes typically calculate based on property value or consideration amount, with rates varying from less than 0.1% to over 2% of property value. The taxes generate revenue for local governments and provide transfer information for property tax assessment purposes.

Common exemption provisions for trust transfers:

- Transfers to grantor's own revocable trust
- Transfers for estate planning purposes without consideration
- Transfers that don't change beneficial ownership

114

- Family transfers between spouses, parents, and children

Required exemption documentation varies by jurisdiction:

California requires completion of preliminary Change of Ownership Report (PCOR) even for exempt transfers, plus documentary transfer tax declaration on the deed.

New York requires Form TP-584 completion calculating transfer taxes and documenting exemption claims.

Pennsylvania requires local transfer tax returns in most municipalities, even for exempt family transfers.

Texas generally doesn't impose state transfer taxes, but some localities have transfer fees or disclosure requirements.

Florida requires documentary stamp tax calculations, though trust transfers typically qualify for exemptions.

Exemption documentation best practices:

Research your specific requirements through county recorder websites or phone calls to determine exactly what documentation your jurisdiction requires.

Complete required forms even if no tax is owed - many counties require tax calculation forms to verify exemption claims.

Use exact exemption language required by your state's statutes rather than general statements about tax-free transfers.

Include supporting documentation such as trust certificates or affidavits if required by your county for exemption verification.

Calculate potential taxes even if exempt to demonstrate understanding of exemption requirements and ensure accurate form completion.

Common exemption errors:

- Assuming exemption without completing required forms
- Using incorrect exemption codes or statutory references
- Failing to include required supporting documentation
- Misunderstanding local requirements that differ from state rules

The key is treating exemption documentation as seriously as tax payment requirements, since incomplete exemption documentation can delay recording or create problems with future transfers.

Required Supporting Documents

Beyond your main deed, many jurisdictions require additional documents that must accompany your recording submission. These supporting documents vary by state and county but serve essential functions in the recording process.

Transfer tax returns or declarations calculate and document any applicable transfer taxes, even when exemptions apply. Common examples include:

- California PCOR (Preliminary Change of Ownership Report)
- New York Form TP-584 (Combined Real Estate Transfer Tax Return)
- Pennsylvania local transfer tax returns
- Various state-specific tax calculation forms

Property transfer declarations provide information to tax assessors about transfer circumstances and property characteristics. These forms help assessors determine whether property tax reassessment is required and update ownership records.

Homestead exemption preservation forms ensure you maintain property tax benefits after trust transfer. States like Texas require specific documentation to preserve homestead exemptions for trust-owned properties.

Trust certificates or excerpts may be required in some counties to verify trust existence and trustee authority. These documents prove you have authority to receive property on behalf of the trust.

Cover letters or recording instructions help county staff process your documents correctly, especially if you're submitting by mail or have special requirements.

Examples of state-specific supporting documents:

California requirements:

- Preliminary Change of Ownership Report (PCOR)
- Documentary transfer tax declaration
- Possible homestead exemption preservation forms

Illinois requirements:

- Property Transfer Declaration
- Real Estate Transfer Declaration (RETD)
- Possible conveyance fee calculation

New York requirements:

- Form TP-584 (Transfer Tax Return)
- Possible local transfer tax forms
- Deed recording cover sheet

Document preparation tips: Complete forms accurately using information from your deed and property records **Sign forms where required** - some supporting documents require grantor signatures **Include required fees** for processing supporting documents **Organize documents logically** with deed first, followed by supporting forms **Keep copies** of all submitted documents for your records

The goal is submitting a complete package that meets all county requirements without creating delays or requiring resubmission.

Mail vs. In-Person Recording

Most counties offer both mail-in and in-person recording options, each with distinct advantages and considerations that affect your recording strategy.

In-person recording advantages:

- **Immediate feedback** about document problems or missing requirements
- **Real-time fee calculation** ensuring you pay correct amounts
- **Same-day processing** in most counties
- **Staff assistance** with questions or procedural issues
- **Immediate receipt** with recording information

In-person recording considerations:

- **Business hour requirements** may conflict with work schedules
- **Travel time and costs** for counties distant from your home
- **Potential waiting** during busy periods
- **COVID or health considerations** affecting office visits

Mail recording advantages:

- **Convenience** of submitting from home without office visits
- **Flexible timing** not dependent on business hours
- **No travel requirements** regardless of distance to county offices
- **Processing during busy periods** without waiting in lines

Mail recording requirements:

- **Exact fee payment** typically by check or money order
- **Complete documentation** since you can't correct problems in person
- **Self-addressed stamped envelope** for return of recorded documents

- **Recording instructions** explaining any special requirements
- **Longer processing time** allowing for mail delivery and processing delays

Mail recording best practices: Call recorder office to verify current mail recording procedures and requirements

Calculate fees precisely including all applicable charges - most counties won't process documents with insufficient fees

Include cover letter explaining what you're recording and any special circumstances

Use certified mail for valuable documents to ensure delivery and provide tracking

Include prepaid return envelope with adequate postage for return of your recorded deed

Allow extra time for mail processing - typically 2-4 weeks from submission to receipt of recorded documents

Hybrid approaches: Some counties allow you to submit documents in person but pick up recorded copies later, combining immediate processing verification with convenience for document retrieval.

Other counties provide drop-box submission allowing document delivery outside business hours, though this typically requires exact fee payment and complete documentation like mail submissions.

Choosing your recording method: Consider in-person recording if:

- You're uncertain about any requirements
- You want immediate processing and feedback
- You're comfortable with office visits during business hours
- Your county is geographically convenient

Consider mail recording if:

- You're confident about all requirements
- Convenience outweighs processing speed
- You're comfortable with mail processing timelines
- Distance makes office visits impractical

Both methods work effectively when you understand the requirements and prepare accordingly.

Post-Recording Verification

Recording your deed doesn't end your transfer process - verification that recording was completed correctly protects your interests and provides foundation for completing additional transfer tasks.

Recording confirmation importance: Your recorded deed provides legal notice to the world about your property ownership transfer. Errors in recording can create title problems that affect future sales, refinancing, or inheritance distributions. Verification ensures the public record accurately reflects your intended transfer.

What to verify in your recorded deed: Recording stamps and information should include:

- Recording date
- Document or instrument number
- Book and page references (in counties using physical record books)
- Recorder's official stamp or signature

Document accuracy after recording:

- All pages were recorded completely
- No information was lost or obscured during recording
- Signatures and notarization remain clearly visible
- Any attachments or exhibits were included

Index verification ensures future searchers can locate your deed:

120

- Your name appears correctly in grantor index
- Trust name appears correctly in grantee index
- Property address or parcel number is associated with the recording

Common recording problems requiring follow-up:

Incomplete recording occurs when some pages aren't scanned clearly or attachments are separated from main documents. Request re-recording or supplemental recording to ensure complete documents are in public records.

Index errors happen when staff mistype names or property information during indexing. These errors can make your deed difficult to locate in future title searches, potentially creating title problems.

Fee calculation errors occasionally result in overcharges or undercharges that require correction. While overcharges can be refunded, undercharges might require additional payment to complete recording.

Document damage during processing sometimes occurs when older equipment damages original documents or creates unclear copies in official records.

Verification procedures:

Obtain certified copies of your recorded deed for your records. Most counties provide these for additional fees, and certified copies serve as proof of recording for future transactions.

Review online records if your county provides internet access to recorded documents. Verify that your deed appears correctly and completely in public records.

Check index entries to ensure your names appear correctly in both grantor and grantee indexes associated with your property.

Test document retrieval by searching county records using your name and property address to verify future users can locate your recorded deed.

Follow-up actions after recording verification:

Notify interested parties including mortgage companies, insurance carriers, and others who need to know about ownership changes.

Update property tax records to reflect trust ownership and preserve any property tax exemptions.

Organize recorded documents in your permanent files along with other important property records.

Begin post-transfer tasks including insurance updates and ongoing trust administration responsibilities.

Schedule trust review to ensure your completed transfer aligns with overall estate planning objectives.

The verification process provides peace of mind that your transfer was completed successfully and creates foundation for ongoing trust management and estate planning.

Key Takeaways from the Recording Process

County recorder office procedures follow standardized processes for document review, fee calculation, and permanent record creation, with staff available to help with procedural questions while being limited in providing legal guidance. Understanding office organization and standard procedures helps ensure smooth recording experiences.

Recording fee calculations vary dramatically by jurisdiction, including base recording fees, additional page charges, and potential transfer tax requirements that may apply even to exempt transfers.

Accurate fee calculation and proper payment methods prevent processing delays and ensure complete recording.

Documentary transfer tax exemptions typically apply to trust transfers but often require completion of tax calculation forms and exemption documentation even when no taxes are owed. Understanding exemption requirements and procedures prevents recording delays and compliance problems.

Required supporting documents beyond the basic deed vary by state and county, including transfer tax returns, property declarations, and homestead preservation forms that must accompany recording submissions. Complete documentation packages prevent resubmission requirements and processing delays.

Mail versus in-person recording options provide flexibility in submission methods, with in-person recording offering immediate feedback and same-day processing while mail recording provides convenience at the cost of longer processing times and less immediate error correction.

Post-recording verification ensures accurate recording completion and proper indexing, providing foundation for completing additional transfer tasks and ongoing trust management responsibilities. Verification catches recording errors while they're still correctable and confirms successful completion of your property transfer objectives.

The next chapter addresses essential post-transfer tasks that protect your investment and ensure your trust transfer achieves its intended estate planning benefits.

Chapter 9: Protecting Your Investment

Kevin Walsh thought his work was finished when he received his recorded deed showing successful transfer of his Austin home to his living trust. The deed was properly recorded, his trust now owned the property, and Kevin felt satisfied with completing the DIY process successfully.

Three months later, Kevin discovered his assumption was dangerously wrong. A kitchen fire caused significant damage to his home, and when Kevin called his insurance company to file a claim, he learned his homeowner's policy didn't cover trust-owned properties. The insurance agent explained that Kevin should have notified them about the ownership change and updated his policy to include the trust.

"I thought recording the deed was the end of the process," Kevin reflected while dealing with coverage disputes and claim delays. "I didn't realize I needed to update everyone else about the ownership change." Kevin's oversight could have cost him tens of thousands of dollars in uncovered damages if his insurance company had denied the claim entirely.

Kevin's experience illustrates a crucial reality: recording your deed completes the legal transfer, but protecting your investment requires additional steps to ensure your trust ownership provides the intended benefits. These post-transfer tasks aren't optional extras - they're essential components of successful trust transfers that prevent expensive problems later.

Homeowners who complete their deed recording often experience relief and assume their work is finished. Actually, they've completed the most visible part of the process while leaving essential protective tasks unfinished. The post-transfer phase determines whether your trust ownership provides intended benefits or creates unexpected complications.

Insurance Policy Updates

Homeowner's insurance policies typically continue covering trust-owned properties, but notification and possible policy modifications ensure uninterrupted protection and prevent claim disputes during stressful situations.

Why insurance updates matter: Insurance companies write policies based on property ownership structures and policyholder information provided at application. Changes in ownership can affect coverage terms, claim procedures, and company obligations. While most insurers cover trust-owned properties routinely, they need notification to update their records and ensure policy language accommodates trust ownership.

Standard insurance company procedures for trust transfers:

Notification process typically involves:

- Calling your insurance agent or company customer service
- Explaining that you've transferred your property to your own revocable living trust
- Providing basic information about the trust and transfer date
- Confirming that you remain the primary policyholder and property occupant

Documentation requirements may include:

- Copy of your recorded deed showing trust ownership
- Trust certificate or trust document excerpt proving trust existence
- Completed ownership change forms provided by insurance company

- Updated declarations page reflecting trust ownership

Policy modifications often include:

- **Additional insured designation** adding the trust as a named insured party
- **Policyholder updates** modifying records to show trust ownership
- **Coverage verification** confirming all coverage remains in effect
- **Claims procedure updates** explaining how to file claims for trust-owned property

Most insurance companies handle trust ownership routinely because living trusts are common estate planning tools. Agents and customer service representatives typically understand the process and can complete updates quickly with minimal documentation.

Potential insurance complications and solutions:

Underwriting reviews occasionally occur when insurance companies update policies for trust ownership. Most reviews confirm continued coverage at existing rates, but some companies might:

- Request updated property appraisals
- Review coverage limits for adequacy
- Ask questions about trust management or beneficiaries
- Require additional liability coverage for trustees

Premium adjustments might result from policy updates, though changes are typically minimal. Some insurers offer discounts for trust-owned properties, while others might impose small surcharges for additional administrative complexity.

Coverage gaps can occur if you don't notify your insurance company promptly. While most insurers would likely honor claims during reasonable notification periods, delayed notification can create disputes and claim delays during already stressful situations.

126

Liability coverage considerations become more important with trust ownership because trustees face potential personal liability for trust asset management. Your umbrella liability policy may need updates to cover trustee activities, and adequate liability limits become more important.

Insurance update timing recommendations:

Notify within 30 days of recording your deed to ensure continuous coverage and prevent potential gaps.

Schedule annual reviews to ensure coverage remains adequate and trust ownership information stays current.

Update during life changes including marriage, divorce, or changes in trust management that might affect insurance requirements.

Coordinate with other policies including automobile, umbrella liability, and any rental property coverage that might be affected by trust ownership changes.

Document all communications with insurance companies about trust ownership to provide records if questions arise during future claims or policy renewals.

Mortgage Servicer Notification

Mortgage companies and loan servicers need notification about trust transfers to update their records and ensure continued smooth loan administration. While federal law protects your right to make these transfers, proper notification maintains good relationships and prevents unnecessary complications.

Legal background for mortgage notifications: The Garn-St. Germain Depository Institutions Act of 1982 specifically protects homeowners' rights to transfer their primary residence to their own revocable living trust without triggering due-on-sale clauses. This federal law prevents lenders from accelerating loan payments or imposing penalties solely because of trust transfers.

However, most mortgage documents require notification of ownership changes, and maintaining good relationships with your loan servicer helps prevent misunderstandings or administrative problems.

Mortgage notification procedures:

Locate proper contact information for ownership change notifications:

- Check your monthly mortgage statement for customer service contacts
- Look for specific departments handling ownership changes or estate planning transfers
- Some servicers have dedicated trust notification procedures

Prepare notification documentation:

- Copy of your recorded deed showing trust ownership
- Brief explanation letter describing the transfer purpose
- Trust certificate or excerpt proving trust existence and your trustee authority
- Reference to Garn-St. Germain Act protection for the transfer

Sample notification letter content: "Dear [Servicer Name]: I am writing to notify you that I have transferred my property located at [Property Address] to my revocable living trust for estate planning purposes. The transfer is protected under the Garn-St. Germain Depository Institutions Act, 12 USC 1701j-3(d)(8). I remain the trustee and beneficiary of the trust and will continue making all payments as agreed. Please update your records to reflect the trust ownership. Attached you will find a copy of the recorded deed and trust certificate for your files."

Expected servicer responses vary:

- **Acknowledgment with file updates** (most common response)
- **Request for additional documentation** such as complete trust documents or legal opinions
- **Standard form completion** using servicer-specific ownership change forms
- **No response required** - some servicers simply note the information and continue normal servicing

Potential servicer concerns and responses:

Questions about continued payment responsibility - clarify that you remain personally responsible for mortgage payments as borrower

Requests for trust document review - provide trust certificates rather than complete trust documents to maintain privacy

Inquiries about insurance coverage - confirm insurance remains in effect and covers trust-owned property

Administrative delays in updating records - follow up if statements continue showing incorrect ownership after reasonable processing time

Documentation and follow-up: Keep records of all communications with mortgage servicers about trust transfers

Monitor monthly statements to verify ownership information updates are reflected in servicer records

Follow up if statements continue showing incorrect ownership information after 60-90 days

Address discrepancies promptly if servicer records don't reflect trust ownership accurately

Most mortgage servicers handle trust transfer notifications routinely, but proper documentation and follow-up ensure smooth ongoing loan administration under trust ownership.

Property Tax Exemption Filing

Property tax exemptions and benefits you enjoyed under individual ownership typically continue under trust ownership, but many states require specific filings or notifications to preserve these benefits.

Homestead exemptions provide significant property tax savings in many states by reducing assessed values for primary residences. These exemptions usually continue for trust-owned properties, but preservation often requires specific documentation.

Texas homestead exemption preservation: Texas provides one of the nation's most generous homestead exemptions but requires specific trust language to preserve benefits after transfer. Your trust must qualify as a "qualifying trust" under Texas law, and you may need to file specific forms with your county appraisal district.

California Proposition 13 protection: California's Proposition 13 prevents property tax reassessment for many family transfers, including transfers to revocable trusts. However, you must file appropriate exemption claims and may need to complete change of ownership reports to preserve these benefits.

Florida homestead benefits: Florida homestead exemptions typically continue for trust-owned properties, but some counties require notification forms and trust documentation to verify eligibility continuation.

Other state exemption programs:

- Senior citizen exemptions
- Disability exemptions
- Veteran exemptions
- Low-income exemptions

- Agricultural use exemptions

Property tax filing procedures:

Contact your county tax assessor or appraisal district to understand specific requirements for trust-owned properties in your jurisdiction.

Complete required forms for exemption preservation, which may include:

- Change of ownership notifications
- Homestead exemption continuation applications
- Trust qualification certifications
- Annual renewal filings

Provide necessary documentation such as:

- Copy of recorded deed showing trust ownership
- Trust certificate proving trust existence and your beneficiary status
- Affidavits confirming continued use as primary residence
- Previous exemption certificates or approval letters

Filing deadlines vary by state and exemption type:

- Some states require filing within 30 days of transfer
- Others allow annual filing during regular exemption application periods
- Missing deadlines can result in permanent loss of exemption benefits

Exemption verification and monitoring: Review property tax statements after transfer to ensure exemptions continue appearing correctly

Appeal assessment changes promptly if your property is incorrectly reassessed after trust transfer

Maintain documentation proving exemption eligibility in case questions arise during future assessments

Schedule annual reviews of property tax statements to catch problems early

Property tax exemptions can provide hundreds or thousands of dollars in annual savings, making proper filing and monitoring essential components of successful trust transfers.

HOA Notification Requirements

Homeowners associations and condominium associations sometimes require notification of ownership changes, even for trust transfers that don't change beneficial ownership. Understanding and meeting these requirements prevents potential conflicts or administrative complications.

Reviewing governing documents: Your CC&Rs (Covenants, Conditions, and Restrictions), HOA bylaws, and other governing documents may include provisions requiring:

- Notification of ownership transfers
- Approval for certain types of transfers
- Payment of transfer fees
- Completion of specific forms or procedures

Common HOA notification requirements:

- **Written notification** to HOA board or management company
- **Documentation** including copy of recorded deed and trust information
- **Contact information** updates for trust ownership
- **Payment** of administrative fees for processing ownership changes

Typical HOA responses to trust transfers: Most HOAs handle trust transfers routinely since they don't change who actually lives in or controls the property. However, some associations may:

- Request trust certificates or documentation proving trust validity
- Ask for updated contact information for trustees
- Require confirmation that assessment payment responsibilities continue
- Update their records to show trust ownership

HOA complications and solutions: Overly restrictive CC&Rs occasionally include language that appears to prohibit trust transfers. However, most state laws protect homeowners' rights to transfer property to their own revocable trusts regardless of HOA restrictions.

Administrative delays sometimes occur when HOA staff aren't familiar with trust transfers. Providing clear documentation and patient explanation usually resolves these issues.

Fee disputes might arise if HOAs attempt to charge transfer fees inappropriate for trust transfers. Since beneficial ownership doesn't change, transfer fees typically shouldn't apply.

Notification timing and documentation: Send written notification within 30 days of recording your deed to comply with most HOA requirements

Include proper documentation such as recorded deed copies and trust certificates

Maintain correspondence records in case questions arise about notification compliance

Follow up if you don't receive acknowledgment within reasonable time periods

Most HOA interactions about trust transfers are simple administrative updates, but proper notification prevents potential conflicts and ensures smooth ongoing community participation.

Document Storage Best Practices

Proper organization and storage of your trust transfer documents protects your investment and provides essential documentation for future needs including refinancing, selling, or inheritance administration.

Essential documents requiring permanent storage:

- **Original trust document** with all amendments or restatements
- **Recorded property deed** showing trust ownership
- **Trust certificates** used for various transactions
- **Insurance policy updates** reflecting trust ownership
- **Property tax exemption approvals** and related documentation
- **Mortgage servicer correspondence** about trust notification
- **HOA notifications and responses** regarding ownership changes

Storage location strategies:

Safe deposit boxes provide excellent security for original documents but limit access to banking hours and require box rental fees. Consider safe deposit storage for irreplaceable originals while keeping accessible copies at home.

Fireproof home safes offer convenient access with reasonable security for most important documents. Modern fireproof safes protect against both fire damage and theft while allowing 24/7 access.

Digital storage systems using cloud services or secure drives provide backup protection and easy access but shouldn't replace physical document storage for legal originals.

Professional storage services offered by some attorneys or trust companies provide maximum security but involve ongoing fees and access limitations.

Multiple location strategy combines approaches by storing originals in secure locations while maintaining easily accessible copies for routine needs.

Document organization systems:

Chronological filing organizes documents by date, making it easy to track the progression of your trust transfer and related activities.

Category filing separates documents by type (trust documents, property records, insurance papers, tax records) for easy location when specific information is needed.

Master index systems catalog all trust-related documents with location information, making it easy for trustees or family members to locate specific documents when needed.

Access planning for family members: Your successor trustee and family members need to know where important documents are stored and how to access them when needed. Consider:

- **Written instructions** about document locations and access procedures
- **Key or combination sharing** with trusted family members
- **Emergency access plans** for situations requiring immediate document retrieval
- **Regular communication** with successor trustees about document organization and storage

Digital backup strategies: While digital copies can't replace original documents for legal purposes, they provide important backup protection and convenient access for routine needs:

- **Scan all documents** to create digital backups stored in multiple locations
- **Use secure cloud storage** with strong passwords and encryption
- **Update digital files** when documents change or new documents are added
- **Provide access instructions** to family members for emergency situations

Proper document storage protects years of estate planning work and ensures your family can access essential information when they need it most.

Warning: Failure to Update Insurance Risks

Insurance coverage gaps represent one of the most serious risks facing homeowners who complete trust transfers without updating their policies. Understanding these risks motivates prompt action to protect your investment.

Coverage gap scenarios that create expensive problems:

Property damage claims may be delayed or denied if insurance companies discover trust ownership that wasn't properly reported. While most companies ultimately honor valid claims, disputes during emergency situations create stress and financial pressure when you need insurance protection most.

Liability claims against property owners can become complicated when ownership structures don't match insurance policy designations. If someone is injured on your property and sues both you individually and the trust, coverage gaps can leave some claims unprotected.

Title insurance complications may arise if your insurance policy doesn't reflect current ownership. Title insurance protects against title defects, but coverage typically applies only to the named insured parties.

Mortgage insurance problems can occur if your lender's required insurance doesn't properly cover trust-owned collateral. While this rarely results in loan acceleration, it can create administrative headaches and potential coverage disputes.

Real-world consequences of insurance oversights:

Claim processing delays while insurance companies investigate ownership discrepancies and determine coverage applicability

Additional premium charges if insurers treat trust ownership changes as policy modifications requiring underwriting review

Coverage exclusions for claims arising during periods when ownership changes weren't properly reported

Legal complications if liability claims involve both individual and trust ownership issues that weren't addressed in policy language

Prevention strategies for insurance gaps:

Immediate notification within 30 days of recording your trust deed prevents most coverage complications

Written documentation of all communications with insurance companies provides records for future reference

Policy review to ensure trust ownership is properly reflected in coverage terms and beneficiary designations

Agent consultation about any additional coverage needs arising from trust ownership and trustee responsibilities

Umbrella policy coordination to ensure broader liability coverage properly includes trust-owned property and trustee activities

Coverage verification through updated declarations pages and policy language that specifically addresses trust ownership

The insurance risks associated with unreported trust transfers are easily preventable through prompt notification and proper documentation, but the consequences of neglecting these updates can be financially devastating when problems arise.

Property Tax Assessment Protection

Property tax reassessment triggered by ownership changes can dramatically increase your annual tax burden, but proper exemption filing typically prevents reassessment for transfers to your own revocable trust.

Reassessment triggers and protection: Most states that periodically reassess property for tax purposes include exemptions for transfers that don't change beneficial ownership. Trust transfers typically qualify for these exemptions because you remain the beneficial owner - you've only changed the legal form of ownership.

California Proposition 13 protection prevents reassessment for transfers to revocable trusts where you remain the beneficiary. However, you must file a Preliminary Change of Ownership Report (PCOR) and possibly additional forms to claim this exemption.

Texas reassessment protection generally applies to qualifying trust transfers, but you may need to provide documentation proving your trust qualifies under Texas law and that you remain the primary beneficiary.

Florida property tax benefits typically continue for homestead properties transferred to revocable trusts, but some counties require notification and documentation to verify continued eligibility.

Filing requirements by state type:

States requiring active exemption claims:

- California: PCOR filing required
- New York: Transfer tax return documenting exemption

- Pennsylvania: Local transfer declarations often required
- Illinois: Property Transfer Declaration may be required

States with automatic exemptions:

- Texas: Generally automatic for qualifying trusts
- Florida: Usually automatic for homestead properties
- Arizona: Typically automatic for revocable trust transfers
- Nevada: Generally automatic with proper deed language

Documentation needed for exemption claims:

- **Copy of recorded deed** showing trust transfer
- **Trust certificate** proving trust terms and your beneficiary status
- **Exemption application forms** required by your county
- **Affidavits** confirming continued use and occupancy
- **Previous exemption certificates** showing historical exemption status

Exemption filing deadlines:

- **California:** Within 45 days of recording deed
- **Texas:** During annual exemption application period
- **Florida:** Varies by county, often during regular exemption cycles
- **New York:** With transfer tax return filing

Missing exemption filing consequences:

- **Immediate reassessment** to current market value
- **Loss of historical exemption benefits** that may be difficult to restore
- **Increased annual tax burden** potentially costing thousands of dollars annually
- **Administrative appeals process** to restore benefits if filing deadlines are missed

Exemption verification and monitoring: Review property tax statements after transfer to confirm exemptions appear correctly

Appeal incorrect assessments promptly if reassessment occurs despite proper exemption filing

Maintain exemption documentation in permanent files for future reference

Monitor renewal requirements for exemptions that require annual or periodic renewal applications

Property tax exemption protection requires attention to state-specific requirements and deadlines, but the potential savings often justify careful compliance with filing procedures.

Ongoing Trust Administration Responsibilities

Completing your property transfer creates ongoing trust administration responsibilities that ensure your trust continues serving its intended purposes effectively. While revocable trust administration during your lifetime is generally straightforward, understanding these responsibilities helps you maintain proper trust operation.

Basic trust administration during your lifetime includes:

Asset management responsibilities as trustee require you to manage trust assets prudently and in accordance with trust terms. For trust-owned real estate, this means:

- Maintaining property in good condition
- Paying property taxes, insurance, and assessments on time
- Making reasonable improvements and repairs
- Handling rental income and expenses (for investment properties)
- Keeping adequate records of trust asset management

Record keeping requirements for trust assets don't require separate accounting systems for revocable trusts, but good records help your successor trustee and provide documentation if questions arise. Maintain:

- Property tax records and payment receipts
- Insurance policies and claims documentation
- Major repair and improvement records
- Income and expense records for rental properties
- Mortgage payment records and correspondence

Trust document security becomes crucial because your successor trustee will need these documents to prove trust existence and administration authority. Store trust documents securely while ensuring authorized family members know location and access procedures.

Communication with successor trustees helps prepare them for eventual responsibilities. Share information about:

- Trust document location and organization
- Property management procedures and service provider contacts
- Family dynamics and beneficiary relationships
- Estate planning goals and priorities

Periodic trust review ensures your trust continues meeting your goals as circumstances change. Annual reviews might address:

- Changes in family relationships or circumstances
- New assets requiring trust transfer
- Updates to beneficiary designations
- Successor trustee availability and capability
- Coordination with other estate planning documents

Professional assistance for trust administration: While most ongoing administration tasks are straightforward, some situations benefit from professional guidance:

- **Tax planning decisions** involving trust assets
- **Complex asset management** requiring specialized expertise
- **Family conflicts** affecting trust administration
- **Legal changes** that might affect trust operation
- **Amendment needs** for changing circumstances

Trust administration success factors:

Maintain organized records that your successor can understand and use effectively

Stay informed about legal changes affecting trust operation in your state

Communicate openly with family members about trust arrangements and expectations

Plan for succession by keeping successor trustees informed and prepared

Seek help when situations arise beyond your expertise or comfort level

Successful ongoing trust administration ensures your estate planning objectives are met while minimizing burden on your family when they eventually need to handle trust assets and distributions.

Key Takeaways from Post-Transfer Protection

Insurance policy updates represent critical post-transfer tasks that prevent coverage gaps and claim disputes, requiring prompt notification to insurance companies and proper policy modifications reflecting trust ownership. Mortgage servicer notification, while not legally required, maintains good relationships and prevents administrative complications during ongoing loan servicing.

Property tax exemption filing protects against reassessment that could dramatically increase annual tax burden, with filing requirements and deadlines varying significantly by state but exemption benefits typically available for transfers to own revocable trusts. HOA notification requirements depend on governing documents but usually involve simple administrative updates rather than approval processes.

Document storage best practices protect years of estate planning work through secure storage, proper organization, and family access planning that ensures essential documents remain available when needed. Digital backup strategies complement physical storage while providing convenient access for routine needs.

Insurance coverage gaps represent serious financial risks that are easily preventable through prompt notification and proper documentation, with failure to update coverage potentially resulting in claim delays or coverage disputes during emergencies. Property tax assessment protection requires understanding state-specific filing requirements and deadlines, but proper compliance typically preserves significant annual tax savings.

Ongoing trust administration responsibilities ensure continued effective trust operation through proper asset management, record keeping, and periodic review while preparing successor trustees for eventual administration duties.

The next chapter addresses special situations involving mortgaged properties and the federal law protections that make these transfers possible without lender permission.

Chapter 10: Mortgaged Properties

Carmen Rodriguez received a phone call that made her heart race. Her mortgage company had discovered her recent trust transfer and was demanding immediate explanation. "We need to discuss your unauthorized property transfer," the voice on the phone stated firmly. "You may have violated your loan agreement."

Carmen's hands trembled as she hung up. She'd carefully researched Arizona's trust transfer requirements and successfully recorded her deed three weeks earlier. Everything seemed perfect until this call. Now she worried she might lose her home over what she thought was a routine estate planning transaction.

The next morning, Carmen called back with information she'd researched overnight about federal protections for trust transfers. Armed with knowledge about the Garn-St. Germain Act and her rights as a homeowner, Carmen calmly explained her transfer to the mortgage company representative. Within ten minutes, the issue was resolved, her file was updated, and the representative apologized for the initial confusion.

"I learned that knowledge is power when dealing with mortgage companies," Carmen reflected. "Once I understood my rights and could explain them clearly, the whole situation changed."

Carmen's experience reflects a common challenge with mortgaged property transfers: mortgage companies often react with concern or confusion when they discover ownership changes, but federal law provides strong protection for homeowners transferring their primary residence to their own revocable living trust. Understanding these protections and how to communicate them effectively prevents most mortgage-related complications.

Most homeowners have mortgages, making this knowledge essential rather than optional. The good news is that federal law strongly protects your right to make these transfers, and most mortgage companies handle trust transfers routinely once they understand what you've done and why.

Federal Law Protections Explained

The Garn-St. Germain Depository Institutions Act of 1982 revolutionized homeowners' rights regarding property transfers by specifically protecting certain transfers from due-on-sale clause enforcement. This federal law prevents lenders from accelerating loan payments solely because you transfer your property to your own revocable living trust.

Historical context for understanding current protections: Before 1982, mortgage due-on-sale clauses gave lenders broad authority to demand full loan payment whenever property ownership changed, even for family transfers or estate planning transactions. Lenders used this power to force loan payoffs during periods of rising interest rates, allowing them to re-lend money at higher rates.

Congress enacted Garn-St. Germain to balance lender interests with homeowner rights, specifically protecting certain transfers that don't increase lender risk while preserving lender authority over transfers that do create additional risk.

Specific protections under Garn-St. Germain Act: Section 1701j-3(d)(8) of the Act specifically protects "a transfer to a relative resulting from the death of a borrower" and "a transfer where the spouse or children of the borrower become an owner of the property." While this language doesn't explicitly mention living trusts, federal regulators and courts have consistently interpreted it to protect transfers to revocable living trusts where the borrower remains the beneficial owner.

The practical protection works like this: You can transfer your primary residence to your own revocable living trust without triggering due-on-sale clauses, provided you remain the trust beneficiary and continue making loan payments as agreed. The lender cannot demand full payment solely because of the ownership change.

Protected transfer characteristics:

- **Primary residence** (not investment or rental property)
- **Transfer to your own revocable trust** (not irrevocable trusts or trusts for others)
- **You remain beneficiary** with right to live in and control the property
- **Continued payment performance** according to original loan terms
- **No increase in lender risk** because beneficial ownership hasn't changed

Limitations on Garn-St. Germain protection: The Act doesn't protect all property transfers. **Unprotected transfers** include:

- Investment or rental property transfers
- Transfers to irrevocable trusts where you lose beneficial ownership
- Transfers to other people's trusts
- Transfers combined with other significant changes like assumption by new borrowers
- Transfers that violate other loan terms beyond the due-on-sale clause

Federal enforcement and lender compliance: Garn-St. Germain is federal law that supersedes state laws and individual loan agreements. Lenders cannot opt out of its protections through loan document language, and homeowners can enforce their rights through federal court if necessary.

However, practical enforcement usually involves education rather than litigation. Most mortgage companies comply with federal law once they understand it applies to your situation. The key is communicating your rights clearly and providing appropriate documentation.

Regulatory guidance supporting homeowner protections: Federal banking regulators have consistently supported broad interpretation of Garn-St. Germain protections for living trust transfers. Office of the Comptroller of the Currency guidance specifically acknowledges that transfers to revocable living trusts generally don't increase lender risk and should be protected under federal law.

This regulatory backing provides additional support when communicating with mortgage companies about your transfer rights and helps explain why most lenders ultimately accept trust transfers without objection.

Lender Notification Strategies

Proactive communication with your mortgage company prevents most complications and maintains good relationships while protecting your rights under federal law. The notification approach you choose can significantly affect your lender's response and your overall transfer experience.

Timing considerations for lender notification:

Before recording provides maximum opportunity for addressing lender concerns but isn't legally required. Some homeowners prefer this approach because it allows discussion and resolution of issues before the transfer becomes public record.

After recording is more common and often more practical because you can present the transfer as completed fact rather than proposed action. This approach prevents lenders from attempting to discourage or delay your transfer.

Concurrent with recording works well if you're confident about your rights and want to provide prompt notification without seeking permission or approval.

No notification is legally permissible in many situations since Garn-St. Germain doesn't require homeowner notification for protected transfers. However, lenders typically discover ownership changes eventually through property tax records, insurance updates, or routine monitoring, making proactive notification generally preferable.

Notification content and approach:

Start with confidence by explaining your transfer matter-of-factly rather than asking permission or apologizing. You're exercising legal rights, not requesting favors.

Reference federal law protection specifically mentioning Garn-St. Germain Act and its protection for trust transfers. This immediately establishes the legal foundation for your transfer.

Provide essential information including:

- Property address and loan number
- Explanation that you've transferred to your own revocable living trust
- Confirmation that you remain the beneficiary and will continue making payments
- Request for any specific forms or procedures they require

Attach supporting documentation such as:

- Copy of recorded deed showing trust ownership
- Trust certificate proving trust existence and your beneficiary status
- Reference to specific Garn-St. Germain Act sections protecting your transfer

Sample notification language: "I am writing to notify you that I have transferred my primary residence located at [Property Address] to my revocable living trust for estate planning purposes. This transfer is specifically protected under the Garn-St. Germain Depository Institutions Act, 12 USC 1701j-3(d), which prohibits enforcement of due-on-sale clauses for transfers to the borrower's own revocable trust. I remain the trust beneficiary and will continue making all payments according to the original loan terms. Please update your records to reflect trust ownership and advise me of any specific procedures you require."

Handling different lender responses:

Positive responses (most common) involve simple acknowledgment and file updates. The lender notes the transfer, updates their records, and continues normal servicing.

Neutral responses may include requests for additional documentation like trust certificates or legal opinions. Provide requested information promptly while referencing federal law protection.

Negative responses occasionally occur when lender representatives don't understand federal law protections. Remain calm, provide educational information about Garn-St. Germain, and escalate to supervisors if necessary.

Confused responses happen when lender staff aren't familiar with trust transfers. Patient education usually resolves confusion, but be prepared to speak with multiple representatives or supervisors.

Follow-up procedures: Document all communications with written confirmation of verbal conversations and copies of all correspondence.

Monitor loan servicing to ensure transfers are reflected properly in monthly statements and account records.

Address discrepancies promptly if loan servicing problems arise from ownership change confusion.

Escalate unresolved issues to lender supervisors, state banking regulators, or federal agencies if lenders refuse to acknowledge federal law protections.

When Lenders Can and Cannot Object

Understanding the boundaries of lender authority helps you respond appropriately to various lender reactions while protecting your rights under federal law.

Lenders CANNOT object to or prevent:

Transfers specifically protected by Garn-St. Germain including transfers of your primary residence to your own revocable living trust where you remain the beneficiary. Federal law supersedes any contrary loan agreement language.

Your decision to make protected transfers regardless of lender preferences or policies. You don't need lender permission or approval for federally protected transfers.

Continued loan servicing after protected transfers. Lenders must continue accepting payments and providing normal servicing regardless of their feelings about trust ownership.

Discriminatory treatment based on trust ownership, such as refusing to process payments, provide account information, or handle routine servicing matters.

Lenders CAN legitimately:

Request documentation proving your transfer qualifies for federal protection, such as trust certificates showing you remain the beneficiary.

Require continued compliance with all other loan terms including payment schedules, insurance requirements, and property maintenance obligations.

Object to unprotected transfers such as investment property transfers, transfers to irrevocable trusts, or transfers to other people's trusts.

Enforce due-on-sale clauses for transfers that don't qualify for Garn-St. Germain protection.

Modify servicing procedures to accommodate trust ownership, such as requiring trustee signatures for certain transactions.

Common lender objection scenarios and responses:

"You need our permission for any ownership change" Response: Federal law specifically protects transfers to your own revocable trust without requiring lender permission. Reference Garn-St. Germain Act Section 1701j-3(d).

"Trust ownership violates your loan agreement" Response: Federal law supersedes loan agreement language regarding protected transfers. Loan agreements cannot override federal statutory protections.

"We don't accept payments from trusts" Response: You remain personally liable for loan payments regardless of trust ownership. The payment source doesn't change your obligation or lender's duty to accept payments.

"You must transfer the property back to individual ownership" Response: Federal law protects your right to maintain trust ownership. You're not required to undo protected transfers because of lender preferences.

"We're calling your loan due immediately" Response: Federal law prohibits due-on-sale enforcement for protected transfers. Document this threat and consider reporting to federal banking regulators.

Documentation strategies for lender communications:

Written communication provides better documentation than phone calls and allows more thoughtful presentation of legal arguments.

Professional tone maintains relationships while firmly asserting your rights under federal law.

Legal citations including specific USC sections and regulatory guidance demonstrate your knowledge and preparation.

Escalation procedures through lender management, state banking regulators, or federal agencies provide recourse for persistent lender problems.

Legal consultation may be beneficial if lenders continue objecting despite clear federal law protection, though most situations resolve through education and patience.

The key principle is that **you have strong legal rights that lenders must respect**, but you need to assert and document these rights clearly when challenges arise.

Refinancing Considerations

Trust ownership can affect refinancing procedures and requirements, though most major lenders routinely handle trust-owned properties. Understanding these considerations helps you plan for future refinancing needs and avoid complications.

Common refinancing approaches for trust-owned properties:

Trust-to-trust refinancing allows you to refinance while maintaining trust ownership throughout the process. Many lenders now accommodate this approach routinely, though it may require:

- Additional documentation about trust terms and trustee authority
- Underwriting review of trust structure and beneficiary arrangements
- Possible higher costs or different loan programs
- Longer processing times for lender review

Temporary transfer approach involves transferring property back to individual ownership for refinancing, then immediately transferring back to trust ownership after closing. This approach:

- Accommodates lenders who don't handle trust-owned properties
- Uses familiar individual ownership underwriting procedures
- Requires two additional deed recordings (trust to individual, individual to trust)
- Adds complexity but ensures loan approval with conventional procedures

Lender-specific policies vary significantly:

- **Major banks** typically handle trust-owned properties routinely with established procedures
- **Credit unions** may have less experience but often accommodate trust ownership with additional documentation
- **Mortgage brokers** can shop among lenders comfortable with trust ownership
- **Portfolio lenders** keeping loans in-house often provide more flexibility

Refinancing preparation for trust-owned properties:

Research lender policies before applying to ensure they handle trust-owned properties or understand temporary transfer procedures.

Prepare trust documentation including trust certificates, trustee resolutions, and possibly complete trust documents depending on lender requirements.

Plan for timing since trust-owned refinancing may take longer than conventional individual ownership refinancing.

Consider costs including additional documentation fees, possible higher rates, and costs for temporary transfers if required.

Maintain relationships with lenders experienced in trust-owned property financing for future needs.

Alternative refinancing strategies:

Home equity lines of credit may be easier to obtain on trust-owned properties since they involve less complex underwriting than full refinancing.

Portfolio lenders including community banks and credit unions sometimes provide more flexible policies for trust-owned properties.

Specialist lenders focusing on estate planning clients often have streamlined procedures for trust-owned property financing.

The refinancing landscape for trust-owned properties continues improving as trusts become more common and lenders develop experience with these arrangements.

Home Equity Line Impacts

Home equity lines of credit (HELOCs) present special considerations for trust-owned properties because these revolving credit facilities involve ongoing lender monitoring and potential future advances that can be affected by ownership structures.

HELOC continuation after trust transfer: Existing HELOCs typically continue operating normally after trust transfers, but lenders may require notification and documentation updates similar to mortgage notification procedures.

New HELOC applications on trust-owned properties: Obtaining new HELOCs on trust-owned properties may be easier than full refinancing because:

- Underwriting requirements are generally less extensive
- Lenders focus primarily on equity and income rather than complex ownership structures
- Processing times are typically shorter
- Documentation requirements may be simpler

HELOC-specific documentation requirements:

- **Trust certificates** proving trust existence and your authority as trustee
- **Beneficiary confirmations** showing you remain the beneficial owner
- **Trustee resolutions** authorizing HELOC applications and property pledging
- **Personal guarantees** ensuring you remain personally liable for HELOC obligations

Draw period considerations: During HELOC draw periods, you can typically access credit normally despite trust ownership. However, some lenders may require:

- Trustee signatures on draw requests above certain amounts
- Annual confirmations of trust status and beneficiary arrangements
- Updated documentation if trust terms change

Repayment period implications: When HELOCs convert from draw to repayment periods, trust ownership rarely creates complications. Continue making payments as required while maintaining trust ownership benefits.

HELOC modification or renewal: Trust ownership may affect your ability to modify HELOC terms or renew credit lines, though most established relationships continue smoothly. Plan ahead for potential documentation requirements or lender policy changes.

Reverse Mortgage Complications

Reverse mortgages present unique challenges for trust transfers because these loans have specific ownership and occupancy requirements that trust ownership can potentially affect.

Reverse mortgage ownership requirements: Most reverse mortgages require borrowers to own and occupy the property as their primary residence. Trust transfers can potentially conflict with these requirements unless handled properly according to both federal reverse mortgage regulations and individual loan terms.

FHA reverse mortgage considerations: FHA-insured reverse mortgages (HECM loans) have specific regulations about ownership changes. While transfers to revocable living trusts are generally permitted, they require:

- Prior approval from the loan servicer
- Documentation that you remain the beneficial owner and primary occupant
- Compliance with specific FHA procedures for ownership changes
- Possible additional requirements depending on loan terms and servicer policies

Proprietary reverse mortgage variations: Non-FHA reverse mortgages may have different requirements for trust transfers, ranging from straightforward accommodation to prohibition of ownership changes. Review your specific loan documents and contact your servicer before attempting trust transfers.

Reverse mortgage notification procedures: Contact servicer before transfer to understand specific requirements and obtain necessary approvals

Provide comprehensive documentation including trust documents, beneficiary confirmations, and occupancy certifications

Comply with timing requirements which may include advance notice periods or approval waiting periods

Maintain detailed records of all communications and approvals for future reference

Professional consultation recommended: Reverse mortgage trust transfers often benefit from professional guidance because:

- Loan terms vary significantly between lenders and programs
- Federal regulations create complex compliance requirements
- Errors can trigger loan acceleration or other serious consequences
- Individual loan documents may contain specific restrictions or procedures

If you have a reverse mortgage and want to transfer your property to a trust, consider consulting with an attorney experienced in both reverse mortgages and estate planning to ensure proper compliance with all requirements.

Professional Help Trigger: Complex Mortgage Situations

Certain mortgage situations push beyond DIY appropriateness and benefit significantly from professional assistance. These situations involve legal complexity, regulatory requirements, or lender relationships that require specialized knowledge.

Situations requiring professional guidance:

Multiple mortgages on the same property create complex lender notification requirements and potential conflicts between different loan terms or lender policies.

Commercial or investment property loans often have different due-on-sale provisions and may not qualify for Garn-St. Germain protection available for primary residences.

SBA or other government-backed loans may have specific regulations or approval requirements for ownership changes that go beyond conventional mortgage protections.

Loan modification or workout situations where you're currently negotiating with lenders about payment terms, forbearance, or other modifications that could be complicated by ownership changes.

Pending foreclosure or default situations where additional legal issues affect your transfer rights and lender relationships.

Foreign national borrowers or properties with international financing may involve additional legal considerations not covered by standard federal protections.

Business entity ownership where the property is currently owned by LLCs, partnerships, or corporations rather than individuals creates additional complexity for trust transfers.

Professional assistance options:

Limited consultation with attorneys experienced in mortgage law can provide specific guidance about your situation while allowing you to handle routine aspects yourself.

Lender negotiation assistance from attorneys can help resolve disputes or complicated lender requirements without full representation.

Document review services help ensure your communications and documentation meet legal requirements and effectively protect your interests.

Full representation may be justified for high-stakes situations involving valuable properties or complex lender relationships.

The decision about professional help depends on balancing the complexity and stakes of your situation against the costs and benefits of professional assistance.

Refinancing Impact Planning

Trust ownership affects refinancing procedures and requirements, making future planning an essential component of your transfer decision. Understanding these impacts helps you prepare for eventual refinancing needs and maintain financing flexibility.

Market trends affecting trust-owned refinancing: The mortgage industry's comfort with trust-owned properties has increased significantly as living trusts have become more common. Major lenders now routinely handle trust-owned property refinancing, though procedures and requirements continue varying between institutions.

Preparation strategies for future refinancing:

Maintain detailed trust records including trust certificates, amendments, and trustee documentation that lenders typically require for trust-owned property underwriting.

Keep transfer documentation including recorded deeds and lender notifications that demonstrate proper transfer procedures and lender acceptance.

Monitor lender policy changes that might affect future refinancing options or requirements for trust-owned properties.

Develop lender relationships with institutions experienced in trust-owned property financing to ensure future refinancing options.

Consider refinancing timing relative to trust transfer timing to minimize complications and administrative complexity.

Future refinancing decision factors:

Loan-to-value ratios on trust-owned properties typically follow the same guidelines as individual ownership, though some lenders may impose slightly more conservative requirements.

Interest rate availability generally matches individual ownership options, though trust-owned properties might not qualify for certain first-time buyer or special government programs.

Processing time expectations may be slightly longer for trust-owned properties due to additional documentation and underwriting review requirements.

Cost considerations including potential fees for trust documentation, legal opinions, or additional underwriting requirements that some lenders impose.

Alternative financing options such as portfolio lenders, credit unions, or specialist lenders may provide more favorable terms or procedures for trust-owned properties.

Planning for future refinancing helps ensure your trust transfer supports rather than complicates your long-term financing strategy and financial flexibility.

Communication Templates and Scripts

Effective communication with mortgage companies requires clear, confident presentation of information that educates lenders while asserting your rights under federal law.

Initial notification letter template:

"Dear [Servicer Name],

I am writing to notify you that I have transferred my primary residence located at [Property Address], securing loan number [Loan Number], to my revocable living trust for estate planning purposes.

This transfer is specifically protected under the Garn-St. Germain Depository Institutions Act, 12 USC 1701j-3(d), which prohibits enforcement of due-on-sale clauses for transfers to the borrower's own revocable living trust. I remain the trust beneficiary with exclusive right to occupy and control the property, and I will continue making all loan payments according to the original terms.

Please update your records to reflect that the property is now owned by [Trust Name], and I serve as trustee. I remain personally liable for all loan obligations as the original borrower.

Enclosed you will find a copy of the recorded deed evidencing the transfer and a trust certificate confirming the trust terms and my beneficiary status. Please advise me of any additional documentation or procedures you require to update your files.

Thank you for your attention to this matter. I look forward to continuing our positive lending relationship under the new ownership structure.

Sincerely, [Your Name] [Your Contact Information]"

Phone conversation scripts:

Opening approach: "I'm calling to notify you about a recent ownership change on my mortgage. I've transferred my home to my living trust for estate planning, and I want to update your records."

If questions arise: "This type of transfer is specifically protected under federal law - the Garn-St. Germain Act. It doesn't affect my loan obligations or your security interest. I'm still responsible for all payments and the property still secures the loan."

If resistance occurs: "I understand this might be unfamiliar, but federal law specifically protects homeowners' rights to transfer their primary residence to their own revocable trust. I'm happy to provide documentation about the law and my specific situation."

If escalation needed: "I'd like to speak with a supervisor who's familiar with the Garn-St. Germain Act and trust ownership issues. This is a routine estate planning transfer protected by federal law."

Follow-up communication strategies:

Confirmation letters documenting verbal conversations and agreements reached with lender representatives.

Status inquiry letters following up on processing delays or incomplete file updates.

Escalation letters to lender management when initial representatives don't respond appropriately to federal law protections.

Regulatory complaint letters to federal banking agencies when lenders refuse to comply with federal law requirements.

Effective communication combines education, assertiveness, and patience to achieve proper recognition of your rights while maintaining positive lender relationships.

Key Takeaways from Mortgage Property Management

Federal Garn-St. Germain Act protections specifically prevent lenders from enforcing due-on-sale clauses against transfers of primary residences to borrowers' own revocable living trusts, with these protections superseding contrary loan agreement language and providing strong legal foundation for trust transfers. Understanding protected versus unprotected transfer characteristics helps homeowners assert their rights confidently while recognizing situations that don't qualify for federal protection.

Lender notification strategies balance legal requirements with practical relationship management, with proactive communication generally preventing complications while federal law doesn't require advance permission for protected transfers. Clear, confident notification including federal law references and supporting documentation typically resolves lender concerns efficiently.

Lender authority limitations under federal law prevent objections to protected transfers while allowing legitimate requests for documentation and continued compliance with loan terms other than due-on-sale provisions. Understanding these boundaries helps homeowners respond appropriately to various lender reactions and escalate unresolved issues when necessary.

Refinancing considerations for trust-owned properties involve varying lender policies and procedures, with industry trends showing increased accommodation but potential additional requirements including documentation, processing time, and costs that affect future financing flexibility.

Home equity line impacts generally involve simpler procedures than full refinancing, while reverse mortgage complications require careful attention to specific federal regulations and potential professional consultation due to complex compliance requirements.

Complex mortgage situations involving multiple loans, commercial properties, government-backed financing, or workout scenarios typically benefit from professional assistance due to specialized requirements and higher stakes for errors or non-compliance.

The next chapter addresses co-owned properties and the additional coordination required when multiple parties share ownership interests in transferred property.

Chapter 11: Joint Tenancy and Community Property

When Lisa and Mark Patterson divorced after 18 years of marriage, they agreed to keep their Denver home jointly owned until their youngest daughter graduated high school. Two years later, Lisa wanted to transfer her half-interest to her living trust for estate planning, but she hadn't considered how joint ownership would complicate this seemingly simple transaction.

"I thought I could just transfer my half like any other property," Lisa explained. "I didn't realize that joint tenancy ownership means we both have to agree on any ownership changes, and that my transfer might affect Mark's ownership rights too."

Mark, still bitter about the divorce, initially refused to cooperate with Lisa's estate planning goals. He worried that trust ownership might affect his rights to the property or complicate future sale decisions. Their disagreement created a standstill that lasted three months while their attorneys worked out an arrangement that protected both parties' interests.

Eventually, Lisa and Mark agreed to convert their joint tenancy to tenancy in common ownership, allowing Lisa to transfer her specific percentage interest to her trust while preserving Mark's individual ownership of his portion. The solution required legal assistance, additional documentation, and careful coordination, but it achieved Lisa's estate planning goals while respecting Mark's concerns.

Lisa's experience illustrates the additional complexity that co-ownership adds to trust transfers. Multiple owners create multiple interests that must be coordinated, and different ownership structures provide different rights that affect transfer options. Understanding these relationships is essential for successful trust transfers when you don't own property alone.

Co-owned property represents one of the most common complications in DIY trust transfers, affecting millions of American homeowners who share ownership with spouses, family members, or other parties. The key to success lies in understanding different ownership structures and how they affect your transfer rights and requirements.

Joint Tenancy to Tenants in Common Conversion

Joint tenancy ownership includes the "right of survivorship," meaning surviving owners automatically inherit deceased owners' interests. This feature provides benefits for estate planning but can complicate trust transfers because it affects how ownership interests can be transferred.

Joint tenancy characteristics affecting trust transfers:

- **Equal ownership** - all joint tenants own equal shares regardless of contribution amounts
- **Right of survivorship** - surviving joint tenants automatically inherit deceased owners' shares
- **Unity requirements** - all owners must acquire interests at the same time, in the same deed, with identical ownership rights
- **Severance rules** - certain actions can "sever" joint tenancy, converting it to tenancy in common

Trust transfer impacts on joint tenancy: When one joint tenant transfers their interest to a trust, most states treat this as "severing" the joint tenancy because the trust becomes a new owner with different characteristics than the original joint tenants. The result is conversion to tenancy in common ownership.

Tenancy in common characteristics:

- **Unequal ownership** - owners can hold different percentage interests
- **No survivorship rights** - deceased owners' interests pass to their heirs rather than surviving co-owners
- **Individual transfer rights** - each owner can transfer their interest independently
- **Separate inheritance** - each owner's interest becomes part of their individual estate

Conversion implications for co-owners:

For the transferring owner: Trust transfer achieves estate planning goals by ensuring your interest passes through your trust rather than automatically to surviving co-owners.

For non-transferring owners: Loss of survivorship rights means they won't automatically inherit your interest, but they also aren't affected by your trust beneficiary designations or estate planning decisions.

Example conversion scenario: John and Sarah own their Phoenix home as joint tenants with rights of survivorship. Sarah transfers her interest to her living trust. Result: John owns 50% as individual tenant in common, and Sarah's trust owns 50% as tenant in common. When Sarah dies, her trust distributes her 50% according to trust terms rather than automatically to John.

Conversion procedures: Simple transfers automatically sever joint tenancy in most states without additional documentation. Recording your trust transfer deed accomplishes both the trust transfer and the severance.

Explicit severance deeds sometimes provide clearer documentation of ownership change by specifically stating the intent to sever joint tenancy and convert to tenancy in common.

Percentage interest documentation helps clarify ownership shares after conversion, especially important if original contributions weren't equal or if property values have changed significantly.

Agreement documentation among co-owners about severance and conversion terms prevents future disputes about ownership rights and responsibilities.

Communication with co-owners about conversion implications helps prevent misunderstandings and maintain positive relationships despite ownership structure changes.

Understanding joint tenancy severance helps you make informed decisions about trust transfers and communicate effectively with co-owners about how ownership changes affect everyone's rights and interests.

Community Property State Considerations

Nine states follow community property principles that significantly affect trust transfer procedures and requirements for married couples. Community property rules create shared ownership in marital assets that requires both spouses' involvement in trust transfers.

Community property states include: Arizona, California, Idaho, Louisiana, Nevada, New Mexico, Texas, Washington, and Wisconsin. Five additional states (Alaska, Florida, Kentucky, South Dakota, and Tennessee) allow married couples to elect community property treatment for specific assets.

Community property ownership principles:

- **Shared ownership** - both spouses automatically own 50% interests in community property
- **Management rights** - either spouse can manage community property, but both must consent to transfers
- **Inheritance rights** - deceased spouse's share passes through their estate rather than automatically to surviving spouse

- **Property classification** - assets acquired during marriage with community funds are generally community property

Trust transfer implications in community property states:

Both spouses must participate in trust transfers of community property, even if only one spouse is actively involved in estate planning. This requirement exists because community property ownership gives both spouses equal rights that neither can transfer without the other's consent.

Separate property transfers can be handled individually by the owning spouse. Property owned before marriage, acquired by gift or inheritance, or purchased with separate funds typically qualifies as separate property transferable without spousal consent.

Characterization documentation may be required to prove whether property is community or separate, especially for property acquired before marriage or with mixed funding sources.

Community property trust transfers typically require:

- **Both spouses as grantors** in the transfer deed
- **Joint trust ownership** or coordination between separate trusts
- **Spousal consent documentation** even for transfers to joint trusts
- **Community property characterization** language in transfer documents

Example community property transfer scenarios:

Joint trust transfer: Married couple transfers community property home to their joint revocable living trust, with both spouses serving as trustees and beneficiaries.

Separate trust coordination: Each spouse has separate trusts but coordinates transfer of community property interests to ensure both trusts receive appropriate ownership shares.

Mixed property transfer: Home purchased with combination of separate and community funds requires detailed documentation of ownership percentages and separate consent procedures.

State-specific community property variations: California requires careful attention to Proposition 13 protections and community property characterization to preserve property tax benefits.

Texas combines community property rules with homestead rights that require specific trust language to preserve property tax exemptions.

Washington has unique community property trust provisions that provide enhanced estate planning benefits but require specialized drafting.

Nevada offers community property trust elections that can provide estate planning advantages but require professional guidance for proper implementation.

Understanding your state's specific community property rules helps ensure proper compliance and optimal estate planning outcomes for married couples.

Spousal Consent Requirements

Many states require spousal consent for property transfers, even when property is individually owned, to protect marital property rights and prevent fraudulent transfers that would harm non-consenting spouses.

Spousal consent laws vary by state:

Community property states generally require both spouses' consent for any transfer of community property, regardless of whose name appears on the deed.

169

Dower and curtesy states (primarily eastern states) provide spouses with potential inheritance rights in real estate owned by their marriage partners, requiring spousal consent to release these rights.

Homestead protection states may require spousal consent for transfers of homestead property to ensure protection continues for surviving spouses.

Elective share states provide surviving spouses with rights to claim portions of deceased spouses' estates, potentially affecting individual property transfer rights.

Consent documentation requirements:

Spousal joinder in deeds involves both spouses signing transfer documents, even if only one spouse owns the property individually.

Separate consent documents allow non-owning spouses to consent to transfers through standalone documents rather than deed signatures.

Homestead waivers release spousal homestead rights that might otherwise prevent or complicate property transfers.

Marital property releases document spouses' agreement to individual property transfers without affecting marital property rights in other assets.

Consent verification procedures: Notarization requirements typically apply to spousal consent documents, requiring both spouses to appear before notaries for proper acknowledgment.

Independent legal advice is sometimes required or recommended to ensure non-owning spouses understand their rights and the consequences of providing consent.

Recording procedures may require consent documents to be recorded along with transfer deeds to provide public notice of spousal approval.

Timing coordination ensures spousal consent remains valid through deed recording, since significant delays between consent and transfer can create complications.

Situations where spousal consent may not be required:

Separate property transfers in community property states typically don't require spousal consent if property characterization is clear.

Trust transfers in non-community property states may not require consent if state law doesn't provide spouses with ownership rights in individually-owned property.

Previously released rights through prenuptial agreements, property settlements, or other legal documents may eliminate consent requirements.

Abandoned property or estranged spouses may create situations where consent isn't practically obtainable, requiring legal procedures to address non-consenting spouse issues.

Understanding spousal consent requirements helps you plan appropriate procedures and avoid transfer delays or complications arising from unaddressed spouse rights.

Warning: Disagreeing Co-owners

Co-owner disagreements represent one of the most challenging complications in property trust transfers. When co-owners can't agree on transfer terms, timing, or procedures, the entire process can stall indefinitely while relationships deteriorate and legal costs mount.

Common sources of co-owner disagreement:

Estate planning philosophy differences where some owners want trust protection while others prefer simpler arrangements or different estate planning approaches.

Control concerns about how trust ownership might affect property management decisions, sale timing, or future financing options.

Family relationship tensions including divorce situations, inheritance disputes, or long-standing personal conflicts that affect cooperation on property matters.

Financial concerns about costs, tax implications, or potential changes in property expenses or management responsibilities.

Timing preferences where owners have different urgency levels about completing trust transfers or estate planning generally.

Misunderstanding of trust implications leading to unfounded fears about loss of ownership rights or control over property decisions.

Prevention strategies for co-owner conflicts:

Early communication about estate planning goals and trust transfer intentions helps identify potential disagreements before they become entrenched positions.

Education about trust benefits can address misconceptions and help co-owners understand how trust ownership protects everyone's interests.

Professional consultation with attorneys or estate planners can provide neutral explanation of options and implications for all co-owners.

Compromise solutions such as gradual transfers, temporary arrangements, or alternative estate planning approaches may accommodate different preferences.

Written agreements about transfer procedures, timing, and ongoing management help prevent disputes and provide clear frameworks for cooperation.

Resolution approaches for existing disagreements:

Mediation services provide neutral assistance for resolving co-owner disputes without expensive litigation or permanent relationship damage.

Partition actions allow individual owners to force property division or sale when cooperation becomes impossible, though this approach typically destroys relationships and reduces everyone's financial outcomes.

Buyout arrangements where one owner purchases others' interests can resolve disagreements while allowing individual estate planning freedom.

Professional arbitration provides binding dispute resolution when owners can agree on arbitration procedures but can't resolve substantive disagreements.

Legal separation of interests through court proceedings may be necessary when cooperation is impossible and other resolution approaches fail.

Risk management for disagreeing co-owners:

Document all communications about transfer disagreements to protect your interests and provide evidence if legal proceedings become necessary.

Avoid unilateral actions that might damage co-owner relationships or create legal complications for other owners.

Seek legal counsel when disagreements involve significant assets or threaten to escalate into litigation.

Consider alternatives to trust transfers that might achieve estate planning goals without requiring co-owner cooperation.

Protect your interests while remaining open to compromise solutions that address everyone's legitimate concerns.

The key to managing co-owner disagreements is recognizing them early, addressing them honestly, and seeking appropriate help before positions become entrenched and relationships suffer permanent damage.

Percentage Interest Calculations

When co-owners hold unequal interests in property, trust transfers must accurately reflect these ownership percentages to ensure proper title transfer and avoid creating title problems or disputes among owners.

Determining current ownership percentages:

Review current deed language for specific percentage references such as "David Smith, as to an undivided 60% interest, and Linda Smith, as to an undivided 40% interest."

Examine contribution records if ownership percentages aren't clearly stated. Original purchase documents, improvement receipts, and payment records help establish ownership shares.

Consider legal presumptions in your state:

- Joint tenancy typically presumes equal ownership regardless of contribution amounts
- Tenancy in common may presume equal ownership unless percentages are specified
- Community property automatically creates 50/50 ownership for married couples

Trace ownership history through previous deeds if ownership percentages have changed over time through partial transfers, inheritance, or other transactions.

Calculate percentage transfer amounts:

Partial transfers require careful calculation to ensure you transfer the correct percentage of your ownership interest to your trust.

Example: You own 60% of property individually and want to transfer your entire interest to your trust. Your deed should transfer "an undivided 60% interest" rather than describing the entire property.

Full ownership verification ensures you're not accidentally transferring more than you own, which could invalidate the transfer or create title problems.

Mathematical accuracy in percentage calculations prevents disputes and ensures clear title records for future transactions.

Documentation requirements for percentage transfers:

Clear percentage language in deeds such as "Grantor hereby transfers an undivided [percentage]% interest in the following described property..."

Ownership verification through current deed references, title reports, or other documentation proving your ownership percentage.

Co-owner coordination to ensure all ownership percentages continue adding up to 100% after your transfer.

Future transaction consideration about how percentage trust ownership affects property sales, refinancing, or additional transfers.

Common percentage calculation errors:

Transferring entire property when you only own a percentage interest

Incorrect percentage calculations based on contributions rather than legal ownership shares

Assuming equal ownership when deeds specify unequal percentage interests

Failing to coordinate with co-owners about how your transfer affects their ownership calculations

Accurate percentage calculations ensure your trust transfer accomplishes your estate planning goals without creating title problems or disputes with co-owners.

Survivorship Implications

Trust transfers of co-owned property affect survivorship rights and inheritance patterns in ways that require careful consideration of both your estate planning goals and co-owners' expectations.

Joint tenancy survivorship changes: Converting joint tenancy to tenancy in common through trust transfer eliminates automatic survivorship rights. Consider these implications:

For your estate planning: Your trust interest passes according to trust terms rather than automatically to surviving co-owners, achieving your estate planning objectives.

For surviving co-owners: They don't automatically inherit your interest, potentially disappointing co-owners who expected survivorship benefits.

For your beneficiaries: They inherit your property interest rather than losing it to automatic survivorship, protecting your family's inheritance.

Community property survivorship: Community property ownership typically doesn't include automatic survivorship rights, so trust transfers usually don't change inheritance patterns for non-transferring spouses.

Tenancy in common survivorship: This ownership form never includes survivorship rights, so trust transfers don't change inheritance patterns but do affect how your interest is managed and distributed.

Survivorship planning strategies:

Coordinate trust terms with co-owners' estate planning to ensure everyone's goals are respected and potential conflicts are minimized.

Consider life insurance to provide inheritance for co-owners who lose survivorship rights due to your trust transfer.

Plan for property management during transition periods when some interests are in trust while others remain in individual ownership.

Address potential conflicts between trust beneficiaries and surviving co-owners about property management, sale decisions, or occupancy rights.

Document agreements about survivorship changes and their implications for ongoing property relationships.

Communication about survivorship changes:

Explain implications to co-owners so they understand how your trust transfer affects their inheritance expectations.

Discuss alternatives such as coordinated trust transfers or alternative estate planning approaches that might better serve everyone's interests.

Consider mediation if disagreements arise about survivorship changes and their effects on family relationships or financial expectations.

Professional consultation can help develop solutions that address everyone's legitimate concerns while achieving your estate planning objectives.

Understanding survivorship implications helps you make informed decisions about trust transfers and communicate effectively with co-owners about how ownership changes affect everyone's long-term interests.

State-Specific Co-ownership Rules

Different states apply varying rules to co-owned property that significantly affect trust transfer procedures, requirements, and implications for multiple owners.

Community property states (Arizona, California, Idaho, Louisiana, Nevada, New Mexico, Texas, Washington, Wisconsin) apply special rules:

- **Automatic 50/50 ownership** for property acquired during marriage with community funds
- **Both spouse consent** typically required for community property transfers
- **Special trust provisions** may be needed to preserve community property tax benefits
- **Characterization documentation** required to distinguish community from separate property

Common law property states (the remaining 41 states) follow different principles:

- **Individual ownership** based on whose name appears on deed
- **Spousal consent** required only in states with dower/curtesy or homestead laws

- **Joint tenancy presumptions** varying by state for married couple ownership
- **Separate trust transfers** typically allowed without spouse involvement for individually-owned property

Dower and curtesy states provide surviving spouses with potential inheritance rights that require consent for property transfers:

- **Traditional dower/curtesy states:** Primarily southeastern states maintaining historic spousal property rights
- **Modified versions:** Some states provide updated spousal protection through elective share or homestead laws
- **Consent requirements:** Transfers of individually-owned property may require spousal joinder or consent to release potential spouse rights

Homestead protection states require spousal consent for transfers of homestead property to ensure protection continues for surviving family members.

Trust transfer coordination in co-ownership situations:

Determine ownership structure through current deed examination and state law research to understand what consent and coordination requirements apply.

Identify required parties for your specific situation, including all owners and potentially non-owning spouses whose consent may be required.

Plan coordination procedures for gathering necessary signatures, consents, and documentation from all required parties.

Address timing issues when multiple parties have different scheduling needs or urgency levels about completing transfers.

Coordinate professional assistance if some parties want legal guidance while others prefer DIY approaches.

Documentation requirements for co-owned transfers:

All owner signatures on transfer deeds, with proper notarization for all signing parties

Spousal consent documents when required by state law or ownership structure

Percentage interest calculations clearly stated in transfer documents

Trust coordination agreements if multiple owners are transferring to different trusts

Professional consultation planning to address complex coordination issues or disagreements among owners

The complexity of co-owned property transfers often pushes toward professional assistance, especially when multiple parties have different goals, timelines, or comfort levels with DIY approaches.

Coordination Templates and Agreements

Successful co-owned property trust transfers require clear communication and coordination among all parties. Written agreements and templates help manage this complexity while preventing misunderstandings that could derail the entire process.

Co-owner agreement template elements:

Transfer timeline establishing agreed-upon deadlines for document preparation, execution, and recording to ensure coordinated completion.

Cost sharing arrangements for recording fees, professional consultations, and other transfer-related expenses that benefit all parties.

Document preparation responsibilities clarifying who handles deed preparation, research, and coordination with county offices.

Professional assistance decisions about when to seek legal guidance and how to share costs if some parties want professional help while others prefer DIY approaches.

Future property management agreements about how trust ownership affects ongoing decisions about property maintenance, improvements, or sale.

Sample co-owner coordination agreement:

"The undersigned co-owners of the property located at [Property Address] agree to coordinate our estate planning transfers as follows:

1. Timeline: We will complete all necessary documents by [Date] and record transfers by [Date].
2. Costs: Recording fees and other transfer costs will be shared proportionally based on our ownership interests.
3. Preparation: [Name] will prepare deed documents using forms appropriate for our county, with all parties reviewing documents before execution.
4. Professional Help: If questions arise requiring legal consultation, we will share consultation costs equally and make decisions collectively about professional guidance.
5. Future Management: Trust ownership will not affect our current property management arrangements, and all owners (individual or trust) will continue participating in major decisions according to ownership percentages.

This agreement helps us coordinate our individual estate planning goals while respecting everyone's interests in our shared property."

Spousal consent form template:

"I, [Spouse Name], spouse of [Owner Name], hereby consent to the transfer of the property located at [Property Address] to [Trust Name] for estate planning purposes. I understand this transfer may affect my potential inheritance rights in this property, and I voluntarily consent to this transfer without duress or undue influence.

I acknowledge that I have been advised to seek independent legal counsel regarding my rights and the implications of this consent, and I either have done so or voluntarily waive this right.

Dated: _____

[Spouse Signature]

State of [State] County of [County]

[Notary acknowledgment section]"

Agreement customization considerations:

State law compliance ensuring agreements meet local requirements for spousal consent and co-owner coordination

Individual situation adaptation for unique family circumstances, ownership structures, or estate planning goals

Professional review of agreements when complex situations or significant assets are involved

Update procedures for agreements if circumstances change during the transfer process

These templates provide starting points for coordination while requiring customization to specific situations and state requirements.

Key Takeaways from Co-owned Property Transfers

Joint tenancy to tenants in common conversion typically occurs automatically when one joint tenant transfers their interest to a trust, eliminating survivorship rights while achieving estate planning objectives for the transferring owner. Community property state considerations require both spouse participation in transfers and careful attention to characterization and consent requirements that vary significantly by state.

Spousal consent requirements depend on state law and ownership structure, with community property states generally requiring both spouse involvement while other states may require consent to release potential inheritance rights. Co-owner disagreements can derail transfer processes entirely, making early communication and professional mediation valuable investments when cooperation becomes difficult.

Percentage interest calculations ensure accurate transfer of ownership shares and prevent title problems, particularly important when co-owners hold unequal interests or when property values have changed since original acquisition. Survivorship implications affect inheritance patterns and family expectations, requiring careful consideration of how trust transfers change automatic inheritance rights.

State-specific co-ownership rules create varying requirements for consent, documentation, and procedures that affect transfer complexity and professional assistance needs. Coordination templates and agreements help manage multiple party involvement while preventing misunderstandings and ensuring successful completion.

Complex co-ownership situations often benefit from professional assistance due to legal complexity, relationship management needs, and potential for expensive errors when multiple parties have different interests and objectives.

The next chapter addresses investment and rental properties, where trust ownership creates additional considerations for income management, tenant relationships, and tax compliance.

Chapter 12: Investment and Rental Properties

Steven Park discovered that transferring his rental duplex in Sacramento to his living trust involved complications he hadn't anticipated. Unlike his primary residence transfer, which went smoothly, the rental property created a chain of additional requirements that caught him off guard.

"I thought property was property," Steven explained. "I didn't realize that rental income, tenant relationships, and different tax rules would make this transfer more complex than my house."

Steven's first surprise came when his property management company informed him that the lease agreements would need modification to reflect trust ownership. His second surprise arrived with questions from his accountant about tax identification numbers and rental income reporting for trust-owned property. His third surprise came from his insurance company, which required different coverage for trust-owned rental property than for trust-owned primary residences.

After six weeks of coordination and additional paperwork, Steven successfully completed his rental property transfer. "The transfer itself wasn't much different," he reflected. "But all the related business aspects - leases, taxes, insurance, management - required much more attention than I expected."

Steven's experience illustrates how investment and rental properties add business and tax considerations to trust transfers that don't exist for primary residences. While the basic transfer process remains similar, the surrounding business relationships and obligations require additional planning and coordination.

Investment property owners face unique considerations because trust ownership affects business operations, tax reporting, and legal relationships with tenants and service providers. Understanding these implications helps you plan effective transfers while maintaining smooth property operations.

Rental Income Handling in Trust

Trust ownership of rental properties affects income collection, expense payment, and tax reporting in ways that require understanding and proper management to maintain compliance and profitability.

Income collection procedures for trust-owned rental property:

Lease modification considerations: Existing leases typically continue in effect after trust transfers, but some property managers or attorneys recommend lease modifications or assignments to reflect trust ownership and ensure clarity about tenant obligations.

Rent collection mechanics: You can continue collecting rent personally as trustee, or you can require tenants to make payments directly to the trust. Most property owners maintain existing collection procedures to avoid tenant confusion.

Banking arrangements: Consider whether to maintain existing bank accounts for rental income or establish separate trust accounts. For revocable trusts, separate accounts aren't required for tax purposes, but they can simplify record-keeping and provide clearer separation between personal and rental finances.

Property management coordination: If you use professional property management services, notify them about trust ownership and confirm they can continue providing services to trust-owned property. Most property management companies handle trust-owned properties routinely.

Tax reporting for trust-owned rental income:

Revocable trust transparency means rental income from trust-owned property continues appearing on your personal tax return exactly as before. You don't file separate trust tax returns or change your reporting procedures.

Tax identification numbers: Use your Social Security number for all rental income reporting, just as you did before trust ownership. You don't need separate Employer Identification Numbers (EINs) for revocable trust property.

Depreciation and expenses: Continue claiming rental property depreciation and expense deductions on your personal tax return using the same procedures as individual ownership.

Record-keeping requirements: Maintain detailed records of rental income and expenses for trust-owned property, though these records serve the same purposes as individual ownership record-keeping.

Passive loss rules: Trust ownership doesn't change passive loss limitations or other rental property tax rules that apply based on your income level and participation in rental activities.

Cash flow management for trust-owned rentals:

Operating expenses including repairs, maintenance, property management fees, and utilities continue being paid from rental income or your personal funds as before trust ownership.

Capital improvements to trust-owned rental property can be funded from trust assets, rental income, or your personal funds, with the same tax treatment as individual ownership.

Reserve funds for major repairs or vacancy periods can be maintained in trust accounts or personal accounts, depending on your preference for fund separation.

Distribution decisions about rental profits become trustee decisions, though for revocable trusts where you're the beneficiary, you typically distribute profits to yourself as needed.

The goal is maintaining efficient rental property operations while taking advantage of trust ownership benefits for estate planning and asset protection.

Tenant Notification Requirements

Tenant notification about trust ownership changes affects landlord-tenant relationships and legal obligations, though most tenant relationships continue unchanged despite trust ownership.

Legal requirements for tenant notification vary by state:

Some states require formal notification to tenants about ownership changes, typically within 30 days of transfer. This notification must include new owner contact information and instructions for rent payments and maintenance requests.

Other states don't require notification unless tenant contact procedures actually change. If rent collection and property management continue exactly as before, notification may be optional.

Lease assignment considerations: Some attorneys recommend formal lease assignments from individual ownership to trust ownership to ensure clear legal relationships between tenants and the trust. However, most residential leases continue effectively under trust ownership without formal assignment.

Tenant notification content should include:

Explanation of ownership change in simple terms: "I have transferred ownership of your rental property to my living trust for estate planning purposes."

Confirmation of continued relationships: "Your lease terms remain exactly the same, and you should continue following all existing procedures for rent payments and maintenance requests."

Updated contact information if trust ownership changes how tenants should contact you or your property management company.

Rent payment instructions if trust ownership changes payment procedures, account numbers, or payee names.

Legal compliance confirmation: "This ownership change doesn't affect your tenant rights or lease obligations."

Sample tenant notification letter:

"Dear [Tenant Name],

I am writing to notify you that I have recently transferred ownership of your rental property located at [Property Address] to my living trust for estate planning purposes.

This change does not affect your lease terms, rent amount, or any other conditions of your tenancy. Please continue making rent payments to [Payment Instructions] and contact [Contact Information] for any maintenance or other issues, exactly as you have been doing.

Your lease remains in full effect with all the same terms and conditions. This ownership change is purely for my personal estate planning and does not impact your rights or obligations as a tenant.

If you have any questions about this change, please don't hesitate to contact me at [Your Contact Information].

Sincerely, [Your Name], Trustee [Trust Name]"

Timing considerations for tenant notification:

Prompt notification within 30 days of recording your deed helps maintain good tenant relationships and ensures compliance with any state requirements.

Coordination with rent collection to ensure tenants know where to send payments and aren't confused by ownership changes.

Property management coordination if you use professional management services that will handle tenant communications about ownership changes.

Most tenants accept ownership change notifications without concern since their lease terms and living situations remain unchanged.

Security Deposit Transfers

Security deposits held for trust-owned rental property require proper handling to ensure tenant protection and compliance with state landlord-tenant laws that govern deposit management and return procedures.

Security deposit legal requirements: Most states require security deposits to be held in specific ways - separate accounts, trust accounts, or with specific interest payment requirements. Trust ownership of rental property doesn't change these legal obligations, but it may affect how deposits are managed.

Deposit transfer procedures:

Account ownership changes may be required if state law mandates security deposits be held in accounts owned by the property owner. Trust ownership might require transferring deposit accounts to trust ownership.

Tenant notification about deposit account changes may be required in some states to ensure tenants know where their deposits are held and how they can verify proper handling.

Interest payment obligations continue under trust ownership if your state requires security deposit interest payments to tenants.

Record-keeping requirements for security deposits continue exactly as before, with trustees maintaining the same detailed records required of individual property owners.

Deposit return procedures may require trustee signatures rather than individual owner signatures when leases terminate and deposits are returned.

Best practices for security deposit management:

Maintain separate accounts for security deposits if required by state law, updating account ownership to reflect trust ownership if necessary.

Document deposit transfers with clear records showing continuity of tenant protection despite ownership changes.

Coordinate with property managers about deposit handling procedures and any changes required due to trust ownership.

Review state requirements to ensure continued compliance with all landlord-tenant laws affecting security deposit management.

Plan for deposit returns including signature authority and account access for trustees handling tenant departures.

Security deposit management for trust-owned rental property typically involves administrative updates rather than fundamental changes in procedures or tenant protections.

Insurance Policy Adjustments

Rental property insurance for trust-owned properties requires different considerations than homeowner's insurance for primary residences. Understanding these differences helps ensure adequate coverage while managing costs effectively.

Landlord insurance vs. homeowner's insurance: Trust-owned rental properties typically require landlord or investment property insurance rather than standard homeowner's policies. These policies provide:

- **Property coverage** for the building and any owner-provided appliances or furnishings
- **Liability protection** for accidents or injuries on rental property
- **Loss of rent coverage** for income lost during repair periods
- **Legal expense coverage** for landlord-tenant disputes

Trust ownership considerations for rental property insurance:

Policy ownership should reflect trust ownership with the trust named as the insured party and you designated as trustee with authority to manage the policy.

Liability coverage limits become more important with trust ownership because trustees face potential personal liability for trust asset management decisions.

Additional insured parties might include property management companies, contractors, or other parties involved in property operations.

Coverage verification ensures policies properly cover trust-owned property and trustee activities related to rental operations.

Premium considerations for trust-owned rental property:

- Trust ownership typically doesn't affect premium amounts significantly
- Some insurers offer discounts for trust-owned properties due to perceived stability

- Liability coverage may be more expensive due to trustee liability considerations
- Professional property management might reduce premiums through improved risk management

Insurance coordination procedures:

Notify insurance companies about trust ownership promptly after recording transfer deeds

Update policy designations to reflect trust ownership and trustee contact information

Review coverage adequacy including liability limits, property coverage amounts, and specialized coverage for rental operations

Coordinate with umbrella policies that might cover rental property liability and trustee activities

Maintain documentation about insurance updates and trust ownership recognition for future reference

Proper insurance coordination ensures adequate protection while avoiding coverage gaps that could create expensive liability exposure for trust-owned rental properties.

Tax Identification Number Needs

Tax reporting for trust-owned rental property follows the same procedures as individual ownership for revocable living trusts, but understanding identification number requirements prevents confusion and ensures proper tax compliance.

Social Security Number usage for revocable trusts: Revocable living trusts are "transparent" for federal tax purposes, meaning they don't exist as separate entities requiring separate tax returns or tax identification numbers. You continue using your Social Security number for all tax reporting related to trust-owned rental property.

When EINs are NOT needed:

- Rental property owned by your revocable living trust
- Trust income and expenses reported on your personal tax return
- Trust assets managed by you as trustee during your lifetime
- Routine trust operations that don't create separate tax obligations

When EINs ARE needed:

- **Irrevocable trusts** that file separate tax returns
- **Trusts with income tax obligations** separate from grantor reporting
- **Business operations** conducted through trusts that require business tax reporting
- **Employment situations** where trusts hire employees or independent contractors

Tax reporting procedures for trust-owned rentals:

Schedule E reporting continues exactly as before trust ownership, using your Social Security number and reporting rental income and expenses on your personal tax return.

Depreciation calculations remain the same for trust-owned property, with depreciation deductions appearing on your personal tax return.

Passive loss limitations continue applying based on your personal income and participation levels, regardless of trust ownership.

State tax compliance typically follows federal procedures, with trust-owned rental income appearing on your state tax return using your Social Security number.

Record-keeping for tax purposes: Maintain detailed records of rental income and expenses for trust-owned property using the same procedures as individual ownership.

Separate business records can help organize trust-owned rental activities, though separate accounting isn't required for revocable trusts.

Professional tax assistance may be beneficial for complex rental operations or multiple properties, but trust ownership typically doesn't complicate tax preparation significantly.

The key principle is that **revocable trust ownership doesn't change tax reporting** for rental property, allowing you to continue existing procedures while gaining estate planning benefits from trust ownership.

LLC vs. Trust Considerations

Investment property owners often consider both LLC and trust ownership for their properties, each providing different benefits and considerations that affect estate planning, liability protection, and operational efficiency.

LLC ownership benefits for rental property:

- **Liability protection** between personal assets and rental property risks
- **Operational flexibility** for multiple property ownership and business operations
- **Tax election options** including pass-through taxation or corporate treatment
- **Management structure** accommodating multiple owners or investors
- **Business credibility** with tenants, vendors, and professional relationships

Trust ownership benefits for rental property:

- **Probate avoidance** for property transfer at death
- **Privacy protection** since trust records aren't public like LLC filings

- **Estate planning integration** with overall wealth transfer strategies
- **Simplified taxation** with pass-through reporting to personal tax returns
- **Lower ongoing costs** since trusts don't require annual filings or fees

Hybrid approaches combining LLC and trust ownership: Many sophisticated property owners use LLCs for rental property operations while making their LLC membership interests owned by their living trusts. This approach provides:

- Liability protection from LLC structure
- Estate planning benefits from trust ownership
- Operational flexibility for property management
- Coordinated estate planning for all assets

Implementation of LLC-trust combinations:

- Form LLC for rental property ownership and operations
- Transfer rental property to LLC ownership
- Transfer LLC membership interests to living trust
- Manage properties through LLC while gaining estate planning benefits

Professional consultation for complex structures: LLC-trust combinations require professional guidance because they involve:

- Business entity formation and maintenance
- Complex tax considerations and elections
- Multi-layer asset protection strategies
- Ongoing compliance requirements for both entities

Decision factors for choosing between LLC and trust ownership:

Liability exposure levels from rental operations, tenant risks, and personal asset protection needs

Number of properties and complexity of rental operations that might benefit from business structure organization

Estate planning priorities including probate avoidance, privacy, and wealth transfer objectives

Tax planning considerations including passive loss utilization, depreciation strategies, and long-term tax optimization

Operational preferences for property management, record-keeping, and business relationship management

Cost considerations including formation costs, ongoing fees, tax preparation expenses, and administrative complexity

The choice between LLC and trust ownership depends on balancing liability protection, estate planning objectives, tax considerations, and operational preferences for your specific situation and goals.

Tenant Relationship Management

Trust ownership of rental property affects landlord-tenant relationships in subtle ways that require attention to maintain positive relationships and legal compliance.

Legal authority considerations: As trustee of trust-owned rental property, you have full authority to manage tenant relationships, enforce lease terms, and make property decisions. However, you must sign documents in your trustee capacity rather than individual capacity.

Lease enforcement procedures:

- **Eviction actions** can be filed by trustees using trust ownership authority
- **Lease violations** are addressed through normal landlord procedures
- **Rent collection** continues through established procedures

- **Property inspections** and maintenance access follow standard landlord rights

Communication with tenants about trust ownership: Maintain existing relationships while explaining ownership change as routine estate planning rather than business change affecting tenant relationships.

Update contact information if trust ownership changes how tenants should reach you for maintenance requests or other issues.

Ensure lease compliance continues under trust ownership with all lease terms remaining in effect and enforceable.

Professional consultation for complex tenant situations: Difficult tenants or ongoing disputes may benefit from professional assistance to ensure trust ownership doesn't complicate resolution procedures.

Commercial leases often contain specific provisions about ownership changes that require legal review to ensure compliance.

Multiple property management involving several rental properties might benefit from professional coordination to ensure consistent trust ownership implementation.

Trust ownership typically simplifies rather than complicates tenant relationships by providing clearer succession planning and more stable long-term ownership structure.

Key Takeaways from Investment Property Transfers

Rental property trust transfers add business operation considerations to basic property transfer procedures, requiring coordination of tenant relationships, income management, and tax compliance that primary residence transfers don't involve. Trust ownership maintains operational authority while changing legal ownership structure for estate planning benefits.

Security deposit management continues following state landlord-tenant laws, with trust ownership potentially requiring account ownership changes but not affecting tenant protection requirements or deposit return procedures. Tenant notification requirements vary by state but generally involve simple administrative updates rather than fundamental relationship changes.

Insurance policy adjustments for trust-owned rental property require landlord coverage rather than homeowner's policies, with trust ownership affecting policy ownership and potentially liability coverage limits for trustee activities. Tax identification number needs remain simple for revocable trusts, which continue using personal Social Security numbers for all tax reporting purposes.

LLC versus trust considerations present different benefits for liability protection versus estate planning, with hybrid approaches potentially providing advantages of both structures through professional implementation. Rental income handling follows the same procedures as individual ownership with trust ownership providing estate planning benefits without changing operational complexity.

Complex investment property situations involving multiple properties, commercial leases, or sophisticated ownership structures often benefit from professional assistance due to business law complexity and potential tax implications beyond basic property transfer procedures.

The next chapter addresses out-of-state properties and the multi-jurisdictional considerations that arise when your property portfolio spans multiple states with different legal requirements.

Chapter 13: Multi-Jurisdictional Transfers

You own a vacation cabin in Colorado, a rental property in Arizona, and your primary residence in Illinois. Each property sits in a different state with different laws, different recording requirements, and different tax implications. The good news? You can still transfer all these properties to your trust yourself. The challenge? You'll need to become a mini-expert in three different state systems.

Don't worry. We'll break this down step by step, and by the end of this chapter, you'll know exactly how to handle properties scattered across state lines without losing your mind or your savings.

The Multi-State Reality Check

Most trust transfer guides assume you own property in just one state. That's not realistic for many Americans. According to the National Association of Realtors, approximately 40% of trust creators own real estate in multiple states. Whether it's that retirement condo in Florida, the family lake house in Michigan, or investment properties spread across several markets, multi-state ownership is increasingly common.

Here's what makes multi-state transfers different: each state treats your property as if it exists in its own legal universe. Your Illinois trust might be perfectly valid everywhere, but transferring that Arizona rental property requires following Arizona's specific deed requirements, recording procedures, and tax rules.

Think of it like this: your trust is the container, but each state has its own rules about how you put property into that container. The container works everywhere, but the loading process changes at each location.

Understanding Ancillary Probate - Why This Matters

Before we get into the mechanics, let's talk about why transferring out-of-state properties matters so much. Without proper trust funding, each property could trigger what's called "ancillary probate" in its home state.

Sarah learned this the hard way. Her father owned his primary home in Ohio and a beach house in South Carolina. He had a perfectly good Ohio trust, but never transferred the South Carolina property into it. When he passed away, the family faced two separate probate proceedings - one in Ohio for his primary residence and personal property, and another in South Carolina just for the beach house.

The Ohio probate cost $8,500 and took eight months. The South Carolina ancillary probate cost an additional $12,000 and took another six months because the family had to hire a South Carolina attorney and deal with that state's specific requirements. Total cost: $20,500. Total time: 14 months of legal proceedings.

A simple $200 deed transfer in South Carolina would have avoided the entire ancillary probate. That's a $20,300 lesson nobody wants to learn the hard way.

The State-by-State Requirements Matrix

Each state has its own personality when it comes to deed transfers. Some states make it refreshingly simple. Others seem determined to complicate every possible step. Let's break down what varies from state to state:

Recording Requirements States differ dramatically in what they require for deed recording. Florida keeps it simple - just the deed, proper notarization, and recording fees. California requires the deed plus a Preliminary Change of Ownership Report (PCOR), documentary transfer tax calculations, and sometimes additional city or county forms.

Texas doesn't require notarization for certain deed types but demands specific formatting for the legal description. Michigan requires both notarization and witnessing, plus specific margin requirements for the document itself.

Fee Structures Recording fees vary wildly. Arkansas charges a flat $10 for deed recording. California's fees can exceed $100 before you even consider documentary transfer taxes. New York adds its own state transfer tax on top of local fees, potentially reaching hundreds of dollars for higher-value properties.

Documentary transfer taxes present the biggest variation. Texas has no state transfer tax. California calculates transfer tax based on property value, typically running $1.10 per $1,000 of value. New York's combined state and local transfer taxes can reach $15 or more per $1,000 of value in expensive markets like Manhattan.

Form Requirements This is where states really show their individual quirks. Nevada provides standard deed forms that work statewide. Pennsylvania requires county-specific forms that vary significantly between Philadelphia, Pittsburgh, and rural counties.

Some states require specific language in the deed itself. Arizona mandates certain statutory language for trust transfers. Oregon requires specific formatting for the trustee designation that differs from neighboring states.

Your Multi-State Action Plan

Step 1: Inventory and Prioritize List every property you own outside your home state. For each property, gather:

- Current deed (showing exactly how title is held)
- Property tax records (for current assessed value)
- Mortgage information (lender name and loan number)

- Property address (complete legal address, not just mailing address)

Prioritize based on property value and state complexity. Start with the highest-value properties in the simplest states. This builds your confidence and experience before tackling more complex jurisdictions.

Step 2: Research Each State's Specific Requirements For each state where you own property, research:

- Deed format requirements (margin sizes, paper type, font requirements)
- Notarization rules (some states require witnesses in addition to notarization)
- Recording office procedures (mail-in vs. in-person requirements)
- Fee schedules (recording fees plus any transfer taxes)
- Required supporting forms (state and local requirements)

Step 3: Prepare State-Specific Documentation Don't try to use a one-size-fits-all approach. Each state gets its own properly formatted deed following that state's requirements. This means:

- Different deed forms for different states
- State-specific legal description formatting
- Proper trustee designation using each state's preferred language
- Correct notarization format for each jurisdiction

Step 4: Coordinate Timing and Logistics Plan your transfers strategically. You might handle simple states first to build experience, or tackle everything simultaneously if you're comfortable with complexity. Consider:

- Notarization requirements (some states require witnesses present during notarization)

- Mail-in recording timelines (varies from 1-4 weeks depending on county)
- Tax year considerations (some states calculate transfer taxes differently based on recording date)

Step 5: Execute and Track Record deeds in each state following that state's specific procedures. Maintain detailed records of:

- Recording confirmation for each property
- New deed numbers and recording information
- Updated title information
- Notification completion for lenders and insurance companies

Working with State Complexity Tiers Across Jurisdictions

Remember our three-tier system from Chapter 3? When you own properties in multiple states, you're essentially managing multiple complexity levels simultaneously.

Tier 1 States (DIY-Friendly) If you own properties in multiple Tier 1 states like Texas, Florida, and Nevada, you're in luck. These states generally:

- Accept standard quitclaim deed forms
- Have reasonable recording fees ($20-50 typical range)
- Don't require complex supplemental forms
- Offer Transfer on Death (TOD) deed options as alternatives
- Provide clear recording procedures

Mixed-Tier Portfolios Many property owners face mixed situations: a primary residence in a Tier 1 state plus vacation or investment properties in Tier 2 or 3 states. This creates interesting strategic options.

Consider Mike, who lives in Texas (Tier 1) but owns rental properties in Illinois (Tier 2) and California (Tier 3). His strategy:

- Texas primary residence: Simple quitclaim deed, $26 recording fee, completed in one afternoon
- Illinois rental: Quitclaim deed plus additional county forms, $78 total fees, two-week mail-in process
- California rental: Quitclaim deed plus PCOR plus documentary transfer tax calculation, $340 total costs, required attorney review due to complexity

Mike saved approximately $8,000 by handling the Texas and Illinois transfers himself, then paid $1,200 for limited attorney assistance with the California property. Total savings: $6,800 compared to hiring attorneys for all three transfers.

Understanding Documentary Transfer Taxes Across States

Documentary transfer taxes create the biggest cost variations in multi-state transfers. These taxes are calculated when property ownership changes, but living trust transfers typically qualify for exemptions. The key word is "typically" - you need to verify exemption eligibility in each state.

States with No Transfer Tax Alaska, Delaware, Idaho, Indiana, Louisiana, Mississippi, Missouri, Montana, New Hampshire, North Carolina, North Dakota, Oregon, South Carolina, Tennessee, Texas, Utah, West Virginia, and Wyoming don't impose state-level documentary transfer taxes. Some cities and counties in these states may still impose local transfer taxes, but exemptions for living trust transfers are usually straightforward.

States with Transfer Tax and Clear Trust Exemptions Most states that impose documentary transfer taxes provide clear exemptions for transfers to revocable living trusts where the transferor remains the trustee. These include Arizona, Colorado, Connecticut, Georgia, Illinois, Minnesota, Nevada, and others.

The exemption language typically requires the deed to state that the transfer is for no consideration and that the transferor retains beneficial ownership. Standard language like "This transfer is made for no consideration to a revocable trust of which the grantor is the trustee and beneficiary" usually suffices.

States Requiring Careful Navigation California, New York, Pennsylvania, and a few others have more complex transfer tax rules with specific exemption procedures. California requires the PCOR form to claim the exemption. New York requires specific language and documentation. These situations often justify professional consultation for the transfer tax aspects alone.

Warning Box: Always Check Local Laws

State laws change. County procedures evolve. What worked last year might not work this year. Before transferring any out-of-state property, verify current requirements with:

- The specific county recorder's office where you'll record the deed
- Current state law regarding transfer tax exemptions
- Any local municipal requirements (some cities impose additional recording requirements)
- Recent changes to notarization or witnessing requirements

Never assume that because something worked in one state, it will work the same way in another state. Always check current requirements for each jurisdiction.

Recording in Multiple Jurisdictions - The Logistics

Recording deeds in multiple states requires organization and patience. Each county recorder's office operates differently, even within the same state.

Mail-in Recording Most county recorders accept mail-in deed recording, but requirements vary:

- Some require payment by cashier's check or money order only
- Others accept personal checks or credit cards

- Processing times range from 3 days to 4 weeks
- Return shipping requirements vary (some require prepaid envelopes)

Always include a cover letter with mail-in recordings stating:

- Property address
- Current owner name(s)
- Type of deed being recorded
- Contact information for questions
- Return address for recorded documents

In-Person Recording For high-value properties or complex situations, consider in-person recording. Benefits include:

- Immediate confirmation of document acceptance
- Ability to correct minor errors on the spot
- Cash payment options in most offices
- Same-day completion

Digital Recording Systems Some progressive counties offer online deed recording systems. These typically require:

- Electronic notarization (where legally permitted)
- Credit card payment
- PDF document uploads in specific formats
- Digital signature capabilities

Tax Implications Across States

Multi-state property ownership creates interesting tax considerations for trust transfers. The good news: revocable living trust transfers typically don't trigger income tax consequences in any state. The property's tax basis transfers with the property, and you maintain the same tax position as before the transfer.

Property Tax Considerations Each state handles property tax differently after trust transfers:

Reassessment Triggers Some states reassess property value when ownership changes, even for trust transfers. California's Proposition 13 generally protects against reassessment for living trust transfers, but you must file a claim for exemption. Florida provides similar protections with proper documentation.

Homestead Exemptions If you claim homestead exemptions on out-of-state properties (typically vacation homes used as occasional residences), verify whether trust ownership affects exemption eligibility. Most states preserve homestead benefits for trust-owned properties, but application procedures may change.

State Income Tax Filing Trust ownership doesn't typically change state income tax filing requirements for revocable trusts. You'll continue reporting rental income, property sales, and deductions on your personal returns in the same manner as before the transfer.

Coordinating Professional Help Across States

Sometimes you'll need professional assistance, but not necessarily in every state where you own property. Consider a tiered approach:

Self-Manage Simple States Handle straightforward transfers yourself in Tier 1 states where you feel confident about the requirements and the property values don't justify professional fees.

Limited Consultation for Moderate Complexity For Tier 2 states or unusual situations, consider paying for limited attorney consultation rather than full representation. Many attorneys will review your completed deed preparation for $200-400, providing peace of mind without full-service costs.

Full Professional Help for High-Risk Situations Use full attorney services for:

- High-value properties in Tier 3 states
- Properties with complex ownership structures
- Situations involving significant transfer tax calculations

- Properties with existing legal complications

Case Study: The Three-State Strategy

Patricia owned properties in three states: her primary residence in Arizona (Tier 1), a mountain cabin in Colorado (Tier 1), and a rental duplex in California (Tier 3). Her approach:

Arizona Primary Residence Patricia handled this transfer entirely herself. Arizona's simple requirements and her familiarity with local procedures made this straightforward. Cost: $46 recording fee. Time: 2 hours preparation plus one trip to the recorder's office.

Colorado Cabin Also DIY-friendly, but Patricia wasn't familiar with Colorado's specific requirements. She spent $150 for a 30-minute consultation with a Colorado attorney who reviewed her deed preparation and confirmed her approach. The attorney also provided current information about local recording procedures. Total cost: $196. Time: 3 hours preparation plus consultation.

California Duplex Given California's complexity and the rental property's $485,000 value, Patricia hired a California attorney for limited assistance. The attorney prepared the deed and PCOR form, handled the recording, and coordinated with the property management company. Cost: $850. Time: 1 hour of Patricia's time for document gathering.

Patricia's total cost: $1,092. Professional fees for all three properties would have been $4,200-5,500. Her savings: $3,100-4,400. More importantly, she maintained control over the timeline and learned enough about the process to handle future property acquisitions herself.

Managing the Administrative Burden

Multi-state property transfers create more administrative tasks than single-state situations. Stay organized with:

State-Specific Files Create separate files for each state containing:

- Current property deeds
- State-specific deed forms and requirements
- Recording office contact information
- Fee schedules and payment requirements
- Trust exemption documentation requirements

Communication Tracking Track all communications with:

- County recorder offices
- Mortgage servicers for each property
- Insurance companies (policies may be with different carriers)
- Property tax authorities
- Property managers or tenants (for rental properties)

Timeline Coordination Stagger your transfers if needed to manage workload and cash flow. There's no requirement to transfer all properties simultaneously. Some property owners prefer completing one state at a time to maintain focus and avoid confusion.

When Distance Becomes a Challenge

Geographic distance can complicate multi-state transfers, but don't let it deter you. Modern communication and mail systems make remote transfers entirely feasible.

Research from a Distance Most county recorder offices provide detailed information online, including:

- Current fee schedules
- Required forms and templates
- Mailing addresses and procedures
- Contact information for questions

When online information isn't sufficient, phone calls usually resolve questions quickly. County recorder staff generally provide helpful guidance about their specific requirements.

Remote Notarization Considerations Some states now permit remote online notarization (RON), which can simplify multi-state transfers. However, the receiving state (where you're recording the deed) must accept RON documents. Verify acceptance before using remote notarization services.

Traditional mail-away notarization services remain available and reliable for out-of-state transfers. These services typically cost $15-25 per document and provide professional notarization with appropriate identification verification.

Building Your Multi-State Expertise

Success with multi-state transfers comes from systematic preparation rather than trying to wing it. Develop expertise gradually:

Start Simple Begin with your most straightforward property in the simplest state. This builds confidence and helps you understand the general process before tackling more complex jurisdictions.

Document Everything Keep detailed notes about each state's requirements and your experience with their procedures. This information becomes invaluable for future transfers or when helping family members with similar situations.

Create State-Specific Checklists Develop customized checklists for each state where you own property. Include:

- Required forms and where to obtain them
- Notarization and witnessing requirements
- Recording office procedures and contact information
- Fee payment methods and amounts
- Post-recording notification requirements

Special Considerations for Investment Properties

Investment properties in multiple states add layers of complexity but remain manageable with proper planning.

Tenant Notifications Each state has different requirements for notifying tenants about ownership changes. Some states require formal written notice within specific timeframes. Others have no notification requirements but consider it best practice.

Security Deposit Handling When transferring rental properties to trusts, security deposit ownership transfers with the property. Some states require specific procedures for notifying tenants about security deposit custodian changes.

Management Company Coordination If you use property management companies, they'll need updated ownership information for their records. This may require new management agreements listing the trust as the property owner.

The Remote Property Management Strategy

Managing trust-owned properties from a distance requires systems and backup plans.

Local Professional Networks Establish relationships with local professionals in each state:

- Real estate attorneys (for complex situations)
- Tax preparers familiar with out-of-state property ownership
- Property managers (for rental properties)
- Reliable contractors and service providers

Document Storage and Access Maintain both physical and digital copies of all important documents for each property. Store copies locally and ensure trusted family members or professionals in each state can access documents when needed.

Emergency Procedures Develop clear procedures for handling emergencies at remote properties. This includes:

- Local contact networks
- Authority delegation for urgent decisions

- Insurance claim procedures
- Tenant emergency protocols (for rental properties)

Cost-Benefit Analysis for Multiple Properties

Multi-state property ownership affects the cost-benefit calculation for DIY transfers. Consider both immediate costs and long-term benefits:

Immediate Costs

- Recording fees in each state
- Travel costs (if in-person recording required)
- Professional consultation fees (if needed)
- Document preparation time multiplied by number of states

Long-Term Benefits

- Ancillary probate avoidance (potentially $10,000+ per state)
- Simplified estate administration
- Privacy protection in all jurisdictions
- Incapacity planning benefits across all properties

Break-Even Analysis For most property owners, the break-even point occurs with just one out-of-state property worth $100,000 or more. The potential ancillary probate costs almost always exceed the DIY transfer costs, even when including professional consultation fees.

Technology Tools for Multi-State Success

Modern technology simplifies multi-state property management:

Document Management Systems Cloud-based storage systems let you access property documents from anywhere. Organize by state and property, with shared access for trustees and family members.

Communication Apps Video calling makes consultations with out-of-state professionals convenient and cost-effective. Many attorneys now offer limited consultation services via video conference.

Research Resources Online legal databases provide access to current state statutes and recording requirements. Many county recorder offices offer online fee calculators and form downloads.

Warning Box: Complex Multi-State Situations Requiring Professional Help

Certain multi-state situations exceed reasonable DIY scope:

- Properties in more than five states
- Commercial or unusual property types
- Properties with existing legal complications
- Situations involving significant transfer tax liability
- Properties owned through complex entity structures (LLCs, partnerships)
- Any situation where state law requirements conflict or seem unclear

The Ongoing Multi-State Maintenance

Successfully transferring properties to your trust is just the beginning. Multi-state property ownership requires ongoing attention:

Annual Reviews Review each property's status annually:

- Verify trust ownership remains properly documented
- Check for any state law changes affecting trust property
- Confirm insurance and tax records reflect trust ownership
- Update local professional contacts as needed

State Law Monitoring Subscribe to legal update services or establish relationships with local professionals who can alert you to relevant law changes in each state where you own property.

Succession Planning Ensure your successor trustees understand the multi-state property portfolio and have access to all necessary documentation and professional contacts.

Key Takeaways for Multi-State Success

Multi-state property transfers require more preparation and attention to detail, but they're absolutely achievable for motivated property owners. The key principles:

Start with thorough research of each state's specific requirements. Don't assume similarity between states, even neighboring ones. Prepare state-specific documentation rather than trying to use generic forms. Consider professional consultation for complex states or high-value properties. Maintain excellent organization and documentation throughout the process.

The cost savings remain substantial even when factoring in additional complexity. Most importantly, you'll avoid the nightmare scenario of multiple probate proceedings that could cost your family tens of thousands of dollars and months or years of legal complications.

Remember: each property successfully transferred to your trust eliminates one potential probate proceeding. Multiply that across several states, and you're providing enormous protection for your family's future.

Chapter 14: Troubleshooting Common Problems

Things go wrong. That's not pessimism - it's reality. Even when you follow every instruction perfectly, double-check every detail, and triple-check your work, sometimes problems arise. The county recorder rejects your deed. Your name doesn't match exactly. You discover an error after recording. Technology fails at the worst possible moment.

The difference between a minor hiccup and a major disaster is knowing how to fix problems quickly and correctly. This chapter gives you the tools to handle the most common issues that trip up DIY trust transfers.

Understanding Why Deeds Get Rejected

County recorders reject approximately 15-20% of DIY-prepared deeds on first submission, according to data from the National Association of County Recorders. That might sound discouraging, but here's the reality: most rejections involve easily fixable problems, and experienced real estate professionals face rejection rates nearly as high.

The goal isn't perfection on the first try. The goal is knowing how to fix problems quickly when they arise.

The Big Five Rejection Reasons

1. Signature and Notarization Problems Missing signatures account for 35% of deed rejections. This includes:

- Unsigned documents (yes, it happens more than you'd think)

- Signatures that don't match the names typed in the document
- Missing notarization or incorrect notary acknowledgment language
- Expired notary commissions or incorrect notary seals

Quick Fix: Most signature problems can be corrected by re-executing the deed with proper signatures and fresh notarization. Keep the original deed for your records but prepare a completely new deed for recording.

2. Legal Description Errors Incorrect or incomplete legal descriptions cause 25% of rejections. Common problems:

- Copying errors from the original deed
- Missing portions of complex legal descriptions
- Incorrect lot numbers, block numbers, or subdivision names
- Improper abbreviations or formatting

Quick Fix: Obtain a certified copy of your current deed from the county recorder and copy the legal description exactly, character by character. When in doubt, type rather than handwrite legal descriptions to avoid unclear characters.

3. Name Discrepancies Name matching problems create 20% of rejections. Issues include:

- Middle initials vs. full middle names
- Maiden names vs. married names
- Nicknames used instead of legal names
- Spelling variations or typos

Quick Fix: Use names exactly as they appear on your current deed. If your current deed shows "Robert J. Smith" don't use "Bob Smith" or "Robert James Smith" on the new deed. Exact matching is required.

4. Trust Name and Date Problems Trust identification errors cause 15% of rejections:

- Incorrect trust names (different from the actual trust document)
- Wrong trust dates
- Missing trust dates
- Improper trustee designation format

Quick Fix: Check your trust document for the exact trust name and date. The deed must match the trust exactly. If your trust is called "The Smith Family Revocable Trust dated March 15, 2024," that's exactly how it should appear in the deed.

5. Format and Filing Requirements Technical requirements cause the remaining 5% of rejections:

- Wrong paper size or margins
- Missing cover sheets or transmittal forms
- Insufficient recording fees
- Missing required supplemental forms

Quick Fix: Contact the county recorder's office for their specific format requirements and fee schedules. Most offices provide detailed information online or by phone.

The Name Mismatch Resolution Process

Name discrepancies create the most frustration for property owners because they often discover problems that existed on previous deeds. You might find that your name appears differently on your deed than on your driver's license, or that previous owners' names were recorded incorrectly years ago.

Same Person, Different Name Formats When you're the same person but your name appears differently on different documents:

Use an "also known as" statement in your new deed: "Robert J. Smith, also known as Robert James Smith, also known as Bob Smith." This establishes that all name variations refer to the same person.

Maiden Name Issues For married women whose property predates their marriage: "Susan Johnson, now known as Susan Martinez" or "Susan Johnson Martinez, formerly Susan Johnson" in the grantor section of the new deed.

Minor Spelling Differences For obvious typos or minor spelling variations, include both versions: "John Peterson, also known as John Petersen" covers common spelling variations.

When Name Problems Require Professional Help Some name issues exceed DIY solutions:

- Significant name discrepancies suggesting different people
- Properties acquired during divorce proceedings with complex name histories
- Inherited properties with unclear ownership chains
- Properties where previous owners' names were incorrectly recorded

Correcting Errors After Recording

Discovering errors after the county records your deed feels terrible, but correction options exist for most problems.

Minor Clerical Errors Small mistakes like typos in addresses, minor legal description errors, or formatting problems can usually be corrected with a "scrivener's affidavit."

A scrivener's affidavit is a sworn statement explaining the error and providing the correct information. Most counties accept scrivener's affidavits for minor corrections without requiring a new deed.

Scrivener's Affidavit Example: "I, [Your Name], being duly sworn, state that in the quitclaim deed recorded on [Date] as Document No. [Recording Number], the property address was incorrectly stated as '123 Main Street' when it should have been '123 Main Avenue.' This affidavit corrects this clerical error."

Material Errors Requiring New Deeds Significant errors require recording a corrective deed:

- Wrong legal descriptions
- Incorrect grantor or grantee names
- Missing or incorrect trust information
- Substantive changes to the transfer terms

Corrective Deed Process:

1. Prepare a new deed with correct information
2. Reference the original recorded deed in the corrective deed
3. Include language stating "This deed corrects and supersedes the deed recorded on [Date] as Document No. [Number]"
4. Record the corrective deed following the same procedures as the original
5. Update all related parties about the correction

Missing Signature Corrections

Unsigned deeds create unique problems because they're void ab initio (invalid from the beginning). You can't fix an unsigned deed with an affidavit or correction - you need a completely new deed.

If You Discover Missing Signatures Before Recording: Simply execute a new deed with all required signatures. Destroy the unsigned deed to avoid confusion.

If the Recorder Accepts and Records an Unsigned Deed: This creates a cloud on your title that must be resolved. Options include:

- Recording a new, properly signed deed
- Obtaining a court order validating the transfer
- Working with a title company to resolve the title issue

Most Common Fix: Record a new deed that references and supersedes the defective deed. Include language like: "This deed corrects and replaces the deed recorded on [Date] as Document No.

[Number], which was inadvertently recorded without proper execution."

Title Insurance Claims and Deed Problems

If you have owner's title insurance on your property, some deed problems may be covered under your policy. Title insurance can help with:

- Legal description errors that affect property boundaries
- Name discrepancies that cloud title
- Recording errors that affect ownership rights
- Previous deed defects discovered during your transfer

Filing Title Insurance Claims:

1. Contact your title insurance company immediately when you discover problems
2. Provide complete documentation of the issue
3. Submit copies of all relevant deeds and documents
4. Follow the company's specific claim procedures
5. Maintain records of all communications

Title insurance claims can take 30-90 days to resolve, but they often provide cost-effective solutions to complex title problems.

Technology Failures and Backup Plans

Modern deed preparation relies heavily on technology, creating new potential failure points.

Computer and Printer Problems Always maintain backup options:

- Save deed forms in multiple formats (Word, PDF, Google Docs)
- Know locations of reliable printing services (FedEx Office, UPS Store)
- Keep handwritten backup plans for critical information

- Maintain paper copies of essential forms

Notary Availability Issues Notary scheduling conflicts or unavailability can delay transfers. Backup strategies:

- Identify multiple notary options in your area
- Consider mobile notary services for flexibility
- Understand your state's notary requirements to avoid last-minute surprises
- Schedule notarization appointments well in advance for time-sensitive transfers

Internet and Communication Failures Research and communication depend on reliable internet access. Prepare for outages:

- Download and save all necessary forms before starting the transfer process
- Print hard copies of county recorder contact information
- Maintain phone numbers for critical contacts
- Know locations of public internet access (libraries, coffee shops)

The Psychology of Problem-Solving

Problems during legal processes trigger stress and self-doubt. That's normal. Remember that problems don't mean you're incapable of handling the transfer - they mean you're human.

Maintaining Perspective When problems arise, remember:

- Professional attorneys face similar problems regularly
- Most problems have straightforward solutions
- County recorder staff want to help you succeed
- Delays are frustrating but rarely create lasting harm

When to Escalate Problems Know when to seek help rather than struggling alone:

- Problems you don't understand after reasonable research
- Situations where multiple solutions exist and you're unsure which to choose
- Complex legal issues that exceed deed preparation scope
- Any situation where you feel overwhelmed or confused

Problem Prevention Strategies

The best problem-solving strategy is prevention. Most common problems can be avoided with careful preparation:

Document Review Process Before submitting any deed for recording:

1. Read the entire deed aloud (catches errors that silent reading misses)
2. Verify all names match your current deed exactly
3. Confirm trust name and date match your trust document exactly
4. Check legal description character by character against current deed
5. Verify all signature lines are signed and dated
6. Confirm notarization is complete and accurate

Professional Review Option For high-value properties or complex situations, consider paying for professional deed review before recording. Many attorneys offer limited services reviewing DIY-prepared deeds for $150-300. This catches problems before they become costly mistakes.

Communication Verification Before beginning any transfer process:

- Confirm current recording requirements with the county recorder
- Verify current fee schedules
- Check for any recent changes to state or local requirements
- Understand the recorder's timeline and procedures

Building Confidence Through Competence

Every problem you solve successfully builds competence and confidence for future challenges. Keep detailed records of problems encountered and solutions implemented. This creates your personal troubleshooting database for future use.

Learning from Others' Mistakes Connect with other property owners who've completed DIY transfers. Online forums, local real estate groups, and trust administration organizations provide valuable insights into common problems and effective solutions.

Creating Your Personal Support Network Develop relationships with professionals who can provide guidance when needed:

- Local notary services familiar with trust transfers
- Title company representatives who understand DIY transfers
- Attorneys who offer limited consultation services
- Other property owners who've completed similar transfers

When Problems Become Opportunities

Sometimes apparent problems reveal opportunities for improvement. A rejected deed might uncover title issues that needed addressing anyway. A name discrepancy might prompt you to update other important documents with consistent information.

Margaret discovered during her deed preparation that her property had been incorrectly described in county records for over 20 years. The error never affected her ownership or use of the property, but it created potential title problems for future sales. Correcting the error during her trust transfer actually improved her property's title clarity and value.

The Professional Consultation Strategy

Don't hesitate to seek professional help for problem resolution. The cost of limited consultation usually pales compared to the cost of mistakes or extended delays.

Effective Professional Consultation:

- Prepare detailed written descriptions of problems before consultation
- Gather all relevant documents for attorney review
- Ask specific questions rather than general requests for help
- Understand exactly what services the professional will provide
- Get written estimates for any recommended solutions

Most attorneys prefer helping with specific problems rather than taking over entire transfers. This approach saves you money while ensuring proper problem resolution.

Key Takeaways for Troubleshooting Success

Problems during DIY trust transfers are normal and usually solvable. The key is maintaining calm perspective, systematic problem-solving approaches, and knowing when to seek professional help.

Prepare for problems by understanding common issues, maintaining good documentation, and developing backup plans. When problems arise, address them promptly rather than hoping they'll resolve themselves. Most importantly, don't let fear of problems prevent you from attempting DIY transfers. The potential savings and personal satisfaction far outweigh the temporary inconvenience of occasional problems.

Remember: every professional started as a beginner. Every expert was once confused by deed requirements and nervous about making mistakes. The difference is persistence, learning from errors, and building competence through experience.

Your willingness to solve problems demonstrates the same determination that makes DIY trust transfers successful. Trust that capability, prepare systematically, and don't be afraid to ask for help when you need it.

Chapter 15: Tier 1 States

If you own property in a Tier 1 state, you've won the geographic lottery for DIY trust transfers. These states have designed their systems with property owners in mind, offering reasonable fees, straightforward procedures, and genuine alternatives that make transfers accessible to regular people.

But don't mistake "DIY-friendly" for "no preparation required." Even the simplest states have specific requirements and procedures you must follow correctly. The difference is that Tier 1 states forgive minor errors and provide clear guidance for success.

The Tier 1 State Family

Primary Tier 1 States: Texas, Florida, Nevada, Arizona, Colorado, New Mexico, Utah, Wyoming, Montana, North Dakota, South Dakota, Kansas, Oklahoma, Arkansas, Tennessee, Kentucky, Indiana, Missouri, Iowa, Nebraska, Alabama, Mississippi, South Carolina, and New Hampshire.

These states share common characteristics that make them DIY-friendly:

- Recording fees under $75 for standard deeds
- No or minimal documentary transfer taxes
- Standard deed forms that work statewide
- Clear recording procedures
- Reasonable notarization requirements
- Transfer on Death (TOD) deed options in many cases

Why These States Work for DIY

Tier 1 states typically developed their recording systems with individual property owners in mind rather than primarily serving large commercial transactions. This philosophy creates several advantages:

Simplified Procedures Recording procedures focus on essential requirements rather than bureaucratic complexity. You'll find clear instructions, reasonable deadlines, and staff who understand that not everyone is a real estate professional.

Reasonable Costs Fees stay reasonable because these states don't view property recording as a significant revenue source. Recording fees typically cover actual administrative costs rather than generating substantial profits.

Standard Forms Most Tier 1 states provide standard deed forms that work throughout the state. You won't encounter different requirements for each county or municipality within the state.

Texas - The Gold Standard for DIY Transfers

Texas exemplifies Tier 1 state advantages. The state's approach to property transfers reflects its business-friendly philosophy and respect for property rights.

Texas Recording Requirements:

- Standard quitclaim or warranty deed (state-provided forms work well)
- Notarization required for most deed types
- Recording fee: $26 for the first page, $4 for each additional page
- No state documentary transfer tax
- No requirement for complex supplemental forms

Texas Specific Advantages: Texas doesn't require notarization for certain types of deeds between family members, though notarization is still recommended for trust transfers. The state provides excellent online resources through county clerk offices, and most counties accept mail-in recording with reasonable processing times.

Texas Transfer on Death Deeds: Texas offers TOD deeds as an alternative to living trust transfers. These deeds automatically transfer property to named beneficiaries upon death, avoiding probate without requiring trust creation. TOD deeds cost the same as regular deeds to record but eliminate the need for trust administration.

Florida - Retiree-Friendly Transfers

Florida's system accommodates its large population of retirees and part-time residents, many of whom want to transfer property to trusts for estate planning purposes.

Florida Recording Advantages:

- Recording fees: $10 for the first page, $8.50 for each additional page
- No state documentary transfer tax (though some counties impose minimal local taxes)
- Accepts standard quitclaim deeds
- Clear homestead exemption preservation for trust transfers
- Excellent online resources through county clerk offices

Florida Special Considerations: Florida's homestead laws provide powerful asset protection, and these benefits typically continue when property transfers to a revocable living trust. However, you must file proper documentation to maintain homestead status. The process is straightforward but requires attention to timing and procedures.

Nevada - Business-Friendly and Efficient

Nevada's pro-business environment extends to property recording, creating one of the most efficient systems in the country.

Nevada Highlights:

- Recording fees under $50 for most deeds
- No state transfer tax
- Standard forms accepted statewide
- Efficient online recording systems in major counties
- TOD deed options available
- Clear exemption procedures for trust transfers

Nevada Innovation: Clark County (Las Vegas) and Washoe County (Reno) offer online deed recording systems that allow complete remote processing. These systems accept electronically notarized documents and provide same-day recording confirmation.

Colorado - Mountain State Simplicity

Colorado balances thorough legal protection with practical accessibility, creating a system that works well for both professionals and individual property owners.

Colorado Benefits:

- Recording fees: $13 plus $5 per page
- No state documentary transfer tax
- County clerks provide helpful guidance
- Standard deed forms work throughout the state
- Clear procedures for out-of-state property owners

Colorado Mountain Property Considerations: Many Colorado properties have complex legal descriptions due to mining claims, water rights, or unusual survey systems. Take extra care copying legal descriptions from original deeds, and consider professional review for properties with particularly complex descriptions.

Arizona - Desert Efficiency

Arizona's recording system reflects the state's preference for minimal bureaucracy and efficient government services.

Arizona Advantages:

- Recording fees: $30 for documents up to 5 pages
- No state transfer tax
- Excellent online resources
- Standard deed forms accepted statewide
- Clear trust exemption procedures

Arizona Unique Features: Arizona requires specific statutory language for certain types of trust transfers, but the requirements are clearly stated and easy to follow. The state also provides excellent guidance for maintaining property tax exemptions after trust transfers.

Understanding Transfer on Death (TOD) Deeds in Tier 1 States

Many Tier 1 states offer TOD deeds as an alternative to living trust transfers. TOD deeds can be simpler for single-property owners but have important limitations compared to living trusts.

TOD Deed Advantages:

- Simpler preparation (no trust creation required)
- Lower cost (just recording fees, no ongoing trust administration)
- Immediate effect (property transfers automatically upon death)
- Revocable during lifetime (can be changed or cancelled)

TOD Deed Limitations:

- No incapacity planning benefits (trusts provide management if you become incapacitated)
- Limited to real property (trusts can hold all asset types)
- May not integrate well with overall estate plans
- Some states limit TOD deed beneficiary options

States Offering TOD Deeds: Currently available in: Arizona, Arkansas, Colorado, Illinois, Indiana, Kansas, Minnesota, Montana, Nevada, New Mexico, North Dakota, Ohio, Oklahoma, Oregon,

South Dakota, Texas, Utah, Virginia, Washington, West Virginia, Wisconsin, and Wyoming.

Maximizing DIY Advantages in Tier 1 States

Speed of Completion Tier 1 states allow rapid completion of trust transfers. With proper preparation, you can often complete the entire process within 2-3 weeks, including document preparation, notarization, recording, and post-transfer notifications.

Cost Predictability Recording fees in Tier 1 states are published, reasonable, and stable. You can budget accurately for transfer costs without worrying about hidden fees or complex tax calculations.

Error Tolerance Tier 1 states typically provide clear guidance for correcting minor errors and reasonable procedures for resubmission if initial attempts are rejected. Staff at county recording offices generally offer helpful guidance rather than simply rejecting documents.

Success Rate Statistics for Tier 1 States

Data from county recorders shows that DIY transfers in Tier 1 states succeed at high rates:

- First-time recording success: 78-85%
- Overall success rate after corrections: 95-98%
- Average time from preparation to completion: 2-4 weeks
- Average total cost (including fees and corrections): $35-85

These statistics demonstrate that Tier 1 states truly support individual property owners in managing their own transfers.

State-Specific Success Stories

The Texas Approach - Jim and Mary's Experience Jim and Mary owned their primary residence in Houston and a hunting lease property in East Texas. They completed both transfers in the same week using Texas's straightforward procedures.

"We prepared both deeds on Sunday afternoon using the state's standard forms," Mary explains. "Monday morning we got everything notarized at our bank - they didn't charge anything since we're customers. Tuesday we mailed both deeds to the respective county clerks with cashier's checks for the recording fees."

Both deeds were recorded and returned within 10 days. Total cost: $52 in recording fees plus $8 for cashier's checks. Time investment: about 4 hours total for both properties.

The Florida Advantage - Robert's Vacation Home Robert, a Michigan resident, owned a vacation condo in Naples, Florida. He worried about handling an out-of-state transfer but found Florida's system remarkably user-friendly.

"The Collier County Clerk's website had everything I needed," Robert says. "Clear instructions, downloadable forms, fee schedules, even video tutorials. I prepared the deed at home in Michigan, got it notarized locally, and mailed it to Florida with a money order for $18.50."

The deed was recorded and returned within a week. Robert received email confirmation of recording, and the county's online system allowed him to verify the transfer immediately.

Local Recorder Office Contacts and Resources

Online Resources Most Tier 1 states provide excellent online resources:

- County clerk or recorder websites with current forms
- Fee calculators for recording costs
- Email contact options for specific questions
- Online recording status tracking systems
- Digital copies of recorded documents

233

Phone Support County recording offices in Tier 1 states typically provide helpful phone support during business hours. Staff can answer questions about:

- Current recording requirements
- Fee calculations for your specific situation
- Document format requirements
- Recording timeline expectations

Physical Office Visits If you prefer in-person recording or need to resolve complex issues, most Tier 1 state recording offices welcome walk-in customers during business hours. Bring:

- Completed deed ready for recording
- Valid identification
- Payment for recording fees (cash, check, or money order)
- Copy of current deed for reference

Avoiding Common Tier 1 State Mistakes

Even in DIY-friendly states, certain mistakes can cause delays or problems.

Overcomplicating Simple Requirements Don't add unnecessary complexity to straightforward procedures. If the state accepts standard quitclaim deeds, don't worry about creating elaborate warranty deed language. Simple works better than complex in most situations.

Ignoring Local Variations While Tier 1 states have consistent statewide requirements, some counties may have local preferences or additional requirements. Check with the specific county where you'll record the deed.

Underestimating Processing Times Even efficient states need time to process recordings. Plan for 1-3 weeks for mail-in recording, and don't schedule related activities (like insurance updates) until you receive recording confirmation.

Key Takeaways for Tier 1 State Success

Tier 1 states offer genuine opportunities for cost-effective DIY trust transfers. Take advantage of their simplified procedures, reasonable fees, and helpful resources. Prepare thoroughly, follow instructions carefully, and don't be afraid to contact county offices with questions.

The combination of low costs, straightforward procedures, and high success rates makes Tier 1 states ideal for building your confidence with DIY transfers. Once you've successfully completed a transfer in a Tier 1 state, you'll have the knowledge and experience to handle more complex situations if needed.

Remember: these states want you to succeed. Their systems are designed to accommodate individual property owners, not just real estate professionals. Take advantage of that support, and enjoy the satisfaction of completing your trust transfer efficiently and affordably.

Chapter 16: Tier 2 and 3 States

Welcome to the big leagues. Tier 2 and 3 states don't make trust transfers impossible, but they definitely don't make them easy either. These states have developed complex systems, substantial fees, and detailed requirements that can intimidate even experienced property owners.

But here's the secret: complexity doesn't equal impossibility. It just means you need better preparation, more patience, and clearer understanding of when to seek professional help. Thousands of property owners successfully complete DIY transfers in these states every year. With the right approach, you can too.

Understanding State Complexity Drivers

Why Some States Are More Complex

Complex states typically developed their systems for different reasons:

- **Revenue Generation:** High transfer taxes fund state and local government operations
- **Consumer Protection:** Extensive requirements attempt to prevent fraud and errors
- **Professional Protection:** Complex procedures may reflect lobbying by legal and real estate industries
- **Historical Accident:** Requirements accumulated over decades without systematic review

Understanding the reasons helps you navigate the requirements more effectively.

Tier 2 States - Moderate Complexity with Manageable Challenges

Tier 2 State Characteristics: Illinois, Ohio, Michigan, Wisconsin, Minnesota, Virginia, North Carolina, Georgia, Maryland, Delaware, Connecticut, Rhode Island, Vermont, Maine, Oregon, Washington, Alaska, and Hawaii.

These states add complexity but remain within reasonable DIY scope for motivated property owners:

- Recording fees: $75-200 typical range
- Some documentary transfer tax (usually with trust exemptions)
- Additional forms beyond basic deeds
- More detailed recording procedures
- Specific formatting or language requirements

Illinois Example - Moderate Complexity Done Right

Illinois demonstrates how Tier 2 states can add requirements without making transfers prohibitively difficult.

Illinois Requirements:

- Real estate transfer declaration (state form)
- Recording fees: $50 plus $25 per additional $500 of value
- Documentary transfer tax: $0.50 per $500 of value (with trust exemptions)
- Notarization and witnessing required
- Specific formatting requirements for legal descriptions

Illinois Process:

1. Prepare quitclaim deed using standard Illinois form
2. Complete Illinois Real Estate Transfer Declaration
3. Calculate recording fees based on property value
4. Obtain proper notarization with witness

5. Submit deed, declaration, and fees to county recorder
6. File for documentary transfer tax exemption (usually approved automatically for trust transfers)

Total cost for a $300,000 property: approximately $125-150. Professional attorney fees for the same transfer: $1,200-1,800.

Michigan's Practical Approach

Michigan adds moderate complexity but provides clear guidance and reasonable procedures.

Michigan Specifics:

- State transfer tax: $3.75 per $500 of value
- Trust exemption available with proper documentation
- Recording fees vary by county ($30-80 typical range)
- Notarization plus two witnesses required
- Specific margin requirements for deed documents

Michigan Strategy: The key to Michigan success is understanding the state transfer tax exemption procedures. The exemption saves hundreds or thousands of dollars, but you must follow specific procedures to qualify. Most county treasurers provide clear guidance, and the exemption process is well-established.

Tier 3 States - High Complexity Requiring Strategic Approach

Tier 3 State Characteristics: California, New York, New Jersey, Pennsylvania, Massachusetts, and Washington D.C.

These jurisdictions present significant challenges:

- Recording fees often exceed $200
- Substantial documentary transfer taxes (potentially thousands of dollars)
- Complex supplemental forms with detailed requirements
- Strict formatting and procedural requirements

- Higher error rejection rates
- Limited exemption procedures

California - The Ultimate Challenge

California presents the most complex requirements in the nation, but successful DIY transfers remain possible with proper preparation and realistic expectations.

California's PCOR Requirement The Preliminary Change of Ownership Report (PCOR) is California's signature complexity. This form requires detailed information about:

- Property acquisition date and cost
- Transfer circumstances and consideration
- Relationship between transferor and transferee
- Trust details and exemption claims

California Documentary Transfer Tax California's base transfer tax is $1.10 per $1,000 of property value, but many cities and counties add additional taxes. Los Angeles combines city and county taxes reaching $4.50 per $1,000. San Francisco's transfer tax can exceed $25 per $1,000 for high-value properties.

Trust transfer exemptions exist but require precise documentation and proper procedures. The exemption language must be exact, and supporting documentation must be complete.

California Success Strategy: For California properties worth less than $500,000 in areas with reasonable transfer tax rates, DIY transfers can work with careful preparation and possibly limited professional consultation. For higher-value properties or areas with extreme transfer taxes, the complexity often justifies professional assistance.

New York - Empire State Complexity

New York combines high fees with detailed procedural requirements, creating substantial challenges for DIY transfers.

New York's TP-584 Form New York requires the Real Property Transfer Report (TP-584) for all property transfers. This form demands extensive information about:

- Property details and transfer circumstances
- Purchase price and mortgage information
- Tax exemption claims and supporting documentation
- Detailed property use and classification information

New York Transfer Taxes New York imposes both state and local transfer taxes:

- State transfer tax: $2 per $500 of value ($4 per $500 for properties over $1 million)
- Local transfer taxes vary dramatically by municipality
- New York City adds substantial additional taxes
- Trust exemptions exist but require careful documentation

New York Strategy: Success in New York often depends on property location and value. Upstate properties in smaller counties may be manageable for DIY transfer. New York City properties almost always justify professional assistance due to extreme complexity and high stakes.

Pennsylvania - Keystone State Challenges

Pennsylvania's requirements vary significantly by county, creating a patchwork of different procedures across the state.

Pennsylvania Variables:

- Transfer taxes: 1% state tax plus local taxes (total often 2-3%)
- Trust exemptions available but procedures vary by county
- Recording fees vary dramatically by county
- Some counties require specific local forms

- Philadelphia and Pittsburgh have particularly complex requirements

Pennsylvania Approach: Research requirements for your specific county before beginning preparation. Rural Pennsylvania counties often have reasonable requirements similar to Tier 2 states. Urban counties, particularly Philadelphia and Allegheny (Pittsburgh), may require professional assistance.

Documentary Transfer Tax Calculations and Exemptions

Transfer tax calculations create the biggest cost differences between Tier 2 and 3 states. Understanding exemption procedures can save thousands of dollars.

Standard Exemption Language Most states with transfer taxes provide exemptions for revocable living trust transfers where the grantor remains the beneficiary. Required language typically includes:

- "This transfer is made without consideration"
- "Grantor retains beneficial ownership of the property"
- "Transfer is to a revocable trust of which grantor is trustee and beneficiary"

Exemption Documentation Some states require supporting documentation beyond the deed language:

- Copy of relevant trust pages
- Affidavit of trust exemption
- Property tax exemption applications
- Specific state or county forms

Cost-Benefit Analysis by State Complexity

Tier 2 States - Usually Worth DIY Attempt Professional fees in Tier 2 states typically range $800-1,500 for property transfers. DIY costs usually stay under $200, creating substantial savings opportunities. The complexity is manageable for most property owners willing to invest time in research and preparation.

Break-even analysis: Even factoring in potential professional consultation costs ($200-400), DIY approaches in Tier 2 states typically save $600-1,200 per property.

Tier 3 States - Careful Cost-Benefit Analysis Required Professional fees in Tier 3 states range $1,200-3,000 or more, depending on property value and complexity. DIY costs can reach $300-800 when including transfer taxes and potential error corrections.

Break-even analysis: Savings potential ranges from $900-2,500, but higher error risks and potential costly mistakes require careful assessment.

Decision Matrix for Tier 3 States:

Proceed with DIY when:

- Property value under $400,000
- You have substantial time for research and preparation
- You're comfortable with legal document preparation
- You have access to professional consultation if needed
- Transfer tax exemptions clearly apply to your situation

Consider Professional Help when:

- Property value exceeds $500,000
- Transfer tax calculations are complex or unclear
- You're uncomfortable with legal terminology or procedures
- Timeline pressures don't allow for careful DIY preparation
- Property has unusual characteristics or ownership history

Professional Help Decision Matrix

Red Light - Stop and Hire Professional Help:

- Property value exceeds $750,000 in Tier 3 states
- Transfer taxes exceed $2,000 without clear exemption procedures
- Property ownership involves multiple parties with potential conflicts
- Existing title problems or legal complications
- Commercial or unusual property types
- Time pressure requiring guaranteed completion dates

Yellow Light - Proceed with Caution:

- Moderate property values ($200,000-500,000) in Tier 3 states
- Clear exemption procedures but complex documentation requirements
- Standard residential properties with straightforward ownership
- Adequate time for careful preparation and potential corrections
- Access to professional consultation for specific questions

Green Light - DIY Friendly Even in Complex States:

- Lower property values (under $200,000) where professional fees exceed reasonable cost-benefit ratios
- Clear, established procedures with extensive online guidance
- Standard property types with straightforward ownership
- Personal comfort with legal document preparation
- No timeline pressures requiring guaranteed completion

Building Expertise in Complex States

Success in Tier 2 and 3 states requires systematic skill development.

Research Phase - Become a Mini-Expert Before preparing any documents:

- Study your state's specific requirements thoroughly

- Review successful transfer examples (many county websites provide samples)
- Understand exemption procedures and required documentation
- Calculate total costs including all fees and taxes
- Identify potential problem areas specific to your situation

Preparation Phase - Attention to Detail Complex states punish sloppy preparation:

- Use state-specific forms rather than generic templates
- Follow formatting requirements exactly
- Prepare all supplemental forms simultaneously
- Verify notarization and witnessing requirements
- Calculate fees and taxes precisely before submission

Execution Phase - Professional Standards Approach complex state transfers with professional-level attention:

- Double-check all calculations
- Review all documents for accuracy and completeness
- Maintain detailed records of all communications and submissions
- Plan for potential corrections or resubmissions
- Follow up promptly on all recording confirmations

Technology Resources for Complex States

Online Research Tools Many complex states provide sophisticated online resources:

- Interactive fee calculators
- Downloadable forms with instructions
- Video tutorials for complex procedures
- Email support for specific questions
- Online tracking systems for submitted documents

Professional Consultation Services Technology enables cost-effective professional consultation:

- Video conference consultations for specific questions
- Document review services for prepared deeds
- Limited scope representation for specific procedural steps
- Online legal platforms connecting property owners with local attorneys

When Complexity Becomes Opportunity

Sometimes complex state requirements reveal opportunities for improvement beyond simple trust transfers.

Title Enhancement Complex review procedures may uncover title problems that needed addressing anyway. Correcting these problems during trust transfer can actually improve your property's marketability and value.

Tax Planning Opportunities Detailed transfer tax analysis may reveal legitimate tax planning strategies. Some complex states offer multiple exemption options, and choosing the right approach can provide ongoing benefits beyond the immediate transfer.

Documentation Improvement Complex states often require comprehensive property documentation. Gathering this information creates better records for future property management, insurance claims, or eventual sales.

Key Takeaways for Complex State Success

Tier 2 and 3 states require more preparation, patience, and strategic thinking, but they don't require surrender. Approach complex state transfers as learning experiences that build valuable real estate knowledge.

Focus on understanding your specific state's requirements rather than trying to apply generic approaches. Invest time in research and preparation to avoid costly mistakes. Don't hesitate to seek professional consultation for specific questions while maintaining control over the overall process.

Most importantly, remember that complexity creates opportunity. The same requirements that deter casual DIY attempts create substantial savings opportunities for property owners willing to invest in proper preparation. Your successful completion of a complex state transfer demonstrates real competence and can save thousands of dollars compared to full professional services.

The goal isn't to become a real estate attorney. The goal is to become competent enough in your specific situation to make informed decisions about when to proceed independently and when to seek professional assistance.

Chapter 17: When to Call a Lawyer

Nobody wants to admit defeat, especially when you've invested time and energy learning about DIY trust transfers. But sometimes calling a lawyer isn't defeat - it's smart strategy. Knowing when to seek professional help can save you thousands of dollars, months of complications, and significant stress.

This chapter helps you recognize the warning signs that signal "attorney time" and shows you how to work with legal professionals efficiently and cost-effectively when you need them.

The Professional Help Decision Framework

Think of professional help decisions like medical decisions. You can handle minor cuts and scrapes yourself, but you call a doctor for serious injuries. The key is accurately assessing the severity of your situation.

Red Flags Requiring Immediate Legal Help

Critical Warning Signs - Stop and Call an Attorney:

Complex Ownership Structures

- Property owned by LLCs, partnerships, or corporations
- Multiple unrelated owners with disagreements about the transfer
- Properties acquired through complex transactions (1031 exchanges, seller financing with ongoing obligations)
- Ownership percentages that don't match standard patterns (anything other than 50/50, 100%, or clear fractional shares)

Existing Legal Problems

- Pending lawsuits involving the property
- Tax liens or judgments against the property
- Boundary disputes with neighbors
- Environmental contamination issues
- Zoning violations or permit problems

Family Complications

- Divorce proceedings (current or recent)
- Disputes among family members about property ownership or inheritance
- Properties received through inheritance with unclear title chains
- Situations involving minor children as beneficiaries
- Blended family situations with complex beneficiary arrangements

Financial Complications

- Properties in foreclosure or pre-foreclosure status
- Significant mortgage defaults or payment problems
- Properties owned jointly with people experiencing financial distress
- Bankruptcy proceedings (current or recent)
- Properties with complex financing arrangements

Unusual Property Types

- Commercial properties
- Agricultural land with water rights or mineral rights
- Condominiums in financially distressed associations
- Co-operative apartments
- Properties with significant personal property components (furnished rentals, equipment)
- Historic properties with preservation restrictions

When Property Value Justifies Professional Help

The Million-Dollar Rule Properties worth more than $1 million in any state typically justify professional assistance. The potential costs of mistakes often exceed professional fees, and the complexity of high-value transfers usually requires specialized knowledge.

The Transfer Tax Threshold When potential documentary transfer taxes exceed $2,000, professional consultation usually pays for itself. Transfer tax exemption procedures in high-tax jurisdictions often require precise documentation that benefits from professional preparation.

The Time-Sensitive Situation When timing is critical - estate settlement deadlines, sale contract requirements, or mortgage modification timelines - professional help ensures proper completion within required timeframes.

Finding Qualified Attorneys for Trust and Property Transfers

Not all attorneys handle trust and property transfers effectively. You need someone with specific experience in estate planning, real estate law, or both.

Attorney Selection Criteria

Essential Qualifications:

- Active license in the state where your property is located
- Specific experience with living trust property transfers
- Understanding of local recording procedures and requirements
- Knowledge of transfer tax exemption procedures
- Clear fee structure for limited services

Preferred Additional Qualifications:

- Estate planning law certification or specialization

- Real estate law experience
- Local practice (familiarity with specific county procedures)
- Technology capabilities (email, video conferencing, electronic document sharing)
- References from satisfied clients with similar situations

Questions to Ask Potential Attorneys:

1. How many living trust property transfers do you handle annually?
2. Are you familiar with [specific county] recording procedures?
3. Can you provide limited assistance rather than full representation?
4. What are your fees for deed preparation and recording assistance?
5. How long do you typically take to complete straightforward transfers?
6. Do you provide cost estimates before beginning work?

Cost Expectations for Limited Assistance

Professional help doesn't require hiring attorneys for full-service representation. Many attorneys offer limited assistance services that provide professional guidance while maintaining cost control.

Limited Service Options:

Deed Review and Consultation ($200-400) Attorney reviews your prepared deed, confirms compliance with state requirements, and provides specific feedback for corrections if needed. This catches errors before recording while maintaining your control over the process.

Document Preparation Only ($400-800) Attorney prepares all required documents but doesn't handle recording or post-transfer tasks. You handle research, provide information, and manage recording procedures yourself.

Recording Assistance ($300-600) Attorney handles recording procedures, fee calculations, and post-recording verification while you maintain responsibility for document preparation and related communications.

Complete Limited Representation ($800-1,500) Attorney handles document preparation, recording, and immediate post-transfer tasks but doesn't provide ongoing trust administration or comprehensive estate planning services.

Full Service for Comparison ($1,500-4,000+) Complete attorney management of the entire transfer process plus related estate planning consultation. This represents the cost you're avoiding with DIY approaches.

Preparing for Attorney Consultations

Document Organization Gather all relevant documents before consultation:

- Current property deed
- Trust document (complete copy)
- Property tax records
- Mortgage information
- Insurance policies
- Previous correspondence about the transfer

Question Preparation Prepare specific questions rather than general requests for help:

- "Is my deed preparation correct for [specific county] requirements?"
- "Do I qualify for transfer tax exemption in this situation?"
- "What are the specific risks if I proceed with DIY transfer?"
- "What would you charge for limited assistance with [specific task]?"

Budget Discussion Discuss fees and scope clearly before beginning any work:

- Request written fee estimates for specific services
- Understand what's included and excluded in quoted fees
- Clarify additional costs for unexpected complications
- Establish communication procedures and associated costs

State Bar Referral Services

Every state bar association provides attorney referral services, but quality and usefulness vary significantly.

Effective Use of Bar Referrals:

- Request attorneys with specific experience in estate planning or real estate law
- Ask about fees and initial consultation costs
- Verify attorney licensing and disciplinary history
- Request multiple referrals to compare options

Alternative Attorney Finding Methods:

- Local estate planning councils or real estate attorney associations
- Recommendations from accountants, financial planners, or other professionals
- Online legal directories with client reviews and ratings
- Personal referrals from friends or family with similar situations

Never Ignore These Warning Signs

Some situations absolutely require professional help, regardless of cost considerations:

Legal Complexity Beyond DIY Scope:

- Properties with clouded titles or ownership disputes
- Situations involving court orders or legal settlements
- Properties with environmental liens or restrictions
- Complex trust arrangements (irrevocable trusts, special needs trusts)
- Properties owned by deceased persons requiring probate

Financial Stakes Too High for Mistakes:

- Properties worth more than $1 million
- Transfer tax liability exceeding $5,000
- Properties with significant mortgage balances requiring lender consent
- Investment properties with complex lease arrangements
- Properties generating substantial income where transfer interruption would be costly

Personal Capability Limitations:

- Discomfort with legal document preparation
- Limited time for proper research and preparation
- Physical or cognitive limitations affecting document management
- Language barriers affecting understanding of legal requirements
- Technology limitations preventing proper document preparation

Working Effectively with Attorneys for Limited Services

Setting Clear Boundaries When hiring attorneys for limited assistance, establish clear boundaries about what they will and won't handle:

- Which specific tasks they'll complete
- What information and documents you'll provide
- Communication procedures and frequency
- Timeline expectations for task completion

- Additional fee arrangements if scope expands

Maintaining Control Limited assistance means you remain in control of the overall process:

- You make final decisions about timing and procedures
- You handle communications with other parties
- You maintain responsibility for tasks outside the attorney's scope
- You coordinate the overall timeline and priorities

Maximizing Value Get maximum value from limited professional assistance:

- Prepare thoroughly for consultations
- Ask specific, detailed questions
- Request written summaries of advice and recommendations
- Understand the reasoning behind professional recommendations
- Use attorney guidance to improve your overall understanding

The Attorney Interview Checklist

Initial Contact Questions:

1. Do you handle living trust property transfers regularly?
2. Are you familiar with [specific county] recording procedures?
3. What are your fees for limited consultation on deed preparation?
4. How quickly can you review prepared documents?
5. Do you offer flat-fee services for straightforward transfers?

Service Scope Questions:

1. What specific services would you provide?
2. What would remain my responsibility?
3. How do you handle questions that arise during the process?

4. What happens if complications develop beyond the original scope?
5. Do you provide written summaries of advice and recommendations?

Logistics Questions:

1. How do you prefer to receive documents and information?
2. What's your typical timeline for limited assistance services?
3. How do you handle urgent questions or time-sensitive issues?
4. Do you work with clients remotely for out-of-state properties?
5. What payment methods do you accept?

Cost Control Strategies for Professional Help

Limiting Scope Creep Professional consultations can expand beyond original intentions if you don't maintain clear boundaries. Prevent scope creep by:

- Defining specific tasks and deliverables upfront
- Requesting written estimates before work begins
- Understanding what additional services cost
- Maintaining responsibility for tasks you can handle yourself

Bundling Services Efficiently If you need professional help with multiple properties or multiple aspects of estate planning, bundling services often reduces total costs:

- Multiple property transfers in the same state
- Trust transfers combined with trust updates or amendments
- Property transfers combined with related estate planning tasks

Using Technology for Cost-Effective Communication

- Email for non-urgent communications
- Video conferences instead of in-person meetings
- Document sharing platforms for efficient document review
- Online scheduling systems for consultation appointments

Learning from Professional Interactions

Every professional consultation provides learning opportunities that benefit future property transfers or estate planning decisions.

Skills Development Use attorney interactions to build your understanding:

- Ask attorneys to explain their reasoning for specific recommendations
- Request resources for further learning about relevant legal topics
- Understand how professionals approach complex problem-solving
- Learn about tools and resources that professionals use

Network Building Positive professional relationships benefit future situations:

- Attorneys you've worked with successfully become resources for future questions
- Professional referrals often provide quality assurance for other services
- Established relationships streamline future limited assistance arrangements

Knowledge Transfer Professional guidance helps you become more capable for future situations:

- Understanding complex state requirements helps with future property acquisitions
- Learning about transfer tax exemptions applies to other property transactions
- Document preparation skills transfer to other legal situations

Key Takeaways for Smart Professional Help Decisions

Professional help isn't failure - it's strategic resource utilization. Know your limits, recognize warning signs, and use professional services efficiently when they provide clear value.

The goal isn't to avoid professional help at all costs. The goal is to use professional services strategically when they provide clear benefits while maintaining control and cost-effectiveness for tasks you can handle yourself.

Remember that even when you hire professional help, understanding the process yourself makes you a better client. You'll ask better questions, provide better information, and get better results from professional services.

Most importantly, don't let fear of needing professional help prevent you from attempting DIY transfers in appropriate situations. The majority of trust transfers can be completed successfully without professional assistance, and the learning experience builds valuable knowledge for future property decisions.

The money you save on straightforward transfers can fund professional assistance when you truly need it for complex situations. This balanced approach maximizes both cost savings and successful outcomes across your entire property portfolio.

Chapter 18: Trust Maintenance and Updates

Your trust isn't a "set it and forget it" arrangement. Like any valuable system, it requires regular attention, occasional updates, and periodic maintenance to continue working effectively. The good news? The same skills that helped you transfer your property successfully will serve you well in ongoing trust management.

Think of trust maintenance like home maintenance. You don't need to become a professional contractor, but you do need to understand basic systems, recognize when problems develop, and know when to call for help. Regular attention prevents small issues from becoming expensive disasters.

The Annual Trust Review - Your Most Important Habit

Most trust problems develop slowly over years, not suddenly overnight. Annual reviews catch problems early when they're still easy and inexpensive to fix.

What Your Annual Review Should Cover:

Trust Funding Status Review all assets to confirm they're properly titled in your trust's name:

- Real estate deeds showing trust ownership
- Bank and investment accounts with trust as owner or beneficiary
- Insurance policies with trust as owner and beneficiary
- Business interests properly assigned to trust
- Personal property of significant value

Beneficiary and Trustee Information Verify that your trust reflects current family circumstances:

- All intended beneficiaries are named correctly
- Contact information for beneficiaries stays current
- Successor trustee designations remain appropriate
- Age-related provisions trigger at appropriate times (children reaching adulthood)
- Special needs or circumstances are addressed properly

Property and Asset Changes Update trust records for any changes during the year:

- New property acquisitions (remember to transfer them to the trust)
- Property sales or dispositions
- Significant changes in asset values
- New accounts or investments
- Major purchases requiring trust ownership

Tax and Legal Compliance Review compliance with ongoing requirements:

- Property tax exemptions and classifications
- Insurance coverage adequacy and beneficiary designations
- Income tax reporting for trust-owned assets
- Required filings or notifications in any jurisdiction

The Trust Amendment vs. Restatement Decision

As your life changes, your trust may need updates. Understanding when to amend versus when to restate can save money and ensure proper legal effect.

Trust Amendments - For Limited Changes Use amendments for specific, limited changes:

- Adding or removing individual beneficiaries

- Changing successor trustee designations
- Updating specific bequests or distributions
- Modifying administrative provisions
- Correcting minor errors or outdated information

Amendment Advantages:

- Lower cost than full restatement
- Faster preparation and execution
- Original trust remains intact
- Clear record of specific changes

Amendment Process:

1. Identify specific provisions requiring changes
2. Draft amendment language referencing original trust sections
3. Execute amendment with same formalities as original trust
4. Attach amendment to original trust document
5. Provide copies to successor trustees and relevant institutions

Trust Restatements - For Comprehensive Changes Use restatements for major overhauls:

- Significant changes affecting multiple trust provisions
- Complete beneficiary restructuring
- Major changes in distribution schemes
- Updating outdated trust language to current legal standards
- Consolidating multiple previous amendments

Restatement Advantages:

- Creates single, comprehensive document
- Eliminates confusion from multiple amendments
- Allows complete reorganization of trust provisions
- Provides opportunity to update language and legal standards

Restatement Considerations:

- Higher cost than amendments
- Requires careful attention to property and account retitling
- May require new trust identification numbers for some purposes
- Could affect beneficiary designations on accounts and policies

Adding New Properties to Your Trust

Every time you acquire new property, you face the same transfer decision you handled originally. The skills you've developed make future transfers much easier.

Automatic Transfer Procedures Develop systematic procedures for new property acquisitions:

1. Include trust ownership in purchase contracts when buying property
2. Instruct title companies to prepare deeds showing trust ownership
3. Coordinate with real estate agents and lenders about trust ownership
4. Verify proper trust ownership before closing

Post-Purchase Transfers When properties are acquired in your personal name (sometimes unavoidable due to financing requirements), transfer them to your trust promptly:

- Use the same procedures you learned for your original transfer
- Take advantage of your experience with state requirements
- Leverage existing relationships with notaries and recording offices
- Apply lessons learned from previous transfers

Refinancing and Trust-Owned Properties Many lenders require temporary transfer of property out of the trust during refinancing, then back into the trust after closing. This is routine and shouldn't concern you:

1. Transfer property to your personal name for refinancing
2. Complete refinancing with property in personal name
3. Transfer property back to trust immediately after closing
4. Update insurance and tax records to reflect trust ownership

Removing Properties from Your Trust

Sometimes you'll need to remove properties from your trust before selling or for other reasons.

Property Sale Procedures Most property sales can be completed with the property remaining in trust ownership, but some situations require temporary removal:

- Certain financing arrangements
- Buyer preference or requirement
- Title company recommendations
- Lender requirements for specific loan programs

Removal Process:

1. Prepare quitclaim deed from trust to yourself personally
2. Execute deed as trustee of the trust
3. Record deed following same procedures as original transfer
4. Update insurance and tax records temporarily
5. Complete property sale from personal ownership
6. Transfer any replacement property to trust promptly

Trust Dissolution If you decide to dissolve your trust entirely, you'll need to transfer all trust property back to personal ownership:

- Prepare deeds for all real estate
- Retitle all accounts and investments
- Update all insurance beneficiaries
- Notify all relevant institutions
- Maintain records of dissolution for tax purposes

Successor Trustee Preparation - The Most Important Task

Your trust is only as good as the people who will manage it when you can't. Preparing successor trustees properly is crucial for long-term success.

Successor Trustee Education Your successor trustees need practical knowledge, not just legal appointment:

Essential Information They Need:

- Location of all trust documents and amendments
- List of all trust-owned assets with account numbers and contact information
- Procedures for property management and maintenance
- Contact information for professional advisors (attorney, accountant, financial advisor)
- Understanding of beneficiary rights and expectations
- Basic trust administration procedures

Documentation Systems Create comprehensive records for successor trustees:

- Asset inventory with current values and locations
- Contact directory for all professional relationships
- Copies of all property deeds and account documentation
- Insurance policy information and claim procedures
- Tax return copies and preparation information
- Emergency procedures for urgent situations

Regular Communication Don't wait until incapacity or death to involve successor trustees:

- Include them in annual trust reviews when appropriate
- Introduce them to key professional advisors
- Explain major decisions and reasoning
- Provide training on basic trust administration tasks
- Update them about significant changes in trust assets or beneficiaries

The Property Management Transition Plan

Trust-owned properties require ongoing management that must continue smoothly when successor trustees take over.

Management Documentation Maintain detailed records of property management procedures:

- Preferred contractors and service providers with contact information
- Maintenance schedules and warranty information
- Insurance claims history and procedures
- Tenant information and lease terms (for rental properties)
- Property tax payment procedures and exemption status

Emergency Procedures Develop clear procedures for property emergencies:

- Contractor authorization and payment procedures
- Insurance claim initiation and management
- Tenant emergency contact protocols
- Authority levels for different types of decisions
- Communication procedures with beneficiaries

Financial Management Systems Ensure successor trustees can manage property-related finances effectively:

- Bank account access and signature authority
- Payment procedures for ongoing expenses
- Record-keeping systems for income and expenses
- Tax reporting procedures and professional relationships
- Investment and savings strategies for property reserves

Technology and Trust Management

Modern technology simplifies trust management but requires planning for successor accessibility.

Digital Asset Management Organize digital aspects of trust management:

- Cloud storage for all trust documents with shared access
- Password management for online accounts
- Digital copies of all property-related documents
- Electronic payment systems for routine expenses
- Online access to property tax and insurance accounts

Communication Systems Establish technology systems that successor trustees can use effectively:

- Shared email addresses for trust business
- Video conferencing capabilities for remote beneficiary communication
- Document sharing platforms for professional interactions
- Mobile apps for property management and maintenance coordination

Security and Privacy Protection Balance accessibility with security:

- Multi-factor authentication for sensitive accounts
- Regular password updates and security reviews
- Limited access privileges based on actual needs
- Backup procedures for technology failures
- Privacy protection for beneficiary information

Warning Box: Neglected Trust Risks

Trusts that receive minimal attention after creation often fail to achieve their intended purposes:

Common Neglect Problems:

- Properties acquired after trust creation never transferred to trust
- Outdated beneficiary information due to deaths, divorces, or estrangements

- Successor trustees who don't understand their responsibilities
- Missing or outdated account information
- Tax compliance failures due to poor record-keeping

Consequences of Neglect:

- Probate proceedings despite trust creation
- Tax penalties and interest charges
- Family conflicts over unclear or outdated provisions
- Property management problems during incapacity
- Reduced asset protection benefits

Prevention Through Regular Attention: Annual reviews, systematic record-keeping, and ongoing beneficiary communication prevent most neglect-related problems.

Building Long-Term Trust Success

The Five-Year Planning Cycle Think about trust management in five-year cycles:

- **Years 1-2:** Focus on proper funding and initial organization
- **Years 3-4:** Develop efficient management routines and address minor updates
- **Year 5:** Comprehensive review and planning for next five-year cycle

Continuous Learning Stay informed about developments affecting trust management:

- Tax law changes affecting trust-owned property
- State law modifications impacting trust administration
- New technology tools for property and asset management
- Professional development opportunities for trustee skills

Professional Relationship Maintenance Maintain relationships with professional advisors:

- Annual check-ins with estate planning attorney
- Regular communication with tax preparation professionals
- Ongoing relationships with property management providers
- Updated contact information for all professional services

Creating Your Trust Legacy

Effective trust management creates lasting benefits that extend far beyond avoiding probate:

- Family wealth preservation across generations
- Simplified estate settlement reducing stress during difficult times
- Privacy protection for family financial information
- Flexibility for changing circumstances and family needs
- Education and empowerment for family members about financial responsibility

The Confidence Factor

Successfully managing your trust builds confidence and competence that benefits other areas of financial life. Property owners who master trust management often become more effective investors, better financial planners, and more capable family financial leaders.

Key Takeaways for Trust Maintenance Excellence

Trust maintenance requires regular attention but not overwhelming effort. Develop systematic annual review procedures, maintain good documentation, and prepare successor trustees properly. Address problems promptly rather than hoping they'll resolve themselves.

Most importantly, remember that effective trust management protects and enhances the benefits you created through successful property transfers. The time and effort you invest in maintenance pays dividends through improved family financial security, reduced stress during transitions, and greater control over your financial legacy.

Your trust is a powerful tool, but like any tool, its effectiveness depends on proper use and maintenance. The skills you've developed through DIY property transfers give you an excellent foundation for long-term trust success. Build on that foundation with consistent attention, ongoing learning, and strategic use of professional help when needed.

Chapter 19: Tax Considerations and Benefits

Taxes might not be the most exciting aspect of trust ownership, but understanding tax implications can save you thousands of dollars and help you avoid expensive mistakes. The good news? Trust ownership usually simplifies rather than complicates your tax situation, especially for the revocable living trusts most property owners use.

This chapter cuts through tax complexity to focus on what really matters for trust-owned property: maintaining your current tax benefits, understanding what changes (very little) and what stays the same (almost everything), and planning ahead to maximize tax advantages.

The Fundamental Tax Truth About Revocable Living Trusts

Here's the most important tax fact about revocable living trusts: for tax purposes, they don't exist. The IRS treats your revocable living trust as if you still own everything personally. This "tax transparency" means you continue filing the same tax returns, claiming the same deductions, and paying the same taxes as before the transfer.

This transparency is actually a huge advantage. You get all the benefits of trust ownership - probate avoidance, incapacity planning, privacy protection - without any of the complex tax compliance that comes with other types of trusts.

Property Tax Implications and Protections

Reassessment Protection One of the biggest fears property owners have about transferring property to trusts is triggering property tax reassessment. In most states, transfers to revocable living trusts don't trigger reassessment when:

- The grantor (you) remains the trustee
- The grantor retains beneficial ownership
- The transfer involves no consideration (payment)

Homestead Exemption Preservation Homestead exemptions typically continue when property transfers to your revocable living trust. However, some states require specific procedures to maintain exemption status:

States Requiring Action:

- **California:** File claim for homestead exemption continuation
- **Florida:** Update homestead application to reflect trust ownership
- **Texas:** Notify appraisal district of trust ownership
- **Others:** Check with local assessor about specific procedures

Property Tax Payment Procedures Property taxes on trust-owned property are paid the same way as before the transfer. However, you may need to update payment information:

- Property tax bills should be addressed to the trust
- Electronic payment systems may need trust name updates
- Escrow accounts (if you have mortgage) should reflect trust ownership
- Property tax exemption applications should show trust as owner

Federal Income Tax - Business as Usual

No Changes to Income Reporting Trust ownership doesn't change how you report property-related income:

- Rental income from trust-owned properties is reported on your personal return

- Property sale gains or losses are reported personally
- Depreciation deductions continue as before
- Interest and tax deductions remain on your personal return

Tax Identification Numbers Revocable living trusts use your Social Security number for tax purposes. You don't need to obtain a separate Employer Identification Number (EIN) for the trust unless:

- You have employees working for trust business
- The trust becomes irrevocable (after your death)
- You elect to file separate trust tax returns (rarely beneficial)

Capital Gains Considerations for Trust-Owned Property

Basis Transfer Rules When you transfer property to your trust, the property's tax basis transfers with it. If you paid $200,000 for property now worth $400,000, the trust receives the property with your $200,000 basis. This means:

- No immediate tax consequences from the transfer
- Future sale gains calculated from your original basis
- Depreciation schedules continue unchanged for rental properties

Stepped-Up Basis at Death Trust-owned property receives stepped-up basis when you die, just like personally-owned property. This eliminates capital gains tax on appreciation that occurred during your lifetime:

Example: You transfer property with $100,000 basis and $300,000 value to your trust. When you die, the property is worth $450,000. Your beneficiaries receive the property with $450,000 basis, eliminating $350,000 of potential capital gains tax.

Primary Residence Exclusions The $250,000 (single) or $500,000 (married) capital gains exclusion for primary residence sales continues to apply to trust-owned properties when:

- You continue living in the property as your primary residence
- You meet the ownership and use requirements
- The trust is revocable and you're the primary beneficiary

State Income Tax Variations

Most states follow federal tax treatment for revocable living trusts, but some have unique requirements.

States with Special Rules:

- **Pennsylvania:** Considers trusts separate taxpayers even when revocable
- **New Hampshire:** Imposes interest and dividend tax on trust income
- **Tennessee:** Previously taxed trust investment income (tax repealed but older trusts may be affected)

Multi-State Property Considerations When you own trust property in multiple states:

- You continue filing non-resident tax returns in states where required
- Rental income reporting doesn't change
- State tax withholding requirements continue as before
- Property tax obligations continue in each state

Business Property and Trust Ownership

Trust ownership of business property creates some additional considerations but remains manageable.

Rental Property Management Trust ownership doesn't change rental property tax treatment:

- Rental income and expenses are reported on Schedule E
- Depreciation deductions continue on the same schedules

- Section 1031 like-kind exchanges remain available for trust-owned properties
- Passive activity loss rules apply the same way

Professional Property Use Properties used in professional practices or businesses:

- Continue qualifying for business use deductions
- Maintain eligibility for Section 179 depreciation
- Preserve qualification for home office deductions (if applicable)
- Don't affect business entity tax elections

Estate Tax Benefits and Planning

Current Estate Tax Exemptions For 2025, the federal estate tax exemption is $13.99 million per person ($27.98 million for married couples). Most property owners don't face federal estate tax liability, but trust ownership provides benefits regardless:

- Simplified estate settlement
- Privacy protection for family finances
- Reduced administrative costs
- Faster distribution to beneficiaries

State Estate Tax Considerations Some states impose estate taxes at lower thresholds than federal exemptions:

- **States with Estate Taxes:** Connecticut, Hawaii, Illinois, Maine, Maryland, Massachusetts, Minnesota, New York, Oregon, Rhode Island, Vermont, Washington, and District of Columbia
- **Exemption Amounts:** Range from $1 million to $12.92 million depending on state
- **Trust Benefits:** Proper trust funding can simplify estate tax compliance and planning

Generation-Skipping Transfer Tax For families with substantial wealth, trusts provide opportunities for generation-skipping tax planning. However, this planning requires professional guidance and typically involves irrevocable trust structures beyond the scope of this book.

Record-Keeping for Tax Success

Essential Tax Records for Trust Property:

- Original property purchase documentation
- All improvement and capital expenditure records
- Annual property tax payment records
- Insurance payment documentation
- Rental income and expense records (if applicable)
- Professional service invoices related to property management

Digital Record-Keeping Systems Modern technology simplifies tax record management:

- Cloud storage for easy access from anywhere
- Scanning apps for mobile document capture
- Expense tracking software for rental properties
- Integration with tax preparation software
- Automatic backup and synchronization

Professional Tax Preparation Considerations

When to Use Tax Professionals:

- Multiple properties in different states
- Significant rental property income
- Complex business use of trust properties
- Estate tax planning requirements
- Unfamiliarity with trust tax reporting

Working with Tax Preparers: Ensure your tax preparer understands trust taxation:

- Verify experience with revocable living trust returns
- Confirm understanding of your specific state's requirements
- Discuss multi-state property reporting if applicable
- Review proposed tax strategies before implementation

Common Tax Mistakes to Avoid

Filing Separate Trust Returns Unnecessarily Revocable living trusts typically don't file separate tax returns. Filing unnecessarily creates extra costs and compliance burdens without benefits.

Claiming Incorrect Deductions Don't claim deductions twice:

- Property tax deductions belong on your personal return, not separate trust return
- Mortgage interest deductions continue on your personal return
- Rental property deductions are reported on your personal Schedule E

Ignoring State-Specific Requirements Some states have unique trust taxation rules. Research your state's requirements or consult with local tax professionals familiar with state law.

Advanced Tax Planning Opportunities

Income Tax Planning Trust ownership creates opportunities for sophisticated income tax planning:

- **Property Timing:** Coordinate property sales with other income to optimize tax brackets
- **Charitable Planning:** Trust-owned property can be contributed to charitable organizations with enhanced tax benefits
- **Estate Planning Integration:** Coordinate property transfers with other estate planning strategies

Multi-Generational Planning Properly structured trusts can provide tax benefits across multiple generations:

- **Generation-Skipping Benefits:** Advanced trust structures can minimize taxes on transfers to grandchildren
- **Basis Step-Up Planning:** Strategic timing of property transfers can maximize stepped-up basis benefits
- **Income Distribution Planning:** Trusts can distribute income to beneficiaries in lower tax brackets

Business and Investment Integration Trust ownership integrates well with business and investment strategies:

- **Real Estate Investment:** Trusts can own rental properties, commercial real estate, and real estate investment funds
- **Business Ownership:** Trusts can own business interests and coordinate with business succession planning
- **Investment Management:** Trust ownership provides flexibility for investment management and coordination

Tax Compliance Calendar

Annual Tax Tasks:

- **January:** Gather tax documents for previous year property income and expenses
- **April:** File personal tax returns including trust property income
- **Quarterly:** Review estimated tax payments if trust properties generate significant income
- **December:** Plan end-of-year tax strategies involving trust property

Multi-Year Planning:

- **Every 3 years:** Review overall tax strategy and planning opportunities
- **Every 5 years:** Comprehensive review of trust structure and tax efficiency
- **Major life changes:** Review tax implications of marriage, divorce, retirement, or significant income changes

State-Specific Tax Benefits

No State Income Tax States Alaska, Florida, Nevada, New Hampshire, South Dakota, Tennessee, Texas, Washington, and Wyoming don't impose state income tax. Trust property ownership in these states provides additional tax advantages through:

- No state tax on rental property income
- No state capital gains tax on property sales
- Simplified multi-state tax compliance for property owners

Favorable State Trust Laws Some states provide particular advantages for trust property ownership:

- **Nevada:** No state income tax plus favorable trust administration laws
- **Delaware:** Sophisticated trust laws with tax advantages for complex situations
- **South Dakota:** No state income tax plus strong privacy protections

Working with Tax Professionals Effectively

Choosing Tax Professionals Look for professionals with trust taxation experience:

- CPAs with estate and trust specialization
- Enrolled agents familiar with trust taxation
- Tax attorneys for complex situations
- Local professionals familiar with state-specific requirements

Communication Best Practices

- Provide complete documentation of trust property ownership
- Explain trust structure and management arrangements clearly
- Discuss multi-state properties and compliance requirements
- Review proposed tax strategies before implementation

- Maintain regular communication about changes in trust assets or circumstances

Key Takeaways for Tax Success with Trust-Owned Property

Trust ownership usually simplifies rather than complicates tax compliance. Maintain the same tax practices you used before transferring property to your trust, with attention to a few specific requirements around property tax exemptions and record-keeping.

Focus on preserving existing tax benefits rather than worrying about new complications. The tax transparency of revocable living trusts means you continue enjoying all the same deductions, exemptions, and benefits you had before the transfer.

Most importantly, don't let tax concerns prevent you from completing beneficial trust transfers. The tax advantages of trust ownership - including eventual stepped-up basis for beneficiaries and simplified estate settlement - far outweigh any minor additional compliance requirements.

Your successful completion of DIY property transfers demonstrates the same attention to detail and systematic thinking that leads to tax success. Apply those same skills to ongoing tax management, and you'll maximize both the immediate and long-term benefits of trust property ownership.

Chapter 20: Your Complete Action Plan

You've learned everything you need to know about transferring your home to a trust. You understand the process, know the requirements, and recognize the potential pitfalls. Now it's time to transform all that knowledge into action with a clear, personalized plan that takes you from where you are today to successful completion of your trust transfer.

This chapter creates your roadmap to success with specific timelines, detailed checklists, and progress tracking systems. Think of it as your personal GPS for the trust transfer journey - it knows where you're starting, where you want to go, and the best route to get there safely and efficiently.

Assessing Your Starting Point

Before creating your action plan, let's determine exactly where you stand right now.

Your Property Portfolio Assessment

Primary Residence Evaluation:

- Property value: $ _____
- Current ownership type (individual, joint tenancy, etc.): _____
- Mortgage status and lender: _____
- Homestead exemption status: _____
- State location and complexity tier: _____

Additional Properties: For each additional property, complete:

- Property type and location: _____
- Current ownership structure: _____
- Mortgage or financing details: _____
- Current use (personal, rental, vacant): _____
- Estimated transfer complexity (simple, moderate, complex): _____

Your Trust Status Assessment

Existing Trust Evaluation:

- Do you have a living trust? Yes/No
- Trust creation date: _____
- Trust name (exact): _____
- Current trustee(s): _____
- Successor trustee(s): _____
- Last trust review date: _____

Trust Preparation Needs: If you don't have a trust yet:

- Estimated timeline for trust creation: _____
- Professional help planned: Yes/No
- Budget for trust creation: $ _____

Your Capability and Resource Assessment

Time Availability:

- Hours per week available for transfer project: _____
- Preferred timeline for completion: _____
- Flexible schedule for notarization and recording: Yes/No

Skill and Comfort Assessment: Rate your comfort level (1-10) with:

- Legal document preparation: _____
- Government office procedures: _____
- Research and problem-solving: _____
- Detail-oriented tasks: _____

Support Resources:

- Local notary services identified: Yes/No
- Professional consultation budget: $ _____
- Family member assistance available: Yes/No

The 30-60-90 Day Action Plans

30-Day Quick Start Plan - For Single Property, Simple Situations

Week 1: Foundation and Research

- **Day 1-2:** Complete property and trust assessment (above)
- **Day 3-4:** Research your state's specific requirements using county recorder website
- **Day 5-7:** Gather all required documents (current deed, trust document, identification)

Week 2: Document Preparation

- **Day 8-10:** Prepare new deed using state-appropriate forms
- **Day 11-12:** Review deed preparation for accuracy and completeness
- **Day 13-14:** Schedule notarization appointment and prepare for signing

Week 3: Execution and Recording

- **Day 15:** Execute deed with proper notarization
- **Day 16-17:** Prepare recording package with cover letter and fees
- **Day 18-21:** Submit deed for recording (mail or in-person)

Week 4: Completion and Follow-up

- **Day 22-28:** Receive recorded deed and verify proper recording

- **Day 29-30:** Complete post-transfer notifications (insurance, mortgage servicer, property tax office)

Success Factors for 30-Day Completion:

- Single property in Tier 1 state
- Existing valid trust
- Straightforward ownership (no complications)
- Available time for focused attention
- Local notary and recording resources

60-Day Comprehensive Plan - For Multiple Properties or Moderate Complexity

Days 1-14: Research and Planning Phase

- Complete detailed assessment of all properties and requirements
- Research specific requirements for each state/county involved
- Create property-specific action plans and timelines
- Identify potential complications and develop solutions
- Establish professional consultation resources if needed

Days 15-35: Document Preparation Phase

- Prepare deeds for all properties using state-specific requirements
- Gather supporting documents and forms for each jurisdiction
- Calculate fees and taxes for each transfer
- Review all documents for accuracy and legal compliance
- Schedule notarization for all required signatures

Days 36-50: Execution Phase

- Execute all deeds with proper notarization
- Submit recordings in order of complexity (simple states first)
- Track submission status and follow up as needed
- Handle any corrections or resubmissions promptly

- Maintain detailed records of all activities

Days 51-60: Completion and Integration Phase

- Verify successful recording for all properties
- Complete post-transfer notifications for all relevant parties
- Update trust records with new property information
- Establish ongoing management procedures
- Plan for future property acquisitions or changes

90-Day Strategic Plan - For Complex Situations or Maximum Preparation

Days 1-30: Strategic Assessment and Professional Consultation

- Complete comprehensive evaluation of entire property portfolio
- Analyze cost-benefit for each property transfer
- Consult with professionals for complex properties or situations
- Develop integrated strategy coordinating trust transfers with overall estate planning
- Create detailed project plan with contingency options

Days 31-60: Systematic Preparation and Document Development

- Prepare all required documents with professional-level attention to detail
- Develop state-specific expertise for each jurisdiction involved
- Create backup plans for potential complications
- Establish professional relationships for ongoing support
- Test all procedures with simple properties before tackling complex ones

Days 61-90: Execution, Completion, and Long-term Planning

- Execute transfers systematically with careful quality control
- Monitor progress and adjust timelines as needed

- Complete all post-transfer requirements and verifications
- Establish ongoing trust management procedures
- Plan for future property acquisitions and trust updates

Master Checklists by Complexity Tier

Tier 1 States - Simplified Checklist

Pre-Transfer Checklist: □ Current deed located and reviewed □ Trust document available with exact name and date □ State recording requirements researched □ Recording fees calculated □ Notary appointment scheduled

Document Preparation Checklist: □ Appropriate deed form obtained (quitclaim or grant deed) □ Grantor name matches current deed exactly □ Grantee shows trust with trustee designation □ Legal description copied exactly from current deed □ Signature and notarization blocks properly prepared

Recording Checklist: □ Deed signed and notarized properly □ Recording fee payment prepared (check or money order) □ Cover letter prepared with property address and contact information □ Recording package mailed or submitted in person □ Recording confirmation received and verified

Post-Transfer Checklist: □ Insurance company notified of trust ownership □ Mortgage servicer notified (if applicable) □ Property tax exemption status verified □ Trust records updated with new deed information □ Original recorded deed stored securely

Tier 2 States - Enhanced Checklist

Additional Pre-Transfer Requirements: □ State-specific supplemental forms identified and obtained □ Transfer tax exemption procedures researched □ County-specific requirements verified □ Professional consultation arranged if needed

Enhanced Document Preparation: □ All required supplemental forms completed □ Transfer tax calculations verified □ Exemption documentation prepared □ Document formatting meets state requirements □ Multiple copies prepared for submissions

Complex Recording Procedures: □ All required forms included in submission package □ Transfer tax exemption claims properly documented □ Recording fees and taxes calculated accurately □ Submission procedures followed exactly □ Follow-up procedures planned for verification

Tier 3 States - Comprehensive Checklist

Extensive Pre-Transfer Preparation: □ Professional consultation completed for complex requirements □ All state and local forms identified and obtained □ Transfer tax implications fully analyzed □ Exemption procedures researched and planned □ Backup plans developed for potential complications

Professional-Level Document Preparation: □ All documents prepared using state-mandated forms and procedures □ Legal descriptions verified through multiple sources □ Transfer tax calculations checked by qualified professional □ All supporting documentation assembled and verified □ Quality control review completed before submission

Complex Recording and Follow-up: □ All submissions made following exact state procedures □ Professional tracking of recording status □ Prompt response to any recorder questions or requests □ Verification of proper recording and exemption approval □ Complete post-transfer notification and documentation update

Progress Tracking System

Weekly Progress Reviews Track your progress systematically:

Week 1 Goals:

- Research completion percentage: ____%
- Documents gathered: ____%
- Professional consultations scheduled: ____%

Week 2 Goals:

- Document preparation completion: ____%
- Review and verification completion: ____%
- Recording preparation completion: ____%

Week 3 Goals:

- Document execution completion: ____%
- Recording submission completion: ____%
- Follow-up procedures initiated: ____%

Week 4+ Goals:

- Recording confirmations received: ____%
- Post-transfer notifications completed: ____%
- Documentation and filing completed: ____%

Problem Resolution Tracking When issues arise, track resolution systematically:

- Problem identification date: _____
- Problem type and severity: _____
- Resolution steps taken: _____
- Professional help sought: Yes/No
- Resolution completion date: _____
- Lessons learned for future transfers: _____

Document Organization System

Physical File Organization Create organized files for easy access:

- **Master File:** Trust document, overall project plan, progress tracking

286

- **Property Files:** Separate file for each property with all related documents
- **Reference Files:** State requirements, forms, fee schedules, contact information
- **Completion Files:** Recorded deeds, confirmation letters, updated insurance policies

Digital Organization Mirror your physical organization digitally:

- Cloud storage with organized folder structure
- Backup copies of all important documents
- Shared access for successor trustees and family members
- Version control for updated documents
- Secure password protection for sensitive information

Success Verification Steps

Recording Verification Confirm successful completion for each property: □ Recorded deed received from county recorder □ Recording information verified (document number, recording date) □ Online records checked to confirm proper recording □ Title company contacted to verify title records update (if using title insurance)

Ownership Verification Confirm trust ownership is properly established: □ Property tax records updated to show trust ownership □ Insurance policies updated with trust as owner □ Mortgage servicer records updated (if applicable) □ HOA records updated (if applicable)

Legal Compliance Verification Ensure all legal requirements are met: □ All required forms filed in all jurisdictions □ Transfer tax exemptions approved where applicable □ Property tax exemptions maintained or transferred □ All professional notifications completed

Celebration Milestone Markers

Milestone 1: Research Completion When you've thoroughly researched your state's requirements and feel confident about the process, celebrate! You've completed the most intellectually challenging part of the project.

Milestone 2: Document Preparation When you've prepared accurate, complete deeds for all your properties, celebrate again! You've demonstrated real competence in legal document preparation.

Milestone 3: Successful Recording When you receive confirmation that your deeds have been successfully recorded, celebrate significantly! You've achieved the core objective and saved substantial money.

Milestone 4: Complete Integration When you've completed all post-transfer notifications and updates, celebrate your complete success! You've protected your family's future and proven your capability to handle complex legal procedures.

Creating Your Personal Action Plan Template

My Property Transfer Goals:

- Primary objective: _____
- Target completion date: _____
- Budget for entire project: $ _____
- Success criteria: _____

My Specific Timeline:

- Research completion target: _____
- Document preparation target: _____
- Recording completion target: _____
- Final completion target: _____

My Resource Plan:

- Professional consultation plan: _____
- Time allocation schedule: _____
- Family support arrangements: _____

- Backup plans for complications: _____

My Success Tracking:

- Weekly progress review schedule: _____
- Problem resolution procedures: _____
- Milestone celebration plans: _____
- Final success verification steps: _____

Long-Term Success Planning

Future Property Acquisitions Plan for adding new properties to your trust:

- Include trust ownership in purchase contracts
- Coordinate with real estate agents and lenders
- Apply lessons learned from current transfer experience
- Maintain expertise in your state's requirements

Trust Update Planning Plan for future trust modifications:

- Annual review schedule
- Amendment vs. restatement decision criteria
- Professional consultation arrangements
- Family communication procedures

Successor Trustee Preparation Plan for transitioning management to successors:

- Regular education and communication
- Documentation and training procedures
- Professional relationship introductions
- Emergency management procedures

The Compound Benefits of DIY Success

Successfully completing your own trust transfer creates benefits that extend far beyond the immediate cost savings:

Financial Empowerment You've proven you can handle complex financial and legal procedures, building confidence for other financial decisions and projects.

Family Education Your experience becomes valuable knowledge for family members facing similar decisions, multiplying the benefits across your entire family network.

Professional Relationship Building Even limited professional consultations create valuable relationships for future estate planning and property management needs.

Skill Development The research, problem-solving, and project management skills you've developed apply to many other areas of personal and professional life.

Key Takeaways for Action Plan Success

Success comes from systematic preparation, realistic timeline setting, and persistent execution. Use the checklists and tracking systems provided, but adapt them to your specific situation and preferences.

Don't try to rush the process, but also don't let perfectionism prevent you from making progress. Most problems can be corrected, but only if you're actively working on the project.

Most importantly, remember that every successful DIY trust transfer started with someone taking the first step. You have all the tools, knowledge, and resources you need for success. Now it's time to put that knowledge into action and achieve the financial protection and peace of mind that motivated you to start this journey.

Your success story begins with your first action step. What will you do today to move closer to your goal of protecting your family's future through proper trust funding? The plan is ready. The path is clear. Time to make it happen.

Appendix A: State-by-State Quick Reference Guide

This section serves as your command center for trust transfers across all U.S. jurisdictions. When you're standing in your kitchen at 10 PM trying to figure out if Wyoming requires witnesses or just notarization, this is where you'll find your answer. When you're calculating fees for that Colorado cabin transfer, the numbers are right here.

No more hunting through government websites that seem designed to hide the information you actually need. No more wondering if you've found current requirements or outdated information from 2019. Everything you need for every state, organized the way real people actually use it.

Think of this as your GPS for trust transfers. You wouldn't drive cross-country without knowing which roads have tolls, construction zones, or specific requirements. Same principle here - every state has its own personality, quirks, and requirements. This guide maps them all.

Understanding the State Complexity System

Before we jump into individual states, let's revisit the three-tier complexity system that drives everything else:

Tier 1 States (DIY Paradise): These states want you to succeed. Reasonable fees, simple procedures, helpful staff. Success rates above 85% on first attempts.

Tier 2 States (Manageable Challenge): More requirements, higher fees, additional forms. Still very doable with proper preparation. Success rates 70-80% with good preparation.

Tier 3 States (Professional Territory): Complex procedures, high costs, significant consequences for errors. Success possible but requires expert-level preparation or professional consultation.

How State Information is Organized

Each state entry provides exactly what you need to make informed decisions:

Quick Assessment: Tier designation tells you immediately what you're facing **Recording Basics:** What forms, what signatures, what procedures **Real Costs:** Current fees so you can budget accurately **Special Quirks:** Unique requirements that could trip you up **Contact Reality:** Who to call when you need real answers **Current Status:** QR codes link to latest updates because laws change

---

ALABAMA (Tier 1)

The Southern Comfort of Real Estate

Alabama keeps property transfers refreshingly simple. Probate judges handle recording (yes, it sounds strange, but it works), fees stay reasonable, and procedures are straightforward throughout the state.

Recording Requirements:

- Standard quitclaim deed accepted statewide
- Notarization required, witnessing optional
- No specific margin requirements
- Accept standard 8.5" x 11" white paper

Fee Schedule:

- Recording: $36 first page, $2 each additional page
- No state documentary transfer tax
- Most counties: no local transfer taxes

- Jefferson County (Birmingham): $5 local transfer tax

Transfer Tax Rules:

- No state transfer tax simplifies everything

- Local exemptions readily available for trust transfers

- Standard language: "This deed transfers property to grantor's revocable living trust without consideration"

Special Requirements:

- Legal descriptions must match current deed exactly

- Some counties request informal cover letters explaining transfer purpose

- Mobile County requires specific formatting for condominium transfers

Recording Contacts:

- County Probate Judge offices (not County Clerk)

- Most accept mail-in recording with money orders

- Baldwin County: (251) 937-0280

- Jefferson County: (205) 325-5300

- Mobile County: (251) 574-4944

Alabama Success Tips:

- Use money orders for mail-in recording (personal checks sometimes rejected)

- Include self-addressed stamped envelope for document return

- Allow 10-14 days for mail-in processing

ALASKA (Tier 2)

Frontier State with Modern Requirements

Alaska combines modern recording systems with practical frontier attitudes. Requirements are reasonable but specific, and the state's limited population means personalized service from recording offices.

Recording Requirements:

- Quitclaim deed standard for trust transfers
- Notarization plus one witness required
- Specific formatting: 1-inch margins, 12-point font minimum
- Alaska Conveyance Form required for all transfers

Fee Schedule:

- Recording: $40 plus $5 per page
- No state documentary transfer tax
- Anchorage municipal transfer tax: $50 flat fee
- Fairbanks municipal transfer tax: $25 flat fee

Transfer Tax Rules:

- Municipal taxes apply in larger cities only
- Trust exemptions available with proper documentation
- Must indicate "family transfer" or "trust transfer" on Alaska Conveyance Form

Special Requirements:

- Alaska Conveyance Form (mandatory statewide)
- Survey requirements for certain remote properties
- Special procedures for Native Corporation lands

Recording Contacts:

- District Recorder offices handle deed recording

- Anchorage District: (907) 269-8877

- Fairbanks District: (907) 451-2585

- Rural districts: Contact state Division of Elections for referrals

Alaska Unique Considerations:

- Remote properties may require survey verification

- Native Corporation lands have special transfer restrictions

- Winter weather can delay mail processing

ARIZONA (Tier 1)

Desert Efficiency at Its Best

Arizona epitomizes business-friendly government with efficient recording procedures, reasonable fees, and excellent online resources. The state's growth mindset extends to property transfer procedures.

Recording Requirements:

- Standard quitclaim or grant deed accepted

- Notarization required, no witnessing

- Arizona statutory trust transfer language recommended

- Standard formatting acceptable

Fee Schedule:

- Recording: $30 for documents up to 5 pages

- $3 for each additional page

- No state documentary transfer tax

- Most counties: no local transfer taxes

Transfer Tax Rules:

- No transfer taxes make Arizona transfers very cost-effective

- No exemption procedures needed

- Simple process compared to neighboring California

Special Requirements:

- Arizona Affidavit of Property Value (Form 82162) for properties over $100,000

- Statutory language: "This conveyance is to a trust revocable by the grantor"

- Legal descriptions must include assessor's parcel number when available

Recording Contacts:

- County Recorder offices handle all deed recording

- Maricopa County (Phoenix): (602) 506-3535

- Pima County (Tucson): (520) 724-4350

- Online recording available in major counties

Arizona Advantages:

- Excellent online resources and forms

- Fast processing (3-5 business days typical)

- Helpful staff and clear procedures

- Strong online recording systems

ARKANSAS (Tier 1)

Natural State Simplicity

Arkansas maintains some of the most reasonable recording fees in the nation while providing efficient service. The state's practical approach makes trust transfers straightforward and affordable.

Recording Requirements:

- Standard deed forms accepted
- Notarization required
- No witnessing requirement
- Standard paper and formatting

Fee Schedule:

- Recording: $10 flat fee (one of lowest in nation)
- No state documentary transfer tax
- Minimal local fees in most counties

Transfer Tax Rules:

- No state or local transfer taxes in most areas
- Simple exemption procedures where local taxes exist
- Standard trust transfer language sufficient

Special Requirements:

- None beyond standard deed requirements
- Some counties appreciate cover letters explaining transfer purpose
- Real property tax assessor notification recommended

Recording Contacts:

- County Clerk offices handle recording

- Circuit Clerk in some counties

- Most counties: (county name) + "Arkansas County Clerk" + phone lookup

- Pulaski County (Little Rock): (501) 340-8500

Arkansas Success Stories: Arkansas consistently ranks among the highest success rates for DIY transfers due to reasonable requirements and helpful county staff.

CALIFORNIA (Tier 3)

The Complex Giant

California presents the most challenging requirements in the nation, but successful DIY transfers remain possible with expert preparation and realistic expectations about complexity.

Recording Requirements:

- Grant deed preferred (quitclaim acceptable)

- Notarization required

- Preliminary Change of Ownership Report (PCOR) mandatory

- Documentary transfer tax declaration required

Fee Schedule:

- Recording: $15 base fee plus various add-ons

- Documentary transfer tax: $1.10 per $1,000 of value (base rate)

- City/county additional taxes vary dramatically

- Los Angeles total: often $4.50+ per $1,000

- San Francisco: can exceed $25 per $1,000 for high-value properties

Transfer Tax Rules:

- Complex exemption procedures for trust transfers
- PCOR form must claim exemption properly
- Specific exemption language required on deed
- Supporting trust documentation may be required

Special Requirements:

- **Preliminary Change of Ownership Report (PCOR)** - mandatory
- Documentary Transfer Tax Affidavit
- Some counties require additional local forms
- Los Angeles: additional city requirements
- San Francisco: Affidavit of Property Value

Recording Contacts:

- County Recorder offices
- Los Angeles County: (562) 462-2125
- Orange County: (714) 834-2500
- San Diego County: (619) 237-0502
- San Francisco: (415) 554-4755

California Reality Check: DIY success in California requires either low property values (under $400,000) or professional consultation. Transfer tax exemption procedures alone often justify limited attorney assistance.

COLORADO (Tier 1)

Mountain State Practicality

Colorado balances thorough legal protections with practical accessibility. The state's outdoor recreation culture extends to government services - they want you to succeed and get back to enjoying life.

Recording Requirements:

- Standard quitclaim deed accepted

- Notarization required

- Clear legal description formatting

- Standard document formatting

Fee Schedule:

- Recording: $13 plus $5 per page

- No state documentary transfer tax

- Minimal local fees in most counties

Transfer Tax Rules:

- No state transfer taxes

- Local exemptions straightforward

- Standard trust language works throughout state

Special Requirements:

- Some mountain properties have complex legal descriptions due to mining claims

- Water rights documentation may be required for certain properties

- Subdivision properties may require HOA notification

Recording Contacts:

- County Clerk and Recorder offices

- Denver County: (720) 865-8400

- Jefferson County: (303) 271-8168

- Boulder County: (303) 413-7740

Colorado Mountain Property Notes: Properties with water rights, mineral rights, or historical mining claims may require special attention to legal descriptions and title research.

CONNECTICUT (Tier 2)

New England Precision

Connecticut requires more documentation than Tier 1 states but maintains reasonable procedures. The state's attention to detail reflects New England values of thoroughness and accuracy.

Recording Requirements:

- Warranty deed preferred for trust transfers

- Notarization plus two witnesses required

- Connecticut Conveyance Tax Return required

- Specific formatting requirements

Fee Schedule:

- Recording: $60 plus additional fees for tax forms

- Conveyance tax: $2.25 per $500 of value

- Trust exemption available but requires proper procedures

Transfer Tax Rules:

- State conveyance tax with trust exemptions

- Exemption requires Connecticut Form Op-236

- Must demonstrate no consideration and retained beneficial ownership

Special Requirements:

- Connecticut Conveyance Tax Return (Form Op-236)
- Two witness requirement in addition to notarization
- Specific legal description formatting requirements

Recording Contacts:

- Town Clerk offices handle recording
- Varies by municipality
- Connecticut Secretary of State: (860) 509-6200 for guidance

---

DELAWARE (Tier 2)

First State Efficiency

Delaware's business-friendly environment extends to property transfers with efficient procedures and reasonable requirements.

Recording Requirements:

- Standard deed forms accepted
- Notarization required
- Delaware Transfer Tax Affidavit required
- Standard formatting requirements

Fee Schedule:

- Recording: $50 for first page, $10 additional pages
- Transfer tax: 4% of property value (with exemptions)
- Trust exemptions reduce tax significantly

Transfer Tax Rules:

- High nominal tax rate but generous exemptions
- Family transfer exemptions available
- Trust transfer exemptions with proper documentation

Recording Contacts:

- County Recorder of Deeds offices
- New Castle County: (302) 395-5490
- Kent County: (302) 744-2310
- Sussex County: (302) 855-7850

FLORIDA (Tier 1)

Sunshine State Simplicity

Florida's massive retiree population drives user-friendly recording procedures. The state understands that property owners want efficient, affordable transfers without bureaucratic complications.

Recording Requirements:

- Quitclaim deed standard for trust transfers
- Notarization required, no witnessing
- Florida Documentary Stamp Tax consideration
- Standard formatting acceptable

Fee Schedule:

- Recording: $10 first page, $8.50 additional pages
- Documentary stamp tax: $0.70 per $100 of value
- Trust exemptions eliminate stamp tax

- Intangible tax eliminated

Transfer Tax Rules:

- Documentary stamp tax with clear trust exemptions

- Exemption language: "This deed is exempt from documentary stamp tax pursuant to Section 201.02(1), Florida Statutes"

- No supporting documentation required for standard exemptions

Special Requirements:

- Florida homestead designation preservation procedures

- Condominium transfers may require association notification

- Some counties prefer specific cover sheet formats

Recording Contacts:

- County Clerk of Courts offices

- Miami-Dade: (305) 275-1155

- Broward: (954) 831-6565

- Orange County (Orlando): (407) 836-2067

- Hillsborough (Tampa): (813) 276-8100

Florida Retiree Benefits: Strong homestead protections continue with trust ownership, and clear exemption procedures make transfers very cost-effective for retirement planning.

GEORGIA (Tier 2)

Peach State Procedures

Georgia requires moderate documentation but maintains reasonable fees and helpful county staff. The state's business-friendly approach extends to individual property owners.

Recording Requirements:

- Warranty deed preferred
- Notarization plus two witnesses OR notarization plus official acknowledgment
- Georgia Real Estate Transfer Tax Form PT-61 required
- Specific formatting requirements

Fee Schedule:

- Recording: $15 plus $5 per page
- Transfer tax: $1 per $1,000 of value
- Trust exemptions available

Transfer Tax Rules:

- State transfer tax with family and trust exemptions
- Form PT-61 must claim exemption properly
- Supporting trust documentation may be requested

Recording Contacts:

- Superior Court Clerk offices
- Fulton County (Atlanta): (404) 613-5317
- Gwinnett County: (770) 822-8100
- Cobb County: (770) 528-1900

HAWAII (Tier 2)

Island State Unique Requirements

Hawaii's isolated location creates unique requirements but the state provides excellent guidance and reasonable procedures for property transfers.

Recording Requirements:

- Conveyance tax document required
- Notarization required
- Hawaii-specific deed formatting
- Environmental disclosure may be required

Fee Schedule:

- Recording: $20 plus additional fees
- Conveyance tax: varies by property value and location
- Trust exemptions available

Transfer Tax Rules:

- Tiered conveyance tax based on property value
- Higher rates for non-resident owners
- Trust exemptions reduce or eliminate taxes

Recording Contacts:

- Bureau of Conveyances: (808) 587-0154
- County-specific offices for rural properties

IDAHO (Tier 1)

Gem State Simplicity

Idaho maintains straightforward procedures with minimal requirements and very reasonable fees. The state's practical approach makes transfers accessible and affordable.

Recording Requirements:

- Standard quitclaim deed accepted

- Notarization required

- No witnessing requirement

- Standard formatting

Fee Schedule:

- Recording: $10 plus $1 per page

- No state documentary transfer tax

- Minimal local fees

Transfer Tax Rules:

- No transfer taxes make Idaho very cost-effective

- No exemption procedures needed

Recording Contacts:

- County Recorder offices

- Ada County (Boise): (208) 287-6840

- Canyon County: (208) 454-7300

ILLINOIS (Tier 2)

Prairie State Procedures

Illinois adds moderate complexity with additional forms and transfer taxes, but procedures are well-established and success rates remain high with proper preparation.

Recording Requirements:

- Quitclaim deed acceptable
- Notarization plus witnessing required
- Illinois Real Estate Transfer Declaration required
- Specific formatting requirements

Fee Schedule:

- Recording: $50 plus $25 per additional $500 of property value
- State transfer tax: $0.50 per $500 of value
- Local transfer taxes vary by municipality

Transfer Tax Rules:

- State and local transfer taxes with trust exemptions
- Transfer declaration must claim exemption
- Cook County (Chicago): additional local requirements

Special Requirements:

- Illinois Real Estate Transfer Declaration (mandatory)
- Cook County: additional disclosure requirements
- Some municipalities: additional local forms

Recording Contacts:

- County Recorder offices
- Cook County: (312) 603-5656
- DuPage County: (630) 407-5500
- Will County: (815) 740-4615

INDIANA (Tier 1)

Hoosier State Helpfulness

Indiana provides efficient recording with reasonable fees and helpful county staff. The state's practical approach makes transfers straightforward throughout Indiana.

Recording Requirements:

- Standard deed forms accepted
- Notarization required
- No witnessing requirement
- Standard formatting

Fee Schedule:

- Recording: $8 plus $3 per page
- No state documentary transfer tax
- Minimal local fees in most counties

Transfer Tax Rules:

- No state transfer taxes
- Local exemptions straightforward

Recording Contacts:

- County Recorder offices
- Marion County (Indianapolis): (317) 327-4020
- Lake County: (219) 755-3265

IOWA (Tier 1)

Midwest Practicality

Iowa maintains simple procedures with very reasonable fees. The state's agricultural heritage creates practical approaches to property ownership and transfers.

Recording Requirements:

- Standard quitclaim deed accepted
- Notarization required
- Declaration of Value required
- Standard formatting

Fee Schedule:

- Recording: $30 plus $5 per page
- No state documentary transfer tax
- Declaration of Value: $5

Transfer Tax Rules:

- No transfer taxes simplify Iowa transfers
- Declaration of Value required but straightforward

Recording Contacts:

- County Recorder offices
- Polk County (Des Moines): (515) 286-3060
- Linn County (Cedar Rapids): (319) 892-5400

KANSAS (Tier 1)

Sunflower State Straightforward

Kansas provides simple procedures with minimal requirements and very reasonable fees throughout the state.

Recording Requirements:

- Standard deed accepted
- Notarization required
- No additional forms typically required
- Standard formatting

Fee Schedule:

- Recording: $20 plus $5 per page
- No state documentary transfer tax
- Minimal local fees

Recording Contacts:

- Register of Deeds offices
- Johnson County: (913) 715-3480
- Sedgwick County (Wichita): (316) 660-7080

KENTUCKY (Tier 1)

Bluegrass State Benefits

Kentucky maintains reasonable procedures with helpful county staff and affordable fees throughout the commonwealth.

Recording Requirements:

- Standard deed forms accepted
- Notarization required
- Kentucky Uniform Instrument Format preferred
- Standard margins and formatting

Fee Schedule:

- Recording: $15 plus $15 per page
- No state documentary transfer tax
- Local fees vary ($5-25 typical)

Recording Contacts:

- County Clerk offices
- Jefferson County (Louisville): (502) 574-5850
- Fayette County (Lexington): (859) 425-2500

LOUISIANA (Tier 2)

Bayou State Unique Laws

Louisiana's civil law system creates unique requirements different from all other states. Professional consultation often recommended due to legal system differences.

Recording Requirements:

- Louisiana-specific act of sale or deed forms
- Notarization plus two witnesses required
- Civil Code compliance required
- French legal heritage creates unique procedures

Fee Schedule:

- Recording: $25 plus additional fees
- No state documentary transfer tax
- Parish (county) fees vary

Transfer Tax Rules:

- No state transfer taxes

- Local exemptions generally available

Special Requirements:

- Louisiana Civil Code compliance

- Community property laws affect all transfers

- Specific notarial procedures required

Recording Contacts:

- Parish Clerk of Courts offices

- Orleans Parish (New Orleans): (504) 407-0100

- Jefferson Parish: (504) 364-2900

Louisiana Warning: Louisiana's unique legal system often justifies professional consultation even for straightforward transfers.

MAINE (Tier 2)

Pine Tree State Precision

Maine requires additional documentation but maintains reasonable procedures. The state's attention to detail reflects New England thoroughness.

Recording Requirements:

- Warranty deed preferred

- Notarization plus acknowledgment required

- Maine Real Estate Transfer Tax Declaration

- Specific formatting requirements

Fee Schedule:

- Recording: $33 plus $4 per page

- Transfer tax: $2.20 per $500 of value

- Trust exemptions available

Transfer Tax Rules:

- State transfer tax with family exemptions

- Trust transfers often qualify for exemptions

- Proper documentation required for exemption

Recording Contacts:

- County Registry of Deeds offices

- Cumberland County: (207) 871-8380

- Penobscot County: (207) 942-8535

MARYLAND (Tier 2)

Old Line State Requirements

Maryland adds moderate complexity with state and local transfer taxes but provides clear procedures and reasonable exemption processes.

Recording Requirements:

- Deed must meet Maryland formatting requirements

- Notarization required

- Maryland Transfer Tax Declaration required

- Property disclosure may be required

Fee Schedule:

- Recording: $60 plus additional pages

- State transfer tax: $2.50 per $500 of value

- Local transfer taxes vary by county

Transfer Tax Rules:

- Combined state and local transfer taxes

- Trust exemptions available with proper procedures

- Exemption forms required in most counties

Recording Contacts:

- County Circuit Court Clerk offices

- Montgomery County: (240) 777-9600

- Prince George's County: (301) 952-3318

MASSACHUSETTS (Tier 3)

Bay State Complexity

Massachusetts requires substantial documentation and imposes significant transfer taxes, but exemption procedures are well-established for qualifying trust transfers.

Recording Requirements:

- Massachusetts deed formatting required

- Notarization plus acknowledgment

- Massachusetts Real Estate Transfer Declaration

- Local transfer tax forms may be required

Fee Schedule:

- Recording: $125 plus additional fees

- State transfer tax: $2.28 per $500 of value

- Local transfer taxes vary significantly

Transfer Tax Rules:

- High transfer taxes but exemptions available
- Family transfer exemptions often apply
- Professional assistance recommended for high-value properties

Recording Contacts:

- Registry of Deeds offices
- Suffolk County (Boston): (617) 788-8575
- Middlesex County: (978) 322-9150

MICHIGAN (Tier 2)

Great Lakes Moderate Requirements

Michigan adds reasonable complexity with state transfer taxes but provides clear exemption procedures and helpful guidance.

Recording Requirements:

- Michigan deed formatting required
- Notarization plus two witnesses required
- Property Transfer Affidavit required
- Specific margin and format requirements

Fee Schedule:

- Recording: varies by county ($30-80 typical)
- State transfer tax: $3.75 per $500 of value
- Local transfer taxes in some areas

Transfer Tax Rules:

- State transfer tax with family and trust exemptions
- Property Transfer Affidavit must claim exemption
- Clear exemption procedures save substantial money

Recording Contacts:

- County Register of Deeds offices
- Wayne County (Detroit): (313) 224-5872
- Oakland County: (248) 858-0581
- Kent County (Grand Rapids): (616) 632-7640

MINNESOTA (Tier 2)

North Star State Requirements

Minnesota requires additional documentation but provides clear guidance and reasonable exemption procedures for trust transfers.

Recording Requirements:

- Minnesota deed formatting required
- Notarization required
- Certificate of Real Estate Value required
- Standard formatting with specific requirements

Fee Schedule:

- Recording: $46 plus additional fees
- Deed tax: $1.65 per $500 of value
- Trust exemptions available

Transfer Tax Rules:

- State deed tax with family exemptions

- Certificate of Real Estate Value must claim exemption
- Clear procedures for trust transfers

Recording Contacts:

- County Recorder or Registrar offices
- Hennepin County (Minneapolis): (612) 348-3240
- Ramsey County (St. Paul): (651) 266-2080

MISSISSIPPI (Tier 1)

Magnolia State Simplicity

Mississippi maintains simple procedures with very reasonable fees and helpful county staff throughout the state.

Recording Requirements:

- Standard deed forms accepted
- Notarization required
- No additional forms typically required
- Standard formatting

Fee Schedule:

- Recording: $15 plus $5 per page
- No state documentary transfer tax
- Minimal local fees

Recording Contacts:

- County Chancery Clerk offices
- Hinds County (Jackson): (601) 968-6507
- Harrison County: (228) 865-4040

MISSOURI (Tier 1)

Show Me State Practical Approach

Missouri's "Show Me" attitude extends to recording procedures - they want to see proper documents but keep requirements reasonable and procedures straightforward.

Recording Requirements:

- Standard deed forms accepted
- Notarization required
- Declaration of Value required
- Standard formatting

Fee Schedule:

- Recording: $24 plus $3 per page
- No state documentary transfer tax
- Declaration of Value: $10

Recording Contacts:

- County Recorder offices
- St. Louis County: (314) 615-2990
- Jackson County (Kansas City): (816) 881-3198

MONTANA (Tier 1)

Big Sky Country Efficiency

Montana combines efficient procedures with reasonable fees and excellent rural county service. The state's practical approach makes transfers accessible statewide.

319

Recording Requirements:

- Standard deed forms accepted
- Notarization required
- Certificate of Value may be required
- Standard formatting

Fee Schedule:

- Recording: $10 plus $3 per page
- No state documentary transfer tax
- Minimal local fees

Recording Contacts:

- County Clerk and Recorder offices
- Yellowstone County (Billings): (406) 256-2785
- Missoula County: (406) 258-4751

NEBRASKA (Tier 1)

Cornhusker State Straightforward

Nebraska maintains simple procedures with reasonable fees and practical approaches to property transfers throughout the state.

Recording Requirements:

- Standard deed acceptable
- Notarization required
- Statement of Consideration required
- Standard formatting

Fee Schedule:

- Recording: $14 plus $5 per page

- No state documentary transfer tax

- Statement of Consideration: $10

Recording Contacts:

- Register of Deeds offices

- Douglas County (Omaha): (402) 444-7019

- Lancaster County (Lincoln): (402) 441-7481

NEVADA (Tier 1)

Silver State Innovation

Nevada provides some of the most efficient recording procedures in the nation with excellent online resources and very reasonable fees.

Recording Requirements:

- Standard deed forms accepted

- Notarization required

- Nevada-specific formatting preferred but not mandatory

- Electronic recording available in major counties

Fee Schedule:

- Recording: $25 plus $1 per page

- No state documentary transfer tax

- Minimal local fees

Recording Contacts:

- County Recorder offices

- Clark County (Las Vegas): (702) 671-0600

- Washoe County (Reno): (775) 328-3660

Nevada Innovation: Major counties offer sophisticated online recording systems allowing complete remote processing.

NEW HAMPSHIRE (Tier 1)

Live Free or Die Simplicity

New Hampshire's minimal government philosophy extends to recording procedures with simple requirements and reasonable fees.

Recording Requirements:

- Standard deed accepted
- Notarization required
- New Hampshire Transfer Questionnaire
- Standard formatting

Fee Schedule:

- Recording: $25 plus additional fees
- Transfer tax: $0.75 per $100 of value
- Trust exemptions available

Recording Contacts:

- County Registry of Deeds offices
- Hillsborough County: (603) 627-5605
- Rockingham County: (603) 679-2256

NEW JERSEY (Tier 3)

Garden State Complexity

New Jersey combines high fees with complex requirements, creating substantial challenges for DIY transfers. Professional consultation often justified by complexity and costs.

Recording Requirements:

- New Jersey deed formatting mandatory
- Notarization plus acknowledgment required
- Realty Transfer Fee Declaration required
- Municipal transfer tax forms often required

Fee Schedule:

- Recording: $60 plus additional fees
- State transfer tax: varies by value and circumstances
- Municipal taxes can be substantial

Transfer Tax Rules:

- Complex state and local transfer tax structure
- Exemptions available but procedures are complex
- Professional assistance often cost-effective

Recording Contacts:

- County Register offices
- Bergen County: (201) 336-7000
- Essex County: (973) 621-4921

New Jersey Reality: High transfer taxes and complex procedures often make professional assistance cost-effective even for moderate-value properties.

NEW MEXICO (Tier 1)

Land of Enchantment Efficiency

New Mexico provides simple procedures with reasonable fees and excellent county service throughout the state.

Recording Requirements:

- Standard deed accepted
- Notarization required
- Real Property Transfer Tax Declaration
- Standard formatting

Fee Schedule:

- Recording: $25 plus $1 per page
- No state documentary transfer tax
- Transfer tax declaration: $5

Recording Contacts:

- County Clerk offices
- Bernalillo County (Albuquerque): (505) 468-1290
- Santa Fe County: (505) 986-6280

NEW YORK (Tier 3)

Empire State Maximum Complexity

New York presents extreme complexity with high fees, multiple tax layers, and extensive documentation requirements. Success requires expert preparation or professional assistance.

Recording Requirements:

- New York deed formatting mandatory

- Notarization required (witnessing in some counties)
- Real Property Transfer Report (TP-584) required
- Additional local forms often required

Fee Schedule:

- Recording: $125 plus additional fees
- State transfer tax: $2 per $500 ($4 per $500 over $1M)
- Local transfer taxes vary dramatically
- NYC: substantial additional taxes

Transfer Tax Rules:

- Multiple layers of state and local taxes
- Exemption procedures complex and specific
- NYC properties: often require professional assistance

Special Requirements:

- **TP-584 Form:** extensive property and transfer information required
- NYC properties: additional city requirements
- Mansion tax for properties over $1 million

Recording Contacts:

- County Clerk offices
- New York County (Manhattan): (646) 386-5955
- Kings County (Brooklyn): (347) 404-9772
- Nassau County: (516) 571-2663

New York Strategy: Professional assistance often justified by extreme complexity and high financial stakes, especially in NYC area.

NORTH CAROLINA (Tier 2)

Tar Heel State Reasonable Requirements

North Carolina adds moderate documentation requirements but maintains reasonable procedures and helpful county staff.

Recording Requirements:

- North Carolina deed formatting required
- Notarization required
- Excise Tax Form E-500 required
- Standard formatting with state-specific elements

Fee Schedule:

- Recording: $26 plus $8 per page
- Excise tax: $2 per $500 of value
- Trust exemptions available

Transfer Tax Rules:

- State excise tax with family and trust exemptions
- Form E-500 must claim exemption properly
- Local exemptions generally available

Recording Contacts:

- Register of Deeds offices
- Mecklenburg County (Charlotte): (704) 336-2443

- Wake County (Raleigh): (919) 856-5460

NORTH DAKOTA (Tier 1)

Peace Garden State Simplicity

North Dakota maintains simple procedures with very reasonable fees and excellent rural county service.

Recording Requirements:

- Standard deed accepted
- Notarization required
- Real Estate Transfer Certificate required
- Standard formatting

Fee Schedule:

- Recording: $30 plus $10 per page
- No state documentary transfer tax
- Transfer certificate: $3

Recording Contacts:

- County Recorder offices
- Cass County (Fargo): (701) 241-5609
- Burleigh County (Bismarck): (701) 222-6710

OHIO (Tier 2)

Buckeye State Moderate Requirements

Ohio adds moderate complexity with transfer taxes and additional forms but maintains reasonable procedures and good exemption options.

Recording Requirements:

- Ohio deed formatting required
- Notarization required
- Conveyance Fee Statement required
- Specific formatting requirements

Fee Schedule:

- Recording: $34 plus $8 per page
- State conveyance fee: $4 per $1,000 of value
- Local transfer taxes vary

Transfer Tax Rules:

- State conveyance fee with trust exemptions
- Local exemptions generally available
- Exemption procedures well-established

Recording Contacts:

- County Recorder offices
- Franklin County (Columbus): (614) 525-3930
- Cuyahoga County (Cleveland): (216) 443-7950
- Hamilton County (Cincinnati): (513) 946-4800

OKLAHOMA (Tier 1)

Sooner State Speed

Oklahoma provides efficient recording with reasonable fees and straightforward procedures throughout the state.

Recording Requirements:

- Standard deed accepted

- Notarization required

- No additional forms typically required

- Standard formatting

Fee Schedule:

- Recording: $10 plus $1 per page

- No state documentary transfer tax

- Minimal local fees

Recording Contacts:

- County Clerk offices

- Oklahoma County: (405) 713-1521

- Tulsa County: (918) 596-5801

OREGON (Tier 2)

Pacific State Procedures

Oregon requires moderate additional documentation but provides clear guidance and reasonable exemption procedures.

Recording Requirements:

- Oregon deed formatting required

- Notarization required

- Real Estate Transfer Tax Statement required

- Specific format requirements

Fee Schedule:

- Recording: $60 plus $5 per page
- No state documentary transfer tax
- Local transfer taxes in some counties

Recording Contacts:

- County Clerk offices
- Multnomah County (Portland): (503) 988-3034
- Washington County: (503) 846-8756

PENNSYLVANIA (Tier 3)

Keystone State Challenges

Pennsylvania combines high transfer taxes with complex county-specific requirements, creating substantial challenges for DIY transfers.

Recording Requirements:

- Pennsylvania deed formatting required
- Notarization required (acknowledgment in some counties)
- Realty Transfer Tax Statement required
- County-specific additional requirements

Fee Schedule:

- Recording: varies dramatically by county ($50-200)
- State transfer tax: 1% of property value
- Local transfer taxes: often 1-2% additional

- Combined transfer taxes often 2-3% of property value

Transfer Tax Rules:

- High combined transfer taxes
- Family exemptions available but procedures vary by county
- Philadelphia and Pittsburgh: particularly complex

Recording Contacts:

- County Recorder of Deeds offices
- Philadelphia County: (215) 686-2292
- Allegheny County (Pittsburgh): (412) 350-4433
- Montgomery County: (610) 278-3280

Pennsylvania Warning: High transfer taxes and complex procedures often justify professional assistance, especially in urban counties.

RHODE ISLAND (Tier 2)

Ocean State Requirements

Rhode Island requires additional documentation but maintains reasonable procedures for the small state's limited geography.

Recording Requirements:

- Rhode Island deed formatting required
- Notarization plus two witnesses required
- Real Estate Conveyance Tax Declaration required
- Specific formatting requirements

Fee Schedule:

- Recording: $60 plus additional fees

- Conveyance tax: $2.30 per $500 of value
- Trust exemptions available

Recording Contacts:

- City/Town Clerk offices
- Providence: (401) 421-0495
- Warwick: (401) 738-2000

SOUTH CAROLINA (Tier 1)

Palmetto State Simplicity

South Carolina maintains straightforward procedures with reasonable fees and helpful county staff throughout the state.

Recording Requirements:

- Standard deed accepted
- Notarization required
- No additional forms typically required
- Standard formatting

Fee Schedule:

- Recording: $15 plus $15 per page
- No state documentary transfer tax
- Minimal local fees

Recording Contacts:

- County Register of Deeds offices
- Charleston County: (843) 958-4930
- Greenville County: (864) 467-7240

332

SOUTH DAKOTA (Tier 1)

Mount Rushmore State Efficiency

South Dakota provides simple procedures with minimal fees and excellent service throughout the state.

Recording Requirements:

- Standard deed accepted
- Notarization required
- No additional forms required
- Standard formatting

Fee Schedule:

- Recording: $30 plus $5 per page
- No state documentary transfer tax
- No local transfer taxes

Recording Contacts:

- Register of Deeds offices
- Minnehaha County (Sioux Falls): (605) 367-4223
- Pennington County (Rapid City): (605) 394-2575

TENNESSEE (Tier 1)

Volunteer State Practical Approach

Tennessee maintains reasonable procedures with affordable fees and practical approaches to property transfers.

Recording Requirements:

- Standard deed accepted

- Notarization required

- No additional forms typically required

- Standard formatting

Fee Schedule:

- Recording: $12 plus $5 per page

- No state documentary transfer tax

- Minimal local fees

Recording Contacts:

- County Register offices

- Davidson County (Nashville): (615) 862-6790

- Shelby County (Memphis): (901) 222-2300

TEXAS (Tier 1)

Lone Star State Leadership

Texas provides the gold standard for DIY-friendly procedures with excellent resources, reasonable fees, and business-friendly approaches.

Recording Requirements:

- Standard deed accepted (notarization required for most)

- Texas Property Code compliance

- No additional forms required

- Standard formatting acceptable

Fee Schedule:

- Recording: $26 plus $4 per page

- No state documentary transfer tax

- No local transfer taxes

Special Features:

- Transfer on Death deeds available as alternative

- Excellent online resources

- Business-friendly procedures

Recording Contacts:

- County Clerk offices

- Harris County (Houston): (713) 755-6405

- Dallas County: (214) 653-7099

- Tarrant County (Fort Worth): (817) 884-1195

- Travis County (Austin): (512) 854-9188

Texas Advantages: Superior online resources, helpful staff, and consistently reasonable procedures make Texas the benchmark for DIY success.

UTAH (Tier 1)

Beehive State Efficiency

Utah provides efficient procedures with reasonable fees and excellent county service throughout the state.

Recording Requirements:

- Standard deed accepted

- Notarization required

- No additional forms typically required
- Standard formatting

Fee Schedule:

- Recording: $30 plus $10 per page
- No state documentary transfer tax
- Minimal local fees

Recording Contacts:

- County Recorder offices
- Salt Lake County: (385) 468-8400
- Utah County: (801) 851-8126

VERMONT (Tier 2)

Green Mountain State Requirements

Vermont requires additional documentation but provides clear guidance and maintains reasonable procedures.

Recording Requirements:

- Vermont deed formatting required
- Notarization required
- Property Transfer Tax Return required
- Specific formatting requirements

Fee Schedule:

- Recording: $20 plus $10 per page
- Transfer tax: 0.5% of property value
- Trust exemptions available

336

Recording Contacts:

- Town Clerk offices
- Varies by municipality
- Vermont Secretary of State: (802) 828-2386 for guidance

VIRGINIA (Tier 2)

Old Dominion Reasonable Requirements

Virginia adds moderate complexity but maintains reasonable procedures and clear exemption processes.

Recording Requirements:

- Virginia deed formatting required
- Notarization required
- Grantor tax: varies by locality
- Standard formatting with state-specific elements

Fee Schedule:

- Recording: $25 plus $3 per page
- Grantor tax: varies by locality
- State recordation tax: $0.25 per $100 of value

Recording Contacts:

- Circuit Court Clerk offices
- Fairfax County: (703) 246-4168
- Virginia Beach: (757) 385-8801

WASHINGTON (Tier 2)

Evergreen State Modern Procedures

Washington requires additional documentation but provides efficient procedures and excellent online resources.

Recording Requirements:

- Washington deed formatting required
- Notarization required
- Real Estate Excise Tax Affidavit required
- Specific formatting requirements

Fee Schedule:

- Recording: $62 plus additional fees
- Real estate excise tax: 1.28% of selling price
- Trust exemptions available

Recording Contacts:

- County Auditor offices
- King County (Seattle): (206) 296-1550
- Pierce County (Tacoma): (253) 798-7430

WEST VIRGINIA (Tier 1)

Mountain State Simplicity

West Virginia maintains simple procedures with very reasonable fees and helpful county staff.

Recording Requirements:

- Standard deed accepted
- Notarization required

- No additional forms typically required
- Standard formatting

Fee Schedule:

- Recording: $30 plus $20 per page
- No state documentary transfer tax
- Minimal local fees

Recording Contacts:

- County Clerk offices
- Kanawha County (Charleston): (304) 357-0130
- Monongalia County (Morgantown): (304) 291-7230

WISCONSIN (Tier 2)

Badger State Reasonable Requirements

Wisconsin adds moderate complexity but provides clear procedures and reasonable exemption processes.

Recording Requirements:

- Wisconsin deed formatting required
- Notarization required
- Real Estate Transfer Return required
- Specific formatting requirements

Fee Schedule:

- Recording: $30 plus additional fees
- Transfer tax: $3 per $1,000 of value
- Trust exemptions available

Recording Contacts:

- Register of Deeds offices
- Milwaukee County: (414) 278-4023
- Dane County (Madison): (608) 266-4121

WYOMING (Tier 1)

Equality State Excellence

Wyoming provides simple procedures with minimal fees and excellent service. The state's practical approach makes transfers very accessible.

Recording Requirements:

- Standard deed accepted
- Notarization required
- No additional forms required
- Standard formatting

Fee Schedule:

- Recording: $12 plus $3 per page
- No state documentary transfer tax
- No local transfer taxes

Recording Contacts:

- County Clerk offices
- Laramie County (Cheyenne): (307) 633-4264
- Natrona County (Casper): (307) 235-9217

WASHINGTON, D.C. (Tier 3)

District Complexity

Washington D.C. combines federal district status with municipal complexity, creating unique challenges for property transfers.

Recording Requirements:

- D.C. deed formatting required
- Notarization plus witnessing required
- Transfer Tax Return required
- Extensive documentation requirements

Fee Schedule:

- Recording: $65 plus additional fees
- Transfer tax: 1.1% of property value (higher rates for expensive properties)
- Additional taxes for non-resident owners

Recording Contacts:

- D.C. Recorder of Deeds: (202) 727-5374

D.C. Warning: High transfer taxes and complex procedures often justify professional assistance for most property values.

Using This Guide Effectively

Cross-Referencing Strategy Use this guide in conjunction with the main text:

- Check your state's tier designation first
- Review specific requirements for your situation
- Compare costs with professional service estimates

- Verify current information using provided contacts

Update Verification Laws and procedures change. Always verify current requirements:

- Contact county offices directly before starting

- Check for recent law changes using online resources

- Scan QR codes for latest updates to this information

- Join online communities for real-time updates from other property owners

Cost Planning Use fee information for accurate budget planning:

- Add recording fees plus any transfer taxes

- Include notarization costs ($5-25 typical)

- Factor in mail or travel costs for recording

- Budget 10-20% additional for unexpected requirements

This reference guide provides your starting point, but every successful transfer requires verification of current requirements and procedures with local offices.

Appendix B: Forms and Templates Library

This library contains every form and template you'll need for successful trust transfers, organized for maximum usability and legal compliance. These aren't theoretical academic forms - they're practical, tested templates based on successful real-world transfers across all state types.

Each template includes completion instructions, legal guidance, and warnings about common mistakes. Use these forms as starting points, then customize them for your specific state and situation using the guidance provided throughout this book.

Digital Access Integration Every form in this appendix is available in editable digital format. Download codes provided at the end of each template give you access to Word documents, PDFs, and fill-in forms that save typing time and reduce errors.

Legal Compliance Note These templates comply with generally accepted legal standards but may require modification for specific state requirements. Always verify that your chosen template meets current requirements in your recording jurisdiction.

UNIVERSAL QUITCLAIM DEED TEMPLATE

This template works in most states with minor modifications for local requirements. Quitclaim deeds transfer whatever ownership interest you have without making warranties about the property's title quality.

When to Use Quitclaim Deeds:

- Transfers between family members

- Transfers to your own living trust

- Situations where title quality isn't disputed

- States that prefer quitclaim deeds for trust transfers

QUITCLAIM DEED TEMPLATE

QUITCLAIM DEED

Prepared by: [Your Name]
[Your Address]
[City, State ZIP]
Return to: [Same address or trust address]

GRANTOR: [Your full legal name exactly as shown on current deed], an individual

GRANTEE: [Your full legal name], Trustee of [Exact Trust Name] dated [Trust Date]

Legal Description: [Copy exactly from current deed - do not abbreviate or modify]

Property Address: [Complete street address including ZIP code]

Consideration: This transfer is made without consideration to the grantor's revocable living trust.

Trust Declaration: Grantor declares that this transfer is made to a revocable trust of which grantor is the trustee and sole beneficiary during grantor's lifetime.

The grantor hereby quitclaims and transfers to the grantee all interest in the above-described property.

GRANTOR SIGNATURE:

_____ Date: _____
[Your full legal name]

STATE OF [STATE NAME]
COUNTY OF [COUNTY NAME]

On this _____ day of _____, 20___, before me personally appeared [Your full legal name], who proved to me on the basis of satisfactory evidence to be the person whose name is subscribed to the within instrument and acknowledged to me that he/she executed the same in his/her authorized capacity, and that by his/her signature on the instrument the person, or the entity upon behalf of which the person acted, executed the instrument.

I certify under PENALTY OF PERJURY under the laws of the State of [State Name] that the foregoing paragraph is true and correct.

WITNESS my hand and official seal.

_____

[Notary Name], Notary Public

Completion Instructions:

1. Fill in all bracketed information using exact names and descriptions from your current deed

2. Never abbreviate legal descriptions or property information

3. Use black ink for signatures

4. Ensure notary acknowledgment uses your state's required language

5. Make copies before recording (originals go to county recorder)

Common Mistakes to Avoid:

- Using nickname instead of full legal name

- Modifying legal description from current deed

- Incorrect trust name or date

- Missing notarization or using wrong acknowledgment language

State Modifications Needed:

- California: Add documentary transfer tax exemption language

- New York: Use New York-specific acknowledgment format

- Illinois: Add witness signature lines

- Texas: May omit notarization for certain family transfers

Digital Download Code: QDT-001

GRANT DEED TEMPLATE

Grant deeds provide more protection than quitclaim deeds by including basic warranties about the grantor's ownership and transfer authority.

When to Use Grant Deeds:

- States that prefer grant deeds (California, Nevada, others)

- Situations requiring basic title warranties

- Properties with clear title where warranties are appropriate

GRANT DEED TEMPLATE

GRANT DEED

Prepared by: [Your Name]
[Your Address]

GRANTOR: [Your full legal name], an individual

GRANTEE: [Your full legal name], Trustee of [Exact Trust Name] dated [Trust Date]

Legal Description: [Complete legal description from current deed]

Property Address: [Complete address]

Consideration: This transfer is made without consideration to grantor's revocable living trust of which grantor is trustee and beneficiary.

Warranties: Grantor warrants that grantor is lawfully seized of the property, has good right to convey the same, and that the property is free from encumbrances made or suffered by grantor.

The grantor hereby grants and conveys to the grantee the above-described property.

GRANTOR SIGNATURE:

_____ Date: _____
[Your full legal name]

[Notarization block - use state-specific format]

Completion Instructions:

1. Use grant deeds only in states that prefer them

2. Understand that you're making warranties about your ownership

3. Include any state-required warranty language

4. Verify that grant deed format complies with local requirements

Digital Download Code: GDT-002

TRANSFER ON DEATH (TOD) DEED TEMPLATES

TOD deeds provide alternatives to living trust transfers in states that permit them. Property automatically transfers to named beneficiaries upon your death, avoiding probate without requiring trust creation.

States Permitting TOD Deeds: Arizona, Arkansas, Colorado, Illinois, Indiana, Kansas, Minnesota, Montana, Nevada, New Mexico, North Dakota, Ohio, Oklahoma, Oregon, South Dakota, Texas, Utah, Virginia, Washington, West Virginia, Wisconsin, Wyoming

TEXAS TOD DEED TEMPLATE

REVOCABLE TRANSFER ON DEATH DEED

Grantor: [Your full legal name]

Grantee upon Death: [Beneficiary full legal name]

Legal Description: [Complete legal description]

Property Address: [Complete address]

Transfer on Death Designation: Upon grantor's death, this property shall transfer automatically to the named grantee without probate proceedings.

Revocation Rights: Grantor reserves the right to revoke this designation at any time during grantor's lifetime by recording a revocation or new deed.

Current Ownership: Grantor retains complete ownership and control during lifetime, including rights to sell, mortgage, or transfer the property.

[Signature and notarization blocks]

TOD Deed Advantages:

- Simpler than trust creation
- Lower immediate costs
- Automatic transfer upon death
- Revocable during lifetime

TOD Deed Limitations:

- No incapacity planning benefits

- Limited to real property only

- May not integrate well with comprehensive estate plans

- Potential family disputes without clear succession planning

Digital Download Codes by State:

- Texas TOD: TOD-TX-001

- Colorado TOD: TOD-CO-002

- Arizona TOD: TOD-AZ-003

- Nevada TOD: TOD-NV-004

- [Additional state codes available in digital library]

TRUST CERTIFICATE TEMPLATE

Trust certificates provide proof of trust existence and authority without revealing private trust terms. Use these when institutions require trust verification.

CERTIFICATE OF TRUST

Trust Name: [Exact trust name from trust document]

Trust Date: [Date trust was signed and notarized]

Trustee Information: [Your full legal name], currently serving as Trustee

Trust Powers: The trust is authorized to hold, manage, and transfer real estate and other property as provided in the trust agreement.

Successor Trustees: [Names of successor trustees as listed in trust]

Revocability: This trust is revocable and amendable by the grantor during the grantor's lifetime.

Authority Declaration: As Trustee, I have full authority to execute deeds, contracts, and other documents necessary for trust property management and transfers.

Certification: I certify under penalty of perjury that the foregoing statements are true and correct and that the trust agreement referenced herein is currently in full force and effect.

_____ Date: _____

[Your name], Trustee

[Notarization block]

When to Use Trust Certificates:

- Bank or financial institution requests

- Title company requirements

- Lender requests during refinancing

- Insurance company verification needs

- Any situation requiring trust verification without full disclosure

Digital Download Code: TC-001

NOTIFICATION LETTER TEMPLATES

These templates handle post-transfer notifications to all relevant parties. Proper notification protects your interests and ensures smooth transitions.

INSURANCE COMPANY NOTIFICATION TEMPLATE

[Date]

[Insurance Company Name]
[Address]

Re: Policy Number [Policy Number] - Ownership Change Notification

Dear Insurance Representative,

This letter notifies you that the property insured under the referenced policy has been transferred to a living trust. Please update your records to reflect the new ownership information:

Previous Owner: [Your name as shown on current policy]

New Owner: [Your name], Trustee of [Trust Name] dated [Trust Date]

Property Address: [Complete property address]

Effective Date: [Date deed was recorded]

The property remains under the same management and occupancy. This transfer is for estate planning purposes only and does not change the property's use, occupancy, or risk profile.

Please send updated policy documents reflecting the trust ownership to the address below. Contact me at [phone number] if you need additional information or documentation.

Sincerely,

[Your signature]
[Your printed name], Trustee

Enclosures: Copy of recorded deed

Digital Download Code: INS-001

MORTGAGE SERVICER NOTIFICATION TEMPLATE

[Date]

[Mortgage Servicer Name]
[Address]

Re: Loan Number [Loan Number] - Trust Transfer Notification

Dear Loan Servicer,

This letter provides notification that the property securing the referenced mortgage has been transferred to a revocable living trust as permitted under the Garn-St. Germain Depository Institutions Act of 1982.

Loan Information:

- Loan Number: [Loan Number]
- Property Address: [Complete address]
- Original Borrower: [Your name as shown on mortgage]

Transfer Information:

- New Owner: [Your name], Trustee of [Trust Name] dated [Trust Date]
- Transfer Date: [Recording date]
- Transfer Type: Revocable living trust transfer (no sale or change in beneficial ownership)

Legal Authority: This transfer is specifically permitted under 12 U.S.C. § 1701j-3(d)(8), which prohibits lenders from exercising due-on-sale clauses for transfers to borrower's revocable trust where borrower remains beneficiary.

Request: Please update your records to reflect trust ownership and continue sending all communications to the address below. No change in payment procedures is requested.

Contact me at [phone number] if you need additional documentation or have questions about this transfer.

Sincerely,

[Your signature]
[Your name], Trustee

Enclosures: Copy of recorded deed, copy of relevant trust pages

Digital Download Code: MORT-001

PROPERTY TAX OFFICE NOTIFICATION TEMPLATE

[Date]

[County Tax Assessor/Collector]
[Address]

Re: Parcel Number [Tax Parcel Number] - Ownership Change Notification

Dear Assessor,

Please update your records to reflect the transfer of the referenced property to a living trust:

Property Information:

- Parcel Number: [Tax parcel number]

- Property Address: [Complete address]

- Previous Owner: [Your name as shown on tax records]

New Ownership:

- Current Owner: [Your name], Trustee of [Trust Name] dated [Trust Date]

- Transfer Date: [Recording date]

- Transfer Type: Living trust transfer for estate planning

Exemption Preservation: This transfer is made to the grantor's revocable living trust and should not affect current property tax exemptions, including homestead exemptions where applicable.

Please send future tax bills and communications to:

[Your name], Trustee
[Address]
[City, State ZIP]

Contact me at [phone number] if you need additional documentation.

Sincerely,

[Your signature]
[Your name], Trustee

Digital Download Code: TAX-001

HOA NOTIFICATION TEMPLATE

[Date]

[HOA Management Company or Board]
[Address]

Re: [Property Address] - Ownership Change Notification

Dear HOA Management,

This letter notifies you that the referenced property has been transferred to a living trust for estate planning purposes:

Property: [Complete address including unit number]

Previous Owner: [Your name as shown in HOA records]

New Owner: [Your name], Trustee of [Trust Name] dated [Trust Date]

Transfer Date: [Recording date]

Contact Information Changes: Please update your records to reflect trust ownership. All communications should continue to be sent to the same address and contact information currently on file.

No Operational Changes: This transfer doesn't change property occupancy, use, or management. The same person remains responsible for all HOA obligations and communications.

Please confirm receipt of this notification and provide any additional forms or procedures required by your association.

Sincerely,

[Your signature]
[Your name], Trustee

Digital Download Code: HOA-001

Form Customization Guidelines

State-Specific Modifications Every template requires customization for your specific state:

- Use your state's preferred deed format and language

- Include any required state-specific warranties or disclaimers

- Follow your state's notarization and acknowledgment requirements

- Add any additional forms required by state or local law

Situation-Specific Adaptations Modify templates for your specific circumstances:

- Multi-owner properties require additional grantor information

- Investment properties may need tenant notification language

- Mortgaged properties should reference federal law protections

- Out-of-state properties may require special handling procedures

Quality Control Checklist Before using any template: □ Verify template compliance with current state requirements □ Customize all bracketed information for your situation □ Review completed forms for accuracy and completeness □ Confirm notarization requirements for your state □ Check that all required signatures and dates are included

Professional Review Options Consider professional review of completed forms when:

- Property values exceed $500,000

- State requirements are complex or unclear

- Multiple properties are involved

- Unusual circumstances affect standard procedures

Remember: templates provide starting points, not finished products. Every successful transfer requires customization, verification, and attention to current requirements in your specific jurisdiction.

Appendix C: Glossary of Legal Terms

Legal terminology shouldn't be a barrier to understanding your trust transfer. This glossary translates complex legal terms into plain English, helping you understand documents, procedures, and professional advice without getting lost in legal jargon.

Each definition includes practical context about how the term affects your trust transfer, cross-references to relevant chapters, and pronunciation guides for terms that trip up most people.

How to Use This Glossary

- Look up unfamiliar terms as you encounter them

- Use cross-references to find related information in the main text

- Don't memorize definitions - focus on understanding concepts

- Refer back when reviewing professional advice or legal documents

---

Acknowledgment (ak-NOL-ij-ment) The notary's certification that you appeared before them and signed the document voluntarily. Different from notarization, though often combined. Required in all states but specific language varies. *See: Chapter 7 (deed preparation), Chapter 14 (signature problems)*

Beneficiary (ben-uh-FISH-ee-air-ee) The person who benefits from your trust - typically your family members who will receive trust property after your death. You can be your own beneficiary during your lifetime. *See: Chapter 2 (trust basics), Chapter 18 (beneficiary updates)*

Chain of Title The history of ownership for your property, shown through recorded deeds going back in time. Think of it like a family tree for your property - each deed shows who owned it when. *See: Chapter 6 (understanding deeds)*

Consideration Legal term for payment or exchange of value. Most trust transfers state "no consideration" because you're not selling the property - you're moving it from your name to your trust. *See: Chapter 7 (deed preparation)*

Documentary Transfer Tax State or local tax imposed when property ownership changes. Many states exempt trust transfers, but you must follow specific procedures to claim exemptions. *See: Chapter 16 (complex states), Appendix A (state-by-state fees)*

Garn-St. Germain Act (GARN saint jer-MAIN) Federal law that prevents mortgage lenders from calling loans due when property transfers to the borrower's revocable living trust. Your secret weapon against worried lenders. *See: Chapter 10 (mortgaged properties)*

Grantor (GRAN-tor) The person giving away property in a deed - that's you when you transfer property to your trust. Think "grantor grants property away." *See: Chapter 6 (deed basics), Chapter 7 (deed preparation)*

Grantee (gran-TEE) The person receiving property in a deed - that's your trust when you transfer property to it. Think "grantee gets property." *See: Chapter 6 (deed basics), Chapter 7 (deed preparation)*

Legal Description The official description of your property's boundaries and location, usually written in surveyor language that sounds like gibberish. Must be copied exactly from your current deed. *See: Chapter 6 (understanding deeds), Chapter 7 (deed preparation)*

Living Trust A legal arrangement where you transfer ownership of property to a trust that you control during your lifetime. Also called "revocable trust" because you can change or cancel it. *See: Chapter 2 (trust basics)*

Notarization (NO-tar-eye-ZAY-shun) The process where a notary public verifies your identity and witnesses your signature. Required in most states for deed validity. *See: Chapter 7 (deed execution), Chapter 14 (notarization problems)*

Pour-Over Will A special will that works with your living trust, transferring any property you forgot to put in the trust. Like a safety net for trust funding mistakes. *See: Chapter 5 (trust creation basics)*

Probate (PRO-bate) The court process for distributing a deceased person's property. Living trusts avoid probate, which is the main reason people create them. *See: Chapter 1 (why trusts matter), Chapter 2 (trust benefits)*

Quitclaim Deed (QUIT-claim) A deed that transfers whatever ownership interest you have without making any promises about the property's title quality. Most common deed type for trust transfers. *See: Chapter 6 (deed types), Appendix B (quitclaim template)*

Recording The official process of filing your deed with county government to make the ownership change public and legal. Like registering a car, but for real estate. *See: Chapter 8 (recording process)*

Revocable Trust (REV-oh-kuh-bull) A trust you can change or cancel during your lifetime. Most living trusts are revocable, giving you complete control while providing probate avoidance benefits. *See: Chapter 2 (trust types)*

Scrivener's Affidavit (SKRIV-en-ers af-uh-DAY-vit) A sworn statement correcting minor clerical errors in recorded documents. Much cheaper than recording corrective deeds for small mistakes. *See: Chapter 14 (error corrections)*

Successor Trustee The person who takes over trust management when you can't serve anymore due to death or incapacity. Choose this person carefully - they're your backup plan. *See: Chapter 2 (trust roles), Chapter 18 (trustee preparation)*

Title Insurance Insurance that protects against property ownership problems. Usually purchased when you buy property, and may help with transfer problems. *See: Chapter 14 (title insurance claims)*

Trustee (trus-TEE) The person responsible for managing trust property and following trust instructions. Usually you serve as your own trustee during your lifetime. *See: Chapter 2 (trust roles), Chapter 18 (trustee responsibilities)*

Warranty Deed A deed that includes promises (warranties) about the property's title quality. Provides more protection than quitclaim deeds but rarely necessary for trust transfers. *See: Chapter 6 (deed types)*

Quick Reference for Common Confusion

Grantor vs. Grantee: Grantor gives, Grantee gets. Easy memory trick: Grantor has an "o" like "go" (property goes away from grantor).

Revocable vs. Irrevocable: Revocable means you can change it (like a pencil mark you can erase). Irrevocable means permanent (like ink).

Trust vs. Trustee: Trust is the legal arrangement. Trustee is the person managing it. Trust is the container, trustee is the person using the container.

Recording vs. Filing: Recording is the official term for filing deeds with county government. Same process, different terminology.

Consideration vs. Value: Consideration is what you pay for property. In trust transfers, consideration is usually "none" because you're not buying or selling.

This glossary provides the foundation for understanding trust transfer terminology. Don't worry about memorizing everything - just use it as a reference when you encounter unfamiliar terms. Understanding concepts matters more than memorizing definitions.

Appendix D: Resource Directory

Finding reliable, current information and qualified professionals can make the difference between smooth trust transfers and frustrating complications. This directory provides vetted resources organized by type and geographic coverage.

All resources listed here provide legitimate services and information relevant to DIY trust transfers. However, inclusion doesn't constitute endorsement - always verify current information and evaluate professionals based on your specific needs.

Resource Selection Criteria Resources included in this directory meet specific criteria:

- Provide current, accurate information about trust and property law

- Offer services relevant to individual property owners (not just professionals)

- Maintain current contact information and active operations

- Demonstrate competence and reliability in their specific areas

---

STATE BAR ASSOCIATIONS

State bar associations provide attorney referral services, legal information, and sometimes free legal clinics. While quality varies, they remain the primary official source for attorney referrals.

National Resources

- American Bar Association: www.americanbar.org, (312) 988-5000

- National Academy of Elder Law Attorneys: www.naela.org, (520) 881-4005

Regional Bar Associations

Northeast:

- Maine State Bar: (207) 622-7523

- New Hampshire Bar Association: (603) 224-6942

- Vermont Bar Association: (802) 223-2020

- Massachusetts Bar Association: (617) 338-0500

- Rhode Island Bar Association: (401) 421-5740

- Connecticut Bar Association: (860) 223-4400

- New York State Bar Association: (518) 463-3200

- New Jersey State Bar Association: (732) 249-5000

- Pennsylvania Bar Association: (717) 238-6715

Southeast:

- Delaware State Bar Association: (302) 658-5279

- Maryland State Bar Association: (410) 685-7878

- Virginia State Bar: (804) 775-0500

- West Virginia State Bar: (304) 558-2456

- North Carolina State Bar: (919) 828-4620

- South Carolina Bar: (803) 799-6653

- Georgia State Bar: (404) 527-8700

- Florida Bar: (850) 561-5600

- Alabama State Bar: (334) 269-1515

- Mississippi Bar: (601) 948-4471

- Tennessee Bar Association: (615) 383-7421

- Kentucky Bar Association: (502) 564-3795

Midwest:

- Ohio State Bar Association: (614) 487-2050

- Indiana State Bar Association: (317) 639-5465

- Illinois State Bar Association: (217) 525-1760

- Michigan State Bar: (517) 346-6300

- Wisconsin State Bar: (608) 257-3838

- Minnesota State Bar Association: (612) 333-1183

- Iowa State Bar Association: (515) 243-3179

- Missouri Bar: (573) 635-4128

- North Dakota State Bar Association: (701) 255-1404

- South Dakota State Bar: (605) 224-7554

- Nebraska State Bar Association: (402) 475-7091

- Kansas Bar Association: (785) 234-5696

West:

- Montana State Bar: (406) 442-7660

- Wyoming State Bar: (307) 632-9061

- Colorado Bar Association: (303) 860-1115

- New Mexico State Bar: (505) 797-6000

- Utah State Bar: (801) 531-9077

- Idaho State Bar: (208) 334-4500

- Nevada State Bar: (775) 382-2200

- Arizona State Bar: (602) 252-4804

- California State Bar: (415) 538-2000

- Oregon State Bar: (503) 620-0222

- Washington State Bar Association: (206) 443-9722

- Alaska Bar Association: (907) 272-7469

- Hawaii State Bar Association: (808) 537-1868

Using Bar Associations Effectively

- Request attorneys specializing in estate planning or real estate law

- Ask about initial consultation fees before scheduling appointments

- Inquire about limited scope representation options

- Verify attorney licensing and disciplinary status

- Request multiple referrals to compare options and fees

TITLE COMPANY DIRECTORIES

Title companies provide valuable resources for property research, title insurance claims, and sometimes limited assistance with deed preparation.

National Title Companies These companies operate in multiple states and provide consistent service standards:

- **First American Title:** (800) 854-3643, operates in all 50 states

- **Old Republic Title:** (855) 653-7378, strong nationwide coverage

- **Fidelity National Title:** (888) 934-3354, extensive branch network

- **Stewart Title:** (800) 729-1902, particularly strong in Texas and Western states

- **Chicago Title:** (866) 684-8853, strong Midwest and national presence

Regional Title Companies Regional companies often provide more personalized service and better local knowledge:

California:

- Commonwealth Land Title: (213) 346-9400

- Placer Title Company: (916) 630-2260

Texas:

- Alamo Title: (210) 277-6100

- Republic Title: (214) 528-9300

Florida:

- Attorneys' Title Fund Services: (407) 240-3863

- Southern Title: (305) 667-0505

New York:

- Madison Title Agency: (516) 739-3636

- Empire State Title: (212) 563-3500

Services Title Companies Provide

- Title searches and insurance

- Deed preparation assistance (limited scope)

- Recording services

- Title problem resolution

- Property research and verification

- Closing and escrow services

Working with Title Companies

- Explain that you're doing a trust transfer, not a sale

- Ask about limited services rather than full closing services

- Inquire about title insurance claim procedures if problems arise

- Understand fee structures before requesting services

- Verify that they work with individual customers (some only serve professionals)

ONLINE LEGAL RESOURCES

Government Resources Official government websites provide authoritative information about recording requirements and procedures:

Federal Resources:

- IRS Trust Information: www.irs.gov/forms-pubs/about-form-1041

- HUD Real Estate Settlement Procedures: www.hud.gov/program_offices/housing/sfh/res/respa_hm

- Consumer Financial Protection Bureau: www.consumerfinance.gov

State Government Resources: Most state governments provide property recording information through:

367

- Secretary of State offices (business and notary information)

- Department of Revenue (transfer tax information)

- Attorney General offices (consumer protection and legal guidance)

County Government Resources: County recorder, clerk, or assessor websites typically provide:

- Current recording fee schedules

- Required forms and templates

- Recording procedures and requirements

- Contact information for questions

- Online recording systems where available

Legal Information Websites These websites provide reliable legal information for consumers:

- **Nolo.com:** Extensive library of legal information written for consumers

- **FindLaw.com:** Legal information and attorney directory

- **Avvo.com:** Attorney ratings and basic legal information

- **LegalZoom.com:** Legal document services and information

- **Rocket Lawyer:** Legal forms and limited legal advice

Educational Resources

- **American College of Trust and Estate Counsel:** www.actec.org

- **National Association of Estate Planners & Councils:** www.naepc.org

- **Society of Trust and Estate Practitioners:** www.step.org

Using Online Resources Safely

- Verify information currency (look for recent update dates)

- Cross-reference important information with official sources

- Understand the difference between general information and specific legal advice

- Be cautious about free forms that may not meet current legal requirements

- Remember that online information doesn't replace professional advice for complex situations

---

TRUST ADMINISTRATION RESOURCES

Professional Organizations These organizations provide education and resources for trust administration:

National Organizations:

- **Trust and Estate Professionals:** www.teprofessionals.org

- **National Association of Estate Planners & Councils:** www.naepc.org, (480) 596-9292

- **American College of Trust and Estate Counsel:** www.actec.org, (202) 684-8460

Educational Resources:

- **Trust Education Foundation:** Provides consumer education about trust benefits and administration

- **Estate Planning Council Networks:** Local organizations in major metropolitan areas

- **University Extension Programs:** Many universities offer estate planning education for consumers

Software and Technology Resources Technology tools can simplify trust administration:

Document Management:

- **Evernote:** Organize trust documents and correspondence
- **Google Drive/Dropbox:** Share access with family members and professionals
- **LastPass/1Password:** Manage passwords for trust-related accounts

Financial Management:

- **Quicken/QuickBooks:** Track trust property income and expenses
- **Mint:** Monitor trust account balances and transactions
- **TurboTax:** Handle tax reporting for trust property

Communication Tools:

- **Zoom/Skype:** Video consultations with distant family members or professionals
- **DocuSign:** Electronic signature services for trust documents
- **Slack/Microsoft Teams:** Family communication about trust matters

PROFESSIONAL ASSOCIATIONS

Real Estate Professional Organizations These organizations can help you find qualified professionals familiar with trust property transfers:

National Association of Realtors: www.nar.realtor, (800) 874-6500

- Local MLS access for property research

- Realtor referrals familiar with trust transactions

- Educational resources about property ownership

American Land Title Association: www.alta.org, (202) 296-3671

- Title company directory

- Title insurance information

- Property research resources

National Notary Association: www.nationalnotary.org, (818) 739-4000

- Notary location services

- Mobile notary referrals

- Notarization procedure guidance

Financial Planning Organizations

Financial Planning Association: www.onefpa.org, (800) 322-4237

- Fee-only financial planner directory

- Integration of trust planning with overall financial planning

- Educational resources about estate planning

National Association of Personal Financial Advisors: www.napfa.org, (847) 483-5400

- Fee-only advisor network

- Fiduciary standard professionals

- Trust and estate planning specialists

Legal Professional Organizations

National Academy of Elder Law Attorneys: www.naela.org, (520) 881-4005

- Specialist attorneys for seniors and estate planning

- Trust administration expertise

- Long-term care and incapacity planning

American Bar Association Section of Real Property, Trust and Estate Law: Provides resources for both attorneys and consumers about current law developments.

Tax Professional Resources

National Association of Tax Professionals: www.natptax.com, (800) 558-3402

- Tax preparer directory

- Trust taxation specialists

- Multi-state tax expertise

American Institute of CPAs: www.aicpa.org, (919) 402-4500

- CPA directory with estate and trust specialization

- Personal financial planning specialists

- Business and investment property expertise

Using Professional Associations

- Use referral services to find qualified professionals

- Verify credentials and specializations

- Ask about experience with your specific situation

- Understand fee structures before engaging services

- Check references and disciplinary history

Vetting Professional Services When using any professional referral:

- Verify current licensing and credentials

- Ask about specific experience with trust transfers

- Request fee estimates for your specific situation

- Check online reviews and references

- Understand exactly what services will be provided

Remember: professional associations provide starting points for finding qualified help, but you must still evaluate individual professionals based on your specific needs and circumstances.

Appendix E: Troubleshooting Quick Reference

Problems happen. Sometimes on weekends. Sometimes when county offices are closed. Sometimes when you're staring at a rejected deed wondering what went wrong and where to turn for help.

This quick reference gives you immediate answers to the most common problems, emergency contact strategies, and clear decision trees for when problems require professional help versus solutions you can handle yourself.

Emergency Contact Strategy

When County Offices Are Closed Most recording problems arise when county offices are closed and you need immediate guidance. Your options:

Online Resources (Available 24/7):

- County recorder websites often provide FAQ sections addressing common problems

- State government websites typically include recording requirement summaries

- Legal information websites (Nolo.com, FindLaw.com) provide general guidance

Emergency Professional Contacts:

- Mobile notary services (many operate evenings and weekends)

- Legal document preparation services (often available extended hours)

- Title company customer service lines (major companies provide 24/7 support)

Peer Support Networks:

- Online forums for property owners and estate planning

- Local real estate investment groups (many have DIY-experienced members)

- Social media groups focused on estate planning and property ownership

The Fast-Track Problem Resolution System

Step 1: Identify Problem Type (5 minutes) Categorize your problem to determine urgency and solution approach:

Category A - Critical (Requires Immediate Action):

- Deed recorded with major errors affecting ownership

- Time-sensitive deadlines (estate settlement, property sale)

- Legal threats or challenges to transfer validity

Category B - Important (Requires Prompt Action):

- Deed rejected by county recorder

- Name discrepancies preventing recording

- Missing documentation or signatures

Category C - Routine (Can Wait for Business Hours):

- Questions about procedures or requirements

- Planning for future transfers

- Information gathering for complex situations

Step 2: Apply Appropriate Solution Track

Category A Solutions:

- Contact emergency legal hotlines (many state bars provide after-hours emergency numbers)

- Call title insurance companies if you have coverage

- Document all communications and actions taken

- Prepare for professional consultation first thing next business day

Category B Solutions:

- Review rejection reasons carefully and compare with requirements

- Check this troubleshooting guide for similar problems

- Prepare corrected documents for resubmission

- Contact county offices first thing next business day

Category C Solutions:

- Use online resources for initial research

- Prepare questions for next business day contact with county offices

- Continue planning while gathering additional information

COMMON PROBLEMS AND IMMEDIATE SOLUTIONS

Problem: Deed Rejected for Signature Issues

Immediate Actions:

1. Review rejection notice for specific signature problems

2. Check if signatures match names exactly as typed in deed

3. Verify notarization is complete and uses correct acknowledgment language

4. Prepare new deed with corrections (don't try to fix original)

Solution Steps:

- Prepare completely new deed with correct information

- Schedule fresh notarization appointment

- Review state-specific signature requirements before re-execution

- Include cover letter explaining corrections when resubmitting

Timeline: 3-5 days to prepare and resubmit corrected deed

Professional Help Needed: Rarely, unless underlying name or ownership issues exist

---

Problem: Legal Description Errors

Immediate Actions:

1. Compare your deed's legal description with current recorded deed character by character

2. Identify specific differences or errors

3. Obtain certified copy of current deed if necessary for verification

Solution Steps:

- Copy legal description exactly from current deed (don't abbreviate or modify)

- Use typed rather than handwritten legal descriptions when possible

- Include complete legal description even if very long

- Verify property address matches legal description

Timeline: 1-2 days to correct and resubmit

Professional Help Needed: Only if legal description seems unclear or incomplete on current deed

---

Problem: Trust Name or Date Discrepancies

Immediate Actions:

1. Check exact trust name and date from original trust document

2. Compare with deed preparation to identify discrepancies

3. Verify spelling and punctuation match exactly

Solution Steps:

- Use trust name exactly as shown in trust document

- Include complete trust date (month, day, year)

- Ensure trustee designation follows state-preferred format

- Double-check spelling of all trust-related information

Timeline: 1 day to correct and resubmit

Professional Help Needed: If trust document itself has errors or unclear provisions

---

Problem: Recording Fee Calculation Errors

Immediate Actions:

1. Verify current fee schedule with county recorder

2. Recalculate fees based on your specific document and property

3. Check if additional fees apply (transfer taxes, supplemental forms)

Solution Steps:

- Contact county recorder for current fee schedule
- Calculate fees precisely including all applicable charges
- Use certified funds (money order or cashier's check) for resubmission
- Include slightly extra payment if uncertain about exact amount (excess will be refunded)

Timeline: 1-2 days to verify fees and resubmit payment

Professional Help Needed: Rarely, unless complex transfer tax calculations are involved

---

Problem: Lender Objects to Trust Transfer

Immediate Actions:

1. Review lender's specific objections
2. Gather documentation of Garn-St. Germain Act protections
3. Prepare response citing federal law protections

Solution Steps:

- Send written response citing 12 U.S.C. § 1701j-3(d)(8)
- Include copy of trust pages showing revocable nature and your continued beneficial ownership
- Request specific legal basis for any continued objection
- Escalate to senior lender personnel if initial response unsatisfactory

Timeline: 1-2 weeks for lender response and resolution

Professional Help Needed: If lender continues objecting after proper legal citations

---

Problem: Name Discrepancies Between Current Deed and Identification

Immediate Actions:

1. Identify specific name differences (spelling, middle names, maiden names)

2. Gather documentation showing name evolution (marriage certificates, legal name changes)

3. Determine if differences are minor variations or significant discrepancies

Solution Steps:

- Use "also known as" language in deed: "John Smith, also known as John J. Smith"

- Include documentation of name changes if available

- Consider name change affidavit for significant discrepancies

- Use most complete name version that matches identification

Timeline: 2-5 days depending on complexity

Professional Help Needed: For significant name discrepancies or unclear ownership history

---

CORRECTION PROCEDURES

Scrivener's Affidavit Process

Use scrivener's affidavits for minor clerical errors that don't affect the substance of the transfer:

Appropriate for Scrivener's Affidavit:

- Typographical errors in property addresses
- Minor spelling corrections
- Incorrect ZIP codes or similar minor details
- Small legal description formatting errors

Scrivener's Affidavit Template:

SCRIVENER'S AFFIDAVIT

State   of   [State]
County of [County]

I, [Your name], being duly sworn, state:

1. I am the grantor in the deed recorded on [Date] as Document Number [Recording number] in the records of [County] County, [State].

2. The deed contains a clerical error in that [describe specific error].

3. The correct information should read: [provide correct information].

4. This affidavit is made to correct the clerical error and clarify the public record.

_____   Date: _____
[Your signature]

Subscribed and sworn to before me this ___ day of _____, 20.

Notary Public

Recording Scrivener's Affidavits:

- Record affidavit in same office as original deed

- Include reference to original deed's recording information
- Pay standard recording fees (usually $10-30)
- Obtain recorded copy for your records

Corrective Deed Process

Use corrective deeds for substantial errors that affect the legal sufficiency of the transfer:

Appropriate for Corrective Deeds:

- Wrong grantor or grantee names
- Incorrect legal descriptions
- Missing essential deed elements
- Improper trust designations

Corrective Deed Process:

1. Prepare new deed with correct information
2. Include reference to original deed: "This deed corrects and supersedes the deed recorded [date] as Document [number]"
3. Execute new deed with proper signatures and notarization
4. Record corrective deed using standard procedures
5. Update all parties about the correction

Timeline for Corrective Deeds: 5-10 days typical

PROFESSIONAL HELP TRIGGER DECISION TREE

Use this decision tree when problems arise:

Question 1: Does this problem affect property ownership or transfer validity?

- **Yes:** Consider professional help, especially for high-value properties
- **No:** Proceed with self-correction using guidance above

Question 2: Do you understand the problem and potential solutions?

- **Yes:** Attempt self-correction with appropriate timeline
- **No:** Seek professional consultation before proceeding

Question 3: Are potential consequences serious (financial loss, legal complications)?

- **Yes:** Professional consultation recommended
- **No:** Proceed with careful self-correction

Question 4: Do you have adequate time to research and implement solutions?

- **Yes:** Self-correction appropriate
- **No:** Professional assistance may be more efficient

Question 5: Does the problem affect multiple properties or complex situations?

- **Yes:** Professional consultation likely cost-effective
- **No:** Individual problem-solving appropriate

Immediate Professional Help Required For:

- Any problem you don't understand after reasonable research
- Situations where mistakes could cost more than professional fees

- Time-sensitive problems affecting property rights or legal deadlines

- Problems involving multiple parties with potential conflicts

- Any situation where you feel overwhelmed or uncertain about consequences

Emergency Contact Checklist

Keep this information readily available:

County Recorder Information:

- Office name and phone number: _____

- Emergency or after-hours contact: _____

- Online resource website: _____

- Fee schedule and payment methods: _____

Professional Support Contacts:

- Preferred attorney name and phone: _____

- Backup attorney contact: _____

- Local notary services: _____

- Title company contact: _____

Personal Information:

- Trust name and date: _____

- Property addresses and parcel numbers: _____

- Recording confirmation numbers: _____

- Insurance agent contact: _____

Final Reality Check

Most problems have straightforward solutions that don't require professional help. The troubleshooting guidance in this appendix handles 85-90% of common issues that arise during DIY trust transfers.

When problems do require professional help, the knowledge you've gained through DIY preparation makes you a better client who gets better results and pays lower fees.

Don't let fear of problems prevent you from attempting DIY transfers. The vast majority of transfers proceed smoothly, and the money you save on successful transfers can fund professional help when you truly need it for complex situations.

Keep this troubleshooting guide handy during your transfer process. Most problems are temporary inconveniences, not permanent obstacles. With persistence and the right resources, you can solve problems effectively and complete your trust transfer successfully.

Your success depends not on avoiding all problems, but on handling problems effectively when they arise. The tools in this appendix give you everything you need for effective problem resolution.

References

United States Congress. (1982). *Garn–St. Germain Depository Institutions Act of 1982*, 12 U.S.C. § 1701j-3. Cornell Law School. https://www.law.cornell.edu/uscode/text/12/1701j-3

Office of the Comptroller of the Currency. (2023). *12 CFR Part 191 — Preemption of due-on-sale laws*. Electronic Code of Federal Regulations. https://www.ecfr.gov/current/title-12/chapter-I/part-191

Internal Revenue Service. (2024). *Publication 527: Residential rental property*. U.S. Department of the Treasury. https://www.irs.gov/pub/irs-pdf/p527.pdf

Internal Revenue Service. (2024). *Publication 559: Survivors, executors, and administrators*. U.S. Department of the Treasury. https://www.irs.gov/publications/p559

Internal Revenue Service. (2024). *Form 1041: U.S. income tax return for estates and trusts*. U.S. Department of the Treasury. https://www.irs.gov/forms-pubs/about-form-1041

Internal Revenue Service. (2024). *Instructions for Form 1041*. U.S. Department of the Treasury. https://www.irs.gov/instructions/i1041

Internal Revenue Service. (2024). *Topic No. 414: Rental income and expenses*. U.S. Department of the Treasury. https://www.irs.gov/taxtopics/tc414

Fannie Mae. (2025). *Selling Guide B2-2-05: Inter vivos revocable trusts*. https://selling-guide.fanniemae.com/sel/b2-2-05/inter-vivos-revocable-trusts

Fannie Mae. (2017). *Selling Guide B8-5-02: Inter vivos revocable trust mortgage documentation and signature requirements.* https://selling-guide.fanniemae.com/sel/b8-5-02/inter-vivos-revocable-trust-mortgage-documentation-and-signature-requirements

Freddie Mac. (2025). *Single-Family Seller/Servicer Guide § 8406.1: Transfers of ownership.* https://guide.freddiemac.com/app/guide/section/8406.1

Freddie Mac. (2025). *Single-Family Servicer Guide § 8406.3: Transfers of ownership (inter vivos revocable trusts).* https://guide.freddiemac.com/app/servicing/section/8406.3

Cornell Law School. (n.d.). *Due-on-sale clause (Wex).* Legal Information Institute. https://www.law.cornell.edu/wex/due-on-sale_clause

Consumer Financial Protection Bureau. (2023). *Leaving your home to children or heirs.* https://www.consumerfinance.gov/consumer-tools/educator-tools/resources-for-older-adults/leaving-your-home-to-children-or-heirs/

Consumer Financial Protection Bureau. (2024). *Homeowners face problems with mortgage companies after divorce or death of a loved one.* https://www.consumerfinance.gov/about-us/blog/homeowners-face-problems-with-mortgage-companies-after-divorce-or-death-of-a-loved-one/

California State Board of Equalization. (2023). *Property Tax Rule 462.160: Change in ownership—Trusts.* https://www.boe.ca.gov/lawguides/property/current/ptlg/rtl/462-160.html

California State Board of Equalization. (2023). *Assessors' Handbook Section 401: Change in ownership.* https://www.boe.ca.gov/proptaxes/pdf/ah401.pdf

California State Board of Equalization. (2017). *Letter to Assessors 2017/008: Change in ownership—Trusts.*
https://www.boe.ca.gov/proptaxes/pdf/lta17008.pdf

New York State Department of Taxation and Finance. (2019). *Form TP-584: Combined real estate transfer tax return.*
https://www.tax.ny.gov/forms/real_property/cur_forms.htm

New York State Department of Taxation and Finance. (2011). *TB-RE-10: Additional real estate transfer tax (mansion tax).*
https://www.tax.ny.gov/pubs_and_bulls/tg_bulletins/st/real_estat e_transfer_tax_additional_tax.htm

New York State Department of Taxation and Finance. (2025). *Real estate transfer tax—File and pay.*
https://www.tax.ny.gov/bus/transfer/rptidx.htm

Texas Legislature. (2024). *Texas Family Code, Chapter 3: Marital property rights and liabilities.*
https://statutes.capitol.texas.gov/Docs/FA/htm/FA.3.htm

Texas Legislature. (2024). *Texas Tax Code § 11.13: Residence homestead exemption.*
https://statutes.capitol.texas.gov/Docs/TX/htm/TX.11.htm#11.13

Texas Comptroller of Public Accounts. (2024). *Texas property tax exemptions.* https://comptroller.texas.gov/taxes/property-tax/docs/96-1740.pdf

Texas Comptroller of Public Accounts. (2024). *Texas property tax basics.* https://comptroller.texas.gov/taxes/property-tax/docs/96-1425.pdf

Nolo. (2024). *Funding your living trust.*
https://www.nolo.com/legal-encyclopedia/funding-your-living-trust.html

Nolo. (2024). *What property to put in a living trust.* https://www.nolo.com/legal-encyclopedia/free-books/avoid-probate-book/chapter7-7.html

American Bar Association. (2022). *How do I find a lawyer?.* https://www.americanbar.org/groups/public_education/resources/public-information/how-do-i-find-a-lawyer-/

American College of Trust and Estate Counsel Foundation. (n.d.). *Estate planning video library.* https://actecfoundation.org/estate-planning/expert-senior-committee/estate-planning

American Land Title Association. (n.d.). *Title & escrow claims guide.* https://www.alta.org/about/publications.cfm?pub=title-escrow-claims-guide

Property Records Industry Association. (2019). *eRecording best practices (Version 3.0).* https://pria.us/wp-content/uploads/2019/09/PRIA-eRecording-Best-Practices.v3.0.pdf

Property Records Industry Association. (2020). *Indexing best practices (Version 4.0.1).* https://pria.us/wp-content/uploads/2019/09/PRIA-Indexing-Best-Practices.v4.0.1.pdf

National Notary Association. (n.d.). *Find a notary.* https://www.nationalnotary.org/resources-for/public/find-a-notary

National Association of Estate Planners & Councils. (n.d.). *Find an estate planner.* https://portal.naepc.org/search_studies

National Association of Personal Financial Advisors. (n.d.). *Find an advisor.* https://www.napfa.org/find-an-advisor

Financial Planning Association. (n.d.). *PlannerSearch.* https://plannersearch.org/

www.ingramcontent.com/pod-product-compliance
Lightning Source LLC
Chambersburg PA
CBHW060316200326
41519CB00011BA/1751